POSTMODERNITY USA

Theory, Culture & Society

Theory, Culture & Society caters for the resurgence of interest in culture within contemporary social science and the humanities. Building on the heritage of classical social theory, the book series examines ways in which this tradition has been reshaped by a new generation of theorists. It will also publish theoretically informed analyses of everyday life, popular culture, and new intellectual movements.

EDITOR: Mike Featherstone, *University of Teesside*

Also in this series

Global Culture
Nationalism, Globalization and Modernity
edited by Mike Featherstone

Talcott Parsons
Theorist of Modernity
edited by Roland Robertson and Bryan S. Turner

Images of Postmodern Society
Social Theory and Contemporary Cinema
Norman K. Denzin

Promotional Culture
Advertising, Ideology and Symbolic Expression
Andrew Wernick

Cultural Theory and Cultural Change
edited by Mike Featherstone

Changing Cultures
Feminism, Youth and Consumerism
Mica Nava

Risk Society
Towards a New Modernity
Ulrich Beck

Max Weber and the Sociology of Culture
Ralph Schroeder

POSTMODERNITY USA

The Crisis of Social Modernism in Postwar America

Anthony Woodiwiss

SAGE Publications

London • Newbury Park • New Delhi

First published 1993

SAGE Publications Ltd
6 Bonhill Street
London EC2A 4PU

SAGE Publications Inc
2455 Teller Road
Newbury Park, California 91320

SAGE Publications India Pvt Ltd
32, M-Block Market
Greater Kailash – I
New Delhi 110 048

British Library Cataloguing in Publication Data

Woodiwiss, Anthony
    Postmodernity USA: Crisis of Modernism in Postwar
    America. – (Theory, Culture & Society Series)
    I. Title   II. Series
    973.9
    ISBN 0-8039-8788-9
    ISBN 0-8039-8789-7 pbk

Library of Congress catalog card number 93-083105

Typeset by Mayhew Typesetting, Rhayader, Powys
Printed in Great Britain by the Cromwell Press Ltd,
Broughton Gifford, Melksham, Wiltshire

For Audrey, Roger and Frank
With whom I began to think for myself

CONTENTS

PREFACE

This book has been so long in the writing and so many debts have been incurred that it is hard to know where to start in expressing my thanks. To begin somewhere near the beginning, I wish to thank all those American scholars and friends who so kindly shared their knowledge of their society with me in the course of several extended visits to the United States in the latter half of the 1970s. These and subsequent visits were made possible by financial assistance from the Fuller Fund of the Department of Sociology at the University of Essex. In particular, I would like to thank Alan Wolfe, Bill Tabb, James O'Connor, Roger Friedland, Erik Olin Wright, Wilma Lanier, Frank Munger, Sam Bowles, the Seidman family, Chuck Miller, the DeCesare sisters, and Angela and Ebba Borregaard. In addition, I would like to thank the faculty and students of the Sociology Department of the State University of New York at Stonybrook for making my time there as a visiting professor in 1979–80 truly a year to remember. I am especially grateful to Gerry Zeitz, John Gagnon, Bill Tam, Gene Havens, Linda Brewster Stearns, Norman and Marylyn Goodman, Lewis and Rose Coser, Lyle Hallowell, Marga Logan, Glen Yago, John Logan, Kurt and Gladys Lang, Paget Henry, Ivan Chase and Donna Di Donato.

Thanks to fate or some very bad planning on my part, the final writing up had to take place in Japan during another stint as a visiting professor, this time at Dokkyo University. The fact that it did not prove an impossible task was almost entirely thanks to Professor Ken Arisue of Keio University, who made the contents of his extraordinary library freely available to me. Drafts of sections of the Introduction and the Conclusion were presented to various seminar groups around Japan. I am especially grateful to the following for their most helpful comments: Professors Kato and Watanabe of Hitotsubashi University, Professors Aoki, Harada and Nishizaka of Meiji Gakuin University, Professor Fuse of Hokkaido University, Professor Fuse of Sapporo Gakuin University, and Professor Fuwa of Tohoku University.

Meanwhile, back home and especially at Essex I have been able to depend upon many good friends, a superb group of colleagues and successive generations of talented and tolerant students on my SC 361 course throughout the process of research and writing. Chief amongst those who made a particular contribution to the realization of the current project were: Frank Pearce, Stephen Barr, Sue Aylot, Bob Jessop, Harold Wolpe, Adrian Sinfield, Howard Newby, Diamora Guevara, Mary Girling, Jane Brooks, Roy and Frankie Todd, Brenda Corti, Eleanor Udall, David Rose, Alan Hunt, Jon Stratton, Mike Lane, Joan Busfield,

Stan Cohen, George and Danuta Kolankiewicz, Orly Sullivan, Mike
Woodiwiss, Terry Wordingham, Ray Cooper, Mick Mann, Elaine Stavro
and Mary McIntosh. As ever, my most profound debt is to Kathyanne
Hingwan, who as far as I am concerned is what the Japanese call 'a living
national treasure' – not, I hasten to add, that she too is on her last legs!

In what follows and elsewhere in my work I take a position for which
none of the above have any great responsibility and which may well
appear to many of them to be somewhat bizarre. This position is the
view that a rigorously non-humanist synthesis of certain elements of
Marxism and postmodernism provides the best basis upon which to
advance the cause of sociology. In what follows and elsewhere I have
provided many technical reasons for taking such a position. So far I have
not, however, explained how I came to think of this as a possible stance.

Some twenty-five years ago I was an active member of a political
group called Solidarity, which was the British offshoot of an anti-
Stalinist, French libertarian socialist *groupuscule* known as *Socialisme ou
Barbarie*. Amongst the leading figures in the latter group were Carlos
Castoriadis and Jean-François Lyotard. For the most part and largely
because of our French comrades' penchant for pseudonyms, ordinary
members of the British group like myself did not even know the real
names of these luminaries. Castoriadis, for example, had several
pseudonyms. In Britain he published, if that is the right way to describe
our roneoed productions, under the name of Paul Cardan, a pseudonym
which always connoted to me the name of *the* fashion designer of the
early 1960s, Pierre Cardin.

Guy Debord, the leading thinker of the *Situationistes*, a *groupuscule*
that shared many positions with *Socialisme ou Barbarie* but took some
of them further, was already describing the sort of society within which
such associations might work for washing powders, even if they were not
to do much good for Castoriadis, as 'the society of the spectacle'. Such
a society was one in which, as a consequence of the discovery and
unleashing of the autonomous power of language and of signs more
generally, the ideological realm had come to dominate that of the
economic and so had also become one that Marxism as it then existed
could make little sense of.

I and other members of the British group sought to develop such ideas
by combining them with a Marxisant Weberianism which, despite a
voluntarism on the parts of our French comrades that is seldom acknowledged by their more recent readers, would nevertheless have scandalized
them had they known us any better than we knew them. On this basis
we tried and failed for some six years or so to rouse the people of Leeds
and North London to a level of 'self-activity' that would enable them to
take advantage of their liberal–democratic freedoms.

Eventually I, along with Frank Pearce and a few others, decided to
think again. Thanks largely to Paul Hirst and Harold Wolpe, we discovered Althusser's Marxism. The appeal of this new Marxism lay, of

course, in its strong sense of the resistant, supra-individual nature of society, a sense which chimed nicely with, and promised an explanation for, the disappointments of the political life; provided, that is, that it could be made to allow a greater determinative power to the ideological and to acknowledge a wider variety of political claims (those of the 'new social movements', for example) than the orthodox Marxism out of which it had emerged. The theoretical and political necessities of these provisos were underlined by increasingly frequent visits to the United States, and there were exciting signs that they might eventually be satisfied. We had more or less simultaneously discovered Gramsci, the (post)structuralist tradition and, most difficult of all to accept let alone learn from sociologically, Freud.

In the meantime, I and others had been expelled from Solidarity as 'quasi-*bolsheviki*'. We had argued for democratic control over the roneo machine, amongst other things, and democracy was discovered to require a degree of centralized authority which the more strictly libertarian majority could not accept!

Our erstwhile French comrades continued to move further and further away from Marx and indeed from any form of sociology. Our journeys through the 1970s diverged to such an extent that when my former comrades announced the arrival of 'the postmodern condition' I could only respond with a certain incredulity. Put in the simplest terms, thanks to these comrades, I had long acknowledged the enhanced significance and the autonomy of the ideological realm in advanced capitalist societies; I could not see why this should lead one to think that such societies are no longer susceptible to social scientific explanation.

To be more specific, there seems to me to be no reason why the recognition of the autonomy inherent in the ideological or cultural realm should lead to the adoption of either metatheoretical or substantive idealism. Rather, all this recognition requires is that a realist analytics focused on understanding the complex articulation of the ideological with the other realms of sociality should be substituted for one premissed upon the reduction of the ideal to the economic – hence my commitment to a reconstructed Marxism. Likewise, there seems to me to be no reason why recognition of the autonomy of the ideological should lead to the rejection of the idea that the possibility of social advance is in part dependent upon the democratic transformation of economic relations – hence my continuing commitment to socialism (cp. Bronner, 1990).

INTRODUCTION

Those who have recently commented upon the social condition of the United States have been obsessed with a particular decade, the 1960s. And one metaphor reappears throughout this commentary, that of 'The Fall'. Christian fundamentalists have motivated themselves by speaking of the fall from grace of 'God's own country', which was occasioned by the rise of 'secular humanism' in the 1960s. Cultural historians such as Richard Sennett (1977) and Christopher Lasch (1978) have warned of 'the fall of public man' and the rise of 'a culture of narcissism', both of which first became apparent in the 1960s. Marxists have comforted themselves by emphasizing a 'fall in the rate of profit', which commenced in the mid-1960s and which has yet to wreak its full havoc. In the context of a general argument concerning 'the rise and fall of the great powers', military historian Paul Kennedy (1987) has argued that the reduction in the United States' economic power and the current decline in its geopolitical standing are related. Finally, the postmodernists (Baudrillard, 1988, for example) have announced that the United States is the world's most vibrant cultural desert, and therefore the first society to have survived that fall of 'the great narratives' (positivism, humanism, liberalism, socialism, etc.), which also first became widely apparent in the 1960s (Lyotard, 1984).

This literature has, of course, attracted a point by point rebuttal from those who reject its apocalyptic tone. The mainstream churches have argued that the fundamentalists' fears are greatly exaggerated. Sociologists have reported that there is little evidence of narcissism interfering with the generally beneficial 'habits of the [American] heart' (Bellah et al., 1985: 290). Non-Marxist economists have stressed the resilience and recuperative powers of the market system, especially when the state is withdrawn to its proper 'nightwatchman' role. International relations experts have stressed that, regardless of the decline in the United States' relative economic position, it is nevertheless 'bound to lead' (Nye, 1990), not least because its former chief adversary, the Soviet Union, has declined still further. And, finally, postmodernism has been dismissed as just another intellectual fad.

I will now say something more about the postmodernists' thesis and the most developed, as well as the most sympathetic, effort by a Marxist to rebut it, both of which are specially pertinent to what follows. Despite the fact that he neither invented the term nor claimed a very broad meaning for it, it was Lyotard's (1984) declaration that our condition is now postmodern that made the term one to conjure with. What he did that was new was to declare that postmodernism as a cultural movement was the harbinger of a new social condition and not just of a new aesthetic. Thus, although the significance of the postmodern condition for Lyotard is narrowly metaphysical and, even more narrowly, epistemological, it is by the same token very general: to wit, a condition wherein it is broadly if belatedly recognized that the two major myths that have legitimated scientific, including social scientific, activity for the past 200 years are no longer believed. On the one hand, 'The Myth of Liberation' has been rendered incredible by science's complicity in the great crimes of the twentieth century, namely the Holocaust (see also Bauman, 1989), the gulags and the creation of weapons of indiscriminate mass destruction. On the other, 'The Myth of Truth' has been rendered incredible by the subversive thoughts of philosophers of science (Paul Feyerabend, Thomas Kuhn and René Thom, for example) – by, in other words, the disbelief of those who are supposed to know. The net result of this general incredulity towards metanarratives is that we now live in a world of competing language games, none of which can claim any privilege, and which can only be judged by the criterion of 'performativity'.

Once it had been announced that the forward march of science had halted, it was not surprising that another announcement should soon follow: that the always more problematic forward march of society had halted, too. Nor was it surprising that this announcement should take place in the United States, the society in which, from any sort of radical European point of view, such progress has always been most obviously problematic. It was more surprising that this latter announcement should be made most forcefully by a Marxist. According to the Marxist in question, Frederic Jameson (1984), a survey of recent aesthetic and social criticism reveals multiform 'senses of the end of this or that'. When combined, the results of this criticism produce an account of an aesthetic practice and a culture that: (1) are assertively concerned with surfaces and hence exhibit a certain 'depthlessness'; (2) are voraciously hungry for variations in surface decoration and hence very adept at pastiche; (3) are very much aware of their own depthlessness and hence characterized by a certain 'waning of affect' or a preference for irony over the expression of strong emotion; (4) are markedly predisposed towards, and fascinated with, schizophrenic psychological conditions and fragmentation more generally; and (5) are strikingly utopian on the grounds that what you dream is what you might get.

As I am sure may be gathered from even my very attenuated summary of a rather complex argument, although Jameson accepts that the condition he so brilliantly characterizes exists, he very definitely does not welcome it in the same, sometimes unambiguously joyful, way that some of the postmodernists do. For Baudrillard (1975), the onset of this condition represents the belated but potentially liberating realization that capitalism long ago severed the link between the world of signs and that of objects. Not so for Jameson, and all of postmodernism's critics on the left. Rather, for Jameson, the postmodern condition represents merely the latest stage of capitalist social development – that in which the cultural realm has finally lost all autonomy from the world of commodities. Thus the postmodernists are to be congratulated on their discovery but berated for their reading of its social significance.

This seems an odd stance to take, since it involves accepting the results of a particular body of work while more or less completely rejecting the presuppositions, concepts and methods that made those results possible. A more defensible response on the part of Marxists, or so it would seem to me, would be one which begins by acknowledging the interest of the postmodernists' results, whilst simultaneously recognizing their limitations as a sketch of a *social* condition. Such a response would then continue by investigating the strengths and weaknesses of postmodernism as a social theory, with a view to incorporating the strengths into a deconstructed/reconstructed Marxism (see Woodiwiss, 1990a), and then using the latter to provide a better account of what has been termed 'the postmodern condition'. The remainder of this text is devoted to this latter task.

The present text represents an effort to set out an analysis of the current condition of the United States that once again focuses on the 1960s, but which in contrast to many of those that have preceded it, is neither a jeremiad nor a Panglossian homily. It seems to me that even, or perhaps especially, in their own terms, all is not as it should be for Americans. And I want to argue that the reasons for this are both larger and more subtle than has been suggested hitherto: larger because they appertain to the condition of the social formation as a whole rather than to a single part of it, and more subtle because, by the same token, the pathology involved is not directly observable and therefore may only be known by its often very diffuse effects.

The Rise and Fall of Social Modernism

For reasons that have been outlined elsewhere (Woodiwiss, 1990b: ch. 7) and will be summarized in Chapter 1, I regard the key signs of the 'social modernism' – the policy-determining 'small print' of what might be termed 'managed individualism' – which has been hegemonic in the postwar United States as: 'self-reliance', 'responsible unionism', 'opportunity', 'loyalty' and 'modernity'.

The last of these signs is both synthetic – in that it describes the sort of society in which the others are hegemonic – and also the one through which the ideologues latterly came to know themselves in the course of the 1950s, that is as 'modernizers'. Each of the signs summarizes a discourse which is understood in a Gramscian manner to have a particular referent in certain other discursive and non-discursive structures and relationships: 'self-reliance' in the welfare system, whereby those it interpellates expect or allow state support only where there is either clear entitlement or utter helplessness; 'responsible unionism' in the industrial relations system, whereby those it interpellates expect or accept that the quid pro quo for the right of self-organization is non-interference with managerial prerogatives; 'opportunity' in the social division of labour, whereby those it interpellates insist or believe that material advancement depends upon individual effort and gaining access to a career line; 'loyalty' in the political sphere, whereby those it interpellates insist or accept that allegiance should only be given to those ideas and organizations that positively validate the status quo; and, finally, 'modernity' in the social formation as a whole and as its ostensibly non-ideological, collective self-image.

As is no doubt readily apparent, the interpellative power of social modernism is amplified by the mutually reinforcing character of its component signs, by, in other words, its discursive coherence. For example, self-reliance as the premiss of the welfare system is likely to be attractive to those who believe that unions, if they exist, should be highly responsible, that opportunities are equally available, that only positive views of the existing system are permissible, and that they are living in a new and privileged type of society. Thus, wherever one looks in the signifying chains made possible by social modernist discourse, one sees the same reinforcement of individual signs by the others and the same closure with respect to the possibility of alternatives. On this basis, then, a powerful resistance to interpellations arising from such other discourses as socialism and conservatism was firmly established in the course of the 1950s and remained highly effective until the latter half of the 1970s.

The only additional comment necessary at this point is one on the relationship between social modernism and aesthetic modernism. Social modernism's relationship to its aesthetic namesake (with its anti-organicist and anti-realist stress on, for example, fragmentariness, ambiguity, self-reflexiveness, and the divided self as the sources and ends of creativity) is highly ambivalent (Brick, 1986: *passim*). On the one hand, most, if not all, aesthetic modernisms combined these concerns with a belief in the possibility of social progress in a relationship of means to ends. On the other, as I shall argue in Part I, social modernism has tended to regard preoccupation with the concerns of its aesthetic namesake as a sign that social progress has been achieved and therefore to regard progress as a purely quantitative matter of increasing the numbers of those who could share such preoccupations. Moreover, 'social modernism' here signifies a discourse which, in the name of 'the great narrative' of positivistic science and far less ambivalently than most varieties of aesthetic modernism, claimed to synthesize and so surpass the ideologically tainted social scientific legacy of the past. In short, it signified a new variant of what Mona Harrington has identified as a recurrent American 'myth of deliverance':

At the core of the myth is the conviction that human relations are, by their nature, harmonious, that *serious* conflict in human societies is unnatural and unnecessary. . . And – most important – the principles of natural order, if properly understood and followed, resolve conflict without loss to any legitimate interest. (1986: 16, emphasis in the original)

According to the social modernist variant of this myth, after many false dawns this comforting thought was finally made flesh, so to speak, in the United States in the late 1960s, when the 'New Economists' finally conquered the world of nature by taming and managing economic life, and a 'Great Society' was promised (see below, Chapter 3).

This, then, is the modernist discourse which became a manifest part (it had long been a latent part) of the hegemonic ideology in the late 1950s (cp. Wolfe, 1983). Thus, to repeat, 'modernism' completes as well as summarizes the other four signs and the discourses constructed around them. In so doing it asserts that the United States, as the first fully modern society, was also the first to discover the means whereby the promises of 'the good life' implicit in each of the other four signs might be met. Social modernism may be understood to summarize what, for most Americans (including many domestic critics, see Chapter 5) and in contradistinction to the 'communism' of the former Soviet Union, is admirable about their society.

In the absence of a domestic ideological 'other', the hegemony of social modernism and of the more specific discourses it makes possible remained unchanged, if not unchallenged, from the late 1950s to the late 1980s. If I may be allowed to sociologize Christopher Lasch's psychoanalytic insight, the result was that the United States became transfixed, like Narcissus, by the beauty of its own image. However, because it was trapped within just such a self-referring ideological world, and for other reasons which, unkindly, appear to have been largely economic in character, the same period also saw the United States welsh on the promises that its ideology makes, especially to those ever-present millions who see little of 'the good life'. That is, during this period the United States gave up on even trying to be in fact, as well as in name, what it itself defines as 'modern'. It also gave up on trying to make its most powerful words refer to anything in the extra-ideological world, and so entered that condition that Baudrillard has specified as 'hyperreality': that is, a condition in which it is impossible to check the veracity of any statements about the world; a condition in which, therefore, aesthetic criteria provide the only alternatives to performative ones and which therefore allow one to say only whether or not one likes a particular statement and/or the person making it. This, then, is a condition in which even those conservatives who have consciously rejected social modernism altogether may nevertheless avoid acknowledging that anything has been given up: 'Critics say that America is a lie because its reality falls far short of its ideals. They are wrong. America is not a lie; it is a disappointment. But it can be a disappointment only because it is also a hope' (Huntington, 1981: 262). Not surprisingly, after the failure of their initial batch of nostrums, such conservatives, including President Bush (see Chapter 7), have had great difficulty deciding what to say next.

Also not surprisingly, such a condition, which in a person would evoke both the charge of hypocrisy and an automatic denial, has engendered certain tensions within the hegemonic discourse too, tensions which have destroyed its coherence. The American case, however, is particularly fascinating because the charge of hypocrisy issuing once again, but this time belatedly, from the social and discursive margins of the society (from the supporters of Jesse Jackson's 'Rainbow Coalition', for example), has barely been registered within the terms of the hegemonic discourse. Thus one discovers, as one peruses the pertinent texts, not so much a chorus of denial as a remarkably widespread and prolonged fit of forgetfulness. This lapse is comparable in all ways except one to the forgetfulness which accompanied social modernism's own hegemonic accession ('the end of ideology') and may also, therefore, be referred to by Russell Jacoby's (1977) term, 'social amnesia'.

There is one critical point of difference between the two amnesiac moments. Whilst the earlier one was rooted in optimism and so had a rapturous quality about it, the present one is rooted in pessimism and has a depressive quality about it. Moreover, this depressiveness is so deeply rooted that 'feel-good' presidencies and successful military adventures are able to alleviate it only temporarily and superficially. It springs from an ideological anger denied, at considerable cost to their own plausibility, by the enunciators of the hegemonic discourse. I intend to show that the ultimate source of that anger was as much an endogenous event – the discovery that capitalism *cannot* live up to its promises – as an exogenous one – defeat in Vietnam.

I would like to suggest that this conjunctural condition – deeply rooted but nevertheless particular and perhaps even temporary – has given rise to the pervasive sense that things are either not, or indeed are only, what they seem; and that the postmodernists and others have confused this with an epochal transformation. The condition is far more pronounced in the United States than in Japan (Woodiwiss, 1991: Conclusion) or Western Europe, where either capitalism remains relatively healthy and/or, a strong social democratic presence ensures that a sense of both capitalism's limitations and its 'other' has never been lost (see below, p. 145). In sum, because the difficulties currently faced by the United States have far deeper roots than any supposed plots or stupidity on the part of recent presidential incumbents (cp. Friedman, 1989: 21–4), they cannot be understood or overcome, even if they may yet be relieved, by hoping for deliverance and imagining that it is possible to make a fresh start. Grave as these difficulties are, and perhaps this is the worst thing about them, they have not proved fatal to hopes of deliverance and are unlikely to do so. Purgatory, then, appears to be the fate of the (post)modern society.

It is not my intention here to prove that social modernism was or is hegemonic, nor to demonstrate the street-level existence of the present forgetfulness as regards its promises. As well as my own earlier work on the ideological determinants of the development of postwar labour law (Woodiwiss, 1990b, pt. 4), three authors, on my reading, have between them gone a long way towards establishing both the hegemony of social modernism and the existence of the present forgetfulness, though I do have reservations concerning the explanations they offer for these states of affairs. They are: Loren Baritz in his historical study of what he terms 'the subjective middle class' (1989); Peter Biskind in his detailed analysis of postwar American cinema (1983); and Studs Terkel in his collection of 'vox pops' concerning 'second thoughts on the American Dream' (1988).

Concerning the present forgetfulness, Terkel's text opens as follows:

> In the making of this book. . ., I was burdened with doubts far more disturbing than any I had ever experienced earlier. . . . I was aware of an attribute lacking in the 1980s that had been throbbingly present in the earlier decades, even in the silent 1950s: memory. (1988: 3)

Later, in part quoting from the main body of his text, he says:

> Along with the expunging of memory has come the removal of shame in all spheres of behavior and thought. 'When I was coming up, it was embarrassing to be considered a racist,' observes a young black woman. 'Now it's nothing to be embarrassed about. I think people take pride in it. It's become fashionable to be a bigot.'
> A young blue-collar housewife is ridiculed by her companions, especially her husband, at the neighborhood tavern. 'They think anybody who doesn't agree with Reagan is dumb. Anybody who gets involved is called stupid. They laugh at me all the time.' She has coined a word: ignorance proud.
> Further evidence is offered by a teacher at a midwestern campus. 'It's not just the ignorance that's disturbing. It's the acceptance of ignorance. Its acceptable not to know about serious things. People who are really interested are bores, the kind you turn off, away from at parties.'. . .
> The pert file clerk across the hall lets me know her disdain for unions. Her immediate boss, a young accountant, who describes himself as 'management,' nods solemnly. They put in eight hours a day. When I ask them how their eight-hour day came to be, their fresh faces are pure Mondrian: the absence of any detail – the furrowed brow, the thoughtful squint. (1988: 12–13)

The texts within which the signs of the current amnesiac condition have presented themselves are of many different types. They range from the often finely-honed but seldom moving reassertions of American virtue contained in ceremonial presidential addresses; through some very well-received but curiously weightless sociological tomes, some of whose most strongly felt passages give vent to the *ressentiment* some of their authors still feel towards 'the protest generation'; through the recent and somewhat troubled recantations of some of those who tormented these same professors; to, finally, the ironic, worldly and sometimes elegant circumlocutions of the postmodernists.

Presidents, of course, cannot admit to hypocrisy. Unsurprisingly, sociologists appear to have trouble maintaining their critical stance when considering the texts that issue from the mainstream of their discipline, and some of the authors of these texts (Daniel Bell, 1988, for example) appear to find a strange sense of vindication in the failure of the social modernism, now called simply 'liberalism', they once espoused. This renaming is in itself, of course, symptomatic of the depth of the unconscious self-loathing that pervades the United States today (cp. Thompson, 1989) and which is most often displaced onto its less advantaged members. Liberalism is the ideology with which, for good as well as for ill, its history has been most closely bound up. For liberalism to have gained, since the 1960s and thanks to the likes of William Buckley (1965), a meaning which is more or less the opposite of what it has historically signified, and to have become as a consequence a term of opprobrium (President Bush's 'L-word'), is a striking sign of some discomfort within the hegemonic discourse. In any event, rather than seriously investigate the reasons for this self-loathing, many of even the moderate professoriat prefer to continue to denounce the excesses of those who, they like to imagine, rendered the results of their days of influence less substantial than they had hoped they might have been.

Some former radicals (see, for example, Collier and Horowitz, 1989) appear to feel an equally strange, but in this instance guilty (have the recriminations of their academic fathers finally got to them?), sense of the importance of their own youthful naiveté and occasional wickedness. They prefer to blame themselves and their erstwhile comrades, again instead of seriously investigating the wider causes of their failure to forge and sustain a more generous alternative to social modernism. Finally, smelling all kinds of rats and fixing on the simulation that dominates a society which no longer wants to make something *else* of itself, the postmodernists (Baudrillard, 1988, for example) avoid looking directly at the middle distance and prefer to switch their gaze rapidly between the text at hand and the philosophical or psychological far horizon. The result is that they imagine that 'the entire Enlightenment project', and not simply a minimalist, local variant, has been transcended, when it has simply been given up. Examples of several such texts will be discussed in Chapter 7.

However, although I am critical of those sociologists who have contributed to and colluded in the forgetting of social modernism, and it is hard to resist the temptation to argue with them, such arguments would not pass muster as sociology in my book. Accordingly, I have tried to restrict my consideration of their texts to demonstrating, first, that they are of a piece with the hegemonic discourse and, second, how the forgetting of social modernism works itself out within them. I hope that, if I can demonstrate such a presence and such an occurrence in the texts of authors who must be supposed to have taken particular care to have rendered their texts impervious to such ideological effects, I will have underlined the powerful character of the spell which social modernism and its discontents have cast over the more serious side of the mental life of Americans in the postwar period. To summarize, the aim of what follows is to exemplify and sociologically explain rather than prove, the rise and fall of social modernism.

Towards a Synthesis of Marxism and Postmodernism

At the heart of the explanatory strategy to be deployed below stand the concepts of class and capitalist crisis. Many Americans have long thought these concepts to be inapplicable to their society; in many ways, and largely because of the economic essentialism that underpins most varieties of class and crisis theory, I think that this is a very reasonable thought. However, I wish to suggest that it is no longer reasonable once, with the help of postmodernism's anti-humanism and anti-representationalism, as well as its insistence on the social effectivity of discourse, the concepts of class and capitalist crisis are rethought.

Rethinking Class Theory

The concept of class deployed below is premissed upon the view that most previous theories (Marxist as well as Weberian) have been mistaken in taking individuals and/or groups as the units of class analysis. In my view, to attempt to construct sociological categories by trying to draw lines around groups of people is to embark upon a mistaken and anyway impossible task (*vide* the proliferating intermediary sub-classes to be found within the class schema of the likes of John Goldthorpe, 1980, and Erik Olin Wright, 1985).

It seems to me that individual people are always too unpredictable to be usefully categorized in this way and so provide any sort of firm basis for sociological reasoning. Ultimately this unpredictability may only be elucidated by recourse to psychology. Thus, instead of pursuing this impossible and mistaken end, and in order that it may also contribute something of its own to the elucidation of this unpredictability, sociology should follow Emile Durkheim's advice and concern itself with discovering, and making its analyses in terms of, entities that are social in a *sui generis* sense (Gane, 1988; Pearce, 1989).

This, at least, is what I have attempted to do by rethinking Marx's class theory on a non-representationalist and non-humanist basis (see Woodiwiss, 1990a: pt. 4; compare the independent work of Resnick and Wolff, 1987). For me, the classes of capitalist societies are not in the first instance collectivities of people but rather things in their own right, ensembles of economic, political and ideological structural positions, which are held together by the forces produced by capital's appropriation of surplus labour. Classes as things are, of course, in part embodied by people and corporate entities, but not necessarily by them as whole entities. Thus, people in general (that is, not simply the 'middle classes') and corporate institutions such as companies and trade unions may embody capital in some of their beliefs and behaviours, whilst in others they may embody the working class. Finally, in the absence of additional modes of production, there are only two classes in capitalist societies – the capitalist and the working classes.

The net result of this approach is that one need no longer think, as the hitherto theoretically determinant humanist metaphor of 'class struggle' has for so long directed, in terms of two or more armies confronting one another in an 'arena' or on a field ('terrain'). Rather, one may think of the class structure of capitalist society as a causal mechanism which divides such societies into two as a necessary consequence of the relations of economic possession, disciplinary or political control, and significatory or ideological title which constitute it as a whole.

The intrinsic structural tensions and, therefore, the nature of the continuing, reciprocally structuring effects of the two classes upon one another, and upon the location of the boundary between them, varies from social formation to social formation. This is because, of course, the content of the particular economic, political and ideological structures upon which classes osmotically depend differ, as do their ongoing, relatively autonomous developmental dynamics. Moreover, similarly varying are the additional, osmotic processes (those relating to 'race' and gender, for example) which may come to structure concrete production relations in specific societies. The former set of variations may lead to varying forms and degrees of segmentation within classes and to fractionalization amongst their human and/or institutional embodiments. Similarly, the latter set may lead to classes as a whole, or segments thereof, being overlain, and hence additionally affected, by economic, political or ideological positionings that are not intrinsically pertinent to the appropriation of surplus labour. Nevertheless, these superincumbent positionings will almost always influence, if not the structure of classes themselves, then their social effects, by imposing additional constraints on the nature of the subjects that can embody particular sets or sub-sets of class positionings. (For example, the embodiments of skilled labour power, or indeed capital, may be required to be white, male, Anglo-Saxon protestants with high school diplomas.) Thus, concrete classes and, as will made clear below, the effects of the tensions between them are likely to be marked and affected by such factors as levels of technological development, international and domestic market conditions, and a whole range of political and ideological conditions which might otherwise be thought of as entirely unrelated to class relations.

One result of the increased pertinence of these superincumbent processes in the United States, as elsewhere in the advanced capitalist world, is that they have partially displaced the class structure as a major and direct source of the positionings which determine the life-chances of individuals, and considerably reduced its importance. As against the likes of Daniel Bell (1973), however, it is important to emphasize that this reduction should in no way be taken as indicative of the disappearance of capitalist class relations. These continue to exist no matter how the positionings derived from them come to be embodied by particular human subjects or groups thereof. This reduction and displacement does however, indicate, an undermining of some at least of the commonalities upon which, in the past, solidarities have been constructed between the embodiments of labour power and, indeed, capital. To be more specific, some of the human embodiments of both classes have been separated out on the grounds of one or other non-class criterion and rewarded relatively highly, so that as the members of a supposed 'middle class' they may perform some of the labour necessary to the assembly, deployment and utilization of capital.

What I propose, then, is a new conception of social mobility. The phenomena to which the phrase 'middle class' refers should be re-conceptualized: (1) as a shifting, even permeable boundary zone between the two classes; (2) therefore, as the most critical site of the structuring/destructuring tension that is necessarily produced between the two classes by their shared, constitutive dependence on the appropriation of the fruits of surplus labour; and, finally, (3) as a crucial indicator of the balance of class forces obtaining in any particular society.

To elaborate on the last point, although many of the tasks performed by the embodiments of contradictory positionings may exist because the tasks performed by embodiments of the proletariat have been deskilled, and/or may involve the embodiments of contradictory positionings in exercising control over the group alongside which they were originally positioned, nevertheless any increase in the number of such positionings represents a weakening of capital. This is because, in order to procure their loyalty, payments made to the contradictorily positioned must exceed the value of their labour power. Thus, not only does any increase in the size of the contradictorily positioned labour force make capital's continuing appropriation of surplus labour potentially subject to the wishes of those so positioned, but it also reduces the quantum of capital's revenues available for investment and therefore for its own expanded reproduction. For these reasons, then, the location of the boundary that separates the embodiments of capital from those of labour will migrate up and down the organizational hierarchy and so vary from workplace to workplace as well as over time according to, amongst other factors, the natures of the capitals involved, the market conditions they face, and the balances obtaining between the classes (Woodiwiss, 1990a: 180–1). In the main text I will use the terms 'embourgeoisement' and 'proletarianization' to refer to the upward and downward movements of this boundary respectively.[1]

All of this changes the nature of the questions one asks about the significance for class relations of extra-class phenomena such as the ideological developments of interest here. Specifically, as a sociologist rather than as a politician or, perhaps, as a political scientist, one no longer asks the traditional questions about the effects of ideological developments on the size, composition and morale of the contending class armies. Rather, one asks questions about the effects of ideological developments, such as Thatcherism or Reaganism, on the strength of the forces that bind and separate the two classes economically, politically and ideologically, and therefore explain the ease or difficulty of capital's appropriation of surplus labour (that is, they explain the location of the boundary between them). Putting the point provocatively, one asks the questions of social scientists rather than those of generals.

More specifically, one asks questions about the effects of macro-ideological developments on: (a) capital's economic possession of its means of production (that is, on labour market conditions inside and outside the workplace); (b) capital's political or disciplinary control of its means of production (that is, on disciplinary conditions inside and outside the workplace); and (c) capital's ideological rights of title to its means of production (that is, on significatory conditions inside and outside the workplace).[2] Necessarily, these are also questions about the balance of forces between capital and labour, and they give a new centrality to what has hitherto been known as the theory of crisis. In the absence of an anthropomorphic conception of class, data pertaining to the reasons for increased or decreased tension along the lines of cleavage between the classes become the prime source of evidence for their existence as well as for the state of the balances between them. In sum, even though it may no longer be permissible to picture classes as contending armies, we may nevertheless imagine them to be those entities whose ever-changing relations best explain the increasing and decreasing boundary tensions signified by movements in the average rate of profit, amongst other things. For me, then, class analysis no longer revolves around classifying and counting individual people, but instead involves the invocation of an imagined causal mechanism which partly explains the existence of the particular patterns of positionings applicable to people and institutions.

Rethinking the Theory of Capitalist Crisis

I would like to turn now to the consequences of this rethinking of class for the rethinking of crisis theory. The most important consequence is that, even more emphatically than has been the case hitherto (cp. for example, Castells, 1980; O'Connor, 1984; and Sawyer, 1989: 286ff.), the theory of crisis has to be rethought as a largely sociological rather than economic affair. The principal point to be made is that 'the law of the tendency of the rate of profit to fall' and its 'counteracting influences' do not stand alone under the heading of Marxist crisis theory. Rather, relating as they do to what is literally 'the bottom line', they stand at the end of a chain of reasoning whose critical links, the three principal sites of tension and possible fragility in capitalist economies, are the following: (1) the production process itself, which Marx aptly refers to in *Capital*

(1965) as an 'interruption' in the circuit of capital, since its outcome in terms of the value of labour power is never certain; (2) the interdependent circuits of capital (that is, the monetary and commodity circuits as well as the productive circuit), whose salience has increased immensely with the growth of so-called 'middle-class' positionings; and (3) the similarly interdependent two departments of production (Department I producing producer goods and Department II consumption goods).

In what follows I will seek to demonstrate not only the pertinence of all four of these sites of tension to what has happened in the postwar United States, but also, in line with my general approach, to show that each was affected for good and for ill, so to speak, by class-structurally mediated political and ideological, as well as more narrowly economic, developments. To be specific, I will argue that both the occurrence and the subsequent stabilization of the rather severe profitability crisis which the United States experienced between the mid-1960s and the early 1980s were caused in large part by the rise and fall of social modernism and of the 'new social movements' that accompanied it.

Conclusion

Put briefly, my thesis is as follows:

1   In the latter half of the 1950s, the claim that, because of the self-reliance of its citizens, the responsible nature of its trade unions, its commitment to the broadening of opportunities, the loyalty of its citizenry, and the domesticated nature of its economy, the United States is the most 'modern' (i.e. the best) society in the world became central to its ideology.

2   In the 1960s efforts were made to make the claim to modernity a reality for those who had hitherto been excluded from 'the good life'. These efforts have been given up by successive Administrations since around 1970.

3   Despite this giving up, the claim to modernity has continued to be repeated but the promises made in the name of social modernism have been forgotten with the result that the hegemonic formation is now better termed social (post)modernism.

4   This forgetting may be explained as the result of a new type of capitalist crisis – one still mediated through class relations but brought about as much by ideological and political as by economic factors; specifically, one brought about as much by suppressed anger at capitalism's incapacity to deliver what it promises as by the failure to deliver as such.

5   Thus what we are faced with in the contemporary United States is not an epochal shift to a new kind of society (for example a 'post-industrial' or 'postmodern' society), but rather the aftermath of a new type of capitalist crisis.

Like 'Soviet communism', social modernism promised a good life for all. By and large, those who did not believe its promises did not suffer the same premeditated repression as their Soviet, East European and Asian peers. Nevertheless, the question must be posed as to whether or not history will be any more forgiving of social modernism's sins of omission than it has been of 'communism's' sins of commission? This is the question which, thanks to the discursive seizure the United States has suffered, Americans have forgotten how to ask, since they no longer know what the 'M' word stood for. It remains an open question because what has been forgotten can sometimes be recalled. More important, it should remain an open question if only because any such recall might yet unlock memories that are even more deeply buried – memories of the ideas, hopes and analytical tools that social modernism itself caused to be forgotten as it denied the true extent of the hurts to which it sought to minister.

Notes

1. In order to avoid any confusion, I must emphasize that, according to the present position and *contra* that enunciated by such as G. Marshall et al. (1989: 98–137, 270–5), such movements do not depend upon changes in the levels of skill required of those who are contradictorily positioned, unless such changes are also accompanied by changes in the levels of work autonomy and/or by changes in the size of any loyalty payments included in salaries.

2. At the present time, much highly interesting work is being done in the United States under the heading of 'economic sociology'. Some of this work takes its cue from recent developments in organization theory and, by insisting on what it terms the 'embeddedness' of economic life in its wider social context, develops a very powerful critique of neo-classical economics. Another bloc of such work uses the same notion of 'embeddedness' to develop a Marxist alternative to neo-classicism which, somewhat coyly, it refers to as 'political economy' (see Zukin and DiMaggio, 1990). While I appreciate the substantive contribution made by both groups, a substantial metatheoretical gulf separates my position from theirs, despite their claim to be engaged in 'structural analysis'. Without developing the point, this is because of the humanism and representationalism that is all too apparent in such key concepts and metaphors as 'embeddedness' and 'networks'. This said, I am nevertheless hopeful that work such as mine and that of the 'economic sociologists' might one day become mutually assimilable. In what follows I will be depending upon some of their substantive results, whilst I would hope that, should they chance to read it, the 'economic sociologists' would discover in the present text a non-humanist Marxism that not only, like theirs, refuses economic essentialism, but also suggests an approach to what they term 'embeddedness' that, in a Durkheimian sense, is more strictly sociological than theirs.

One thing that encourages me to think that this is not an entirely forlorn hope is Fred Block's recent book *Postindustrial Possibilities*. At the beginning of his book, Block distances himself quite sharply from the Marxist tradition by explicitly embracing Bell's post-industrialism thesis and with it an almost entirely non-conflictual image of a society that he no longer wishes to term 'capitalist'. Despite his disavowals, it seems to me that Marxist concepts nevertheless continue to animate his text. For example, not only does he deploy a notion of differing degrees of 'marketness' which is remarkably similar in its substantive content to my outlines of the polar modalities of capitalist class relations (Woodiwiss, 1990a: 180–1), but he also arrives at a set of conclusions which would appear to be organized by a very similar, if strangely unconstraining, conception of the capital/labour relation to the one just outlined in the main body of the present text (Block, 1990: 199ff.).

PART I
FINDING SOCIAL
MODERNISM

1

NEW DEAL FIGURATIONS

The United States first thought seriously of itself as *the* modern society in the latter half of the 1950s, under the pressure for ideological self-definition created by the Cold War, but the event which made this thought possible occurred in the 1930s. It was the passage of the 1935 Social Security Act. More than any other single piece of New Deal legislation, this Act fulfilled the promise of 'a reasonable degree of security [for all]' which Roosevelt made in the course of his first acceptance, or 'New Deal', speech. As such, it represented a figuration of the new ideological world which was gradually to emerge in the aftermath of the collapse of liberalism brought about by the Great Depression. This is the world that I (Woodiwiss, 1990b: pts 3, 4), following many others (for example: Kolko, 1967; Radosh and Rothbard, 1972; Sklar, 1988; Weinstein, 1969) have termed 'corporate liberalism', and which was later to be transmuted into that of social modernism. Although he expresses himself in far too humanist a manner for my taste, no one has defined or summarized the manner in which corporate liberalism emerged more concisely than Martin Sklar:

> . . . corporate liberalism emerged not as the ideology of any one class, but rather as a cross-class ideology expressing the interrelations of corporate capitalists, political leaders, intellectuals, proprietary capitalists, professionals and reformers, workers and trade union leaders, populists, and socialists – all those who could, to a greater or lesser extent, identify their outlook, or their interest in administered markets and government regulation, with the rise, legitimation, and institutionalization of the corporate-capitalist order, and hence with the dominant position in the market of the corporate sector of the capitalist class. (1988: 35)

The Formulation of the Social Security Act

The Social Security Act was the emblematic legislative Act of this emergent ideological order. In its origins, its incorporative intent relative to labour, its formulation, the techniques used to gain support for it and get it institutionally established, and in its mode of financing, it was both a figuration of, and a ward of, this order. The origins of the Act may be found in the 'institutional economics' of the Wisconsin School, the most prominent representatives of which were Professors Richard T. Ely and John R. Commons. These were the people who, in the context of Wisconsin's proto-corporate liberal politics, had designed the state's very advanced welfare system – by 1932, it even included unemployment insurance. The writings of this School, and especially of Commons, make the incorporative intent of social security legislation in regard to labour explicit, since in addition to recognizing the direct contribution that such legislation might make to worker loyalty, they are marked by a constant juxtapositioning of suggestions for legislation relating to the improvement of the minimum employment conditions with calls for the routinization of labour relations (cp. Fusfeld, 1972: 108ff.; Piven and Cloward, 1971, chs. 2, 3). The role of the School's work in the formulation of the Act is underlined by the fact that Arthur Altmeyer, who had been Commons' research assistant and had subsequently become a leading figure in the Wisconsin social security bureaucracy, became the chairman of the President's Drafting Committee. And another prominent Wisconsinite, Edwin Witte, latterly became the director of research for the Committee.

The aspirations of the Wisconsin School were no doubt responsible for what Arthur Schlesinger has termed 'the social-democratic tinge' of the New Deal. A consideration of the internal Administration struggle over the Social Security Act makes it clear why this tinge never deepened into an at all 'red' hue. The majority of the Administration did not intend to start any such process, understanding quite clearly that the wider balances of forces would not allow it, even during the Depression. The Wisconsinites and their sympathizers wished to see a fully comprehensive welfare system, which would cover the labour force in respect of all possible harmful eventualities, from industrial injury, through unemployment, to ill health and old age. These were to be financed on an insurance basis. Roosevelt too was committed to this vision – indeed, he coined the phrase 'cradle to the grave insurance' to describe it. (Francis Perkins [1946: 283–4] reports him as subsequently rather peeved when Sir William Beveridge, with whom he discussed these matters, was credited with originating the phrase.)

Harry Hopkins, who was head of the Works Progress Administration and was thereby responsible for the day to day control of the work-relief programme, was the most powerful Administration figure who wished to go beyond the Wisconsin Plan. However, he was unable to change Roosevelt's negative evaluation of what to me is the *sine qua non* of a social democratic welfare system, namely a general right to public assistance (cp. Wedderburn, 1965), or what Roosevelt insisted on calling 'the dole' (Perkins, 1946: 284). Thus the so-called 'Second New Deal', within which the Social Security Bill emerged as the centrepiece, signified not the New Deal's radicalization, as has been commonly supposed, but rather its reaffirmation of such individualist traits as self-reliance and, therefore, of what became known much later as a corporate liberal strategy over a social democratic one (cp. B. Bernstein, 1968: 275ff.; Fraser, 1989; Ferguson, 1989).

Once the advanced position represented by permanent and universal public assistance, as opposed to temporary relief, had been finally rejected, the New Deal's social security programme became particularly vulnerable to the depredations of the federal/state, cross-class and sectionalist coalition politics that are such a deeply embedded and distinctive characteristic of the American polity (for detailed discussions and debate on the pertinence of these politics to the Social Security Bill see: Amenta and Carruthers, 1988; Domhoff, 1970; Quadagno, 1984, 1985; Skocpol and Amenta, 1985). Since there was no longer a great principle at stake, the contents of the bill were whittled down without any particular anguish within the Administration, and indeed with some confidence that by the end of the legislative process it would have become a passable bill, since it should by then no longer offend any but the irreconcilables amongst those who had been initially opposed to it. The principal programmes established by the Act were pension and unemployment schemes, and a system for assisting the blind, the severely disabled and dependent children, as well as old people who were not entitled to the new pensions.

These provisions represented minimalist qualifications to the still sacrosanct value of 'self-reliance', but, in case further reassurance was needed, the temporary nature of the then existing workfare relief programme was reasserted by sharp cutbacks from 1936 on, except in the case of the 'deserving poor' – the old, the blind and the children of one-parent families (Piven and Cloward, 1971: 111ff.). For the same reason, even the payments to be made from the compulsory unemployment insurance scheme were to be available only for the very limited period of sixteen weeks, and were to be set at a level which would be adequate only if the recipients had been in the habit of saving and were capable of 'practical family budgeting', as Secretary Perkins (1946: 285) said in her thoroughly 'progressive' manner. Further, in order not to offend more specific interests, the whole bill was declared inapplicable to agricultural labour, domestic labour and the self-employed, or in other words to approximately 50 per cent of the total labour force and most of its African-American component. Finally, in order to allow the maximum possible flexibility in the light of variations in local circumstances, the financing and administration of the public assistance and unemployment schemes were turned over to the states, who would be free to set their own benefit levels and to administer the schemes according to their own criteria of eligibility, even though it was known that many of the latter would be racist (Altmeyer, 1966: 74ff.; Feagin, 1975: 68ff.; McKinley and Frase, 1970, chs. 4, 5; Steiner, 1966: 85ff.).

Although not even these conciliatory measures satisfied the liberalistic majority, they were sufficient to gain the support of certain important business groups which represented the newer, more internationally oriented industries (Ferguson, 1989). The Republican Party spoke for the majority when it criticized the bill on strikingly sectional grounds for the unfair competition it offered to private insurance companies, and for its undermining of the worker's loyalty to his company. The latter was said to follow from the state's assumption of responsibilities which even in the breach, the companies claimed were theirs (Altmeyer, 1966: 37). (After the war a very similar and even more aggressively expressed defence was used very successfully to counter an effort to establish an equivalent to the British National Health Service; see Starr, 1982 and Wolfe, 1981b: 104.) On the other hand, such organizations as the Business Advisory Council, which represented the views of some of the nation's largest corporations, and the Rockefeller Foundation took the Administration's wider view and strongly supported the bill (Domhoff, 1970: 212ff.).

The Ideological Significance of the Social Security Act

The rationale given for the Social Security Act was overwhelmingly paternalistic. This may be seen most clearly in the arguments used to justify what might otherwise appear to be one of its more obviously redistributive elements, namely its stipulation of employer-only contributions to the unemployment insurance scheme. This appearance vanishes, however, once one realizes two things. Firstly, the employer-only nature of the contributions is in large part an illusion. The Act allows employers a 90 per cent tax-offset in relation to their contributions, and consequently unemployment insurance is largely financed out of general tax revenues, and in such a way as to increase markedly their regressivity. In addition, the general nature of the consumption and employment relationships allows employers to 'shift back' any remaining costs either onto consumers in the form of higher prices or onto their employees by paying lower wages than they otherwise might (Rimlinger, 1971: 221ff.). Secondly, there was very little specific agitation on this point from either labour or other social groups, and certainly nothing comparable to that represented by the Townsend Movement in relation to pensions. The non-social-democratic nature of organized labour meant that it had little interest in the politicization of state finance that would be necessary to uncover the illusion of the employer-only contributions, and unorganized labour had altogether more pressing problems to attend to.

The net effect was the establishment of a system which would allow future Administrations to work out a strategy for dealing with unemployment with virtually only business to worry about. No ideological hostages to fortune had been offered in terms of shared responsibilities and shared rights between capital and labour. More immediately, the Roosevelt Administration was free to convince capital on hardheaded, cost-accounting terms, which were more likely to be convincing to business leaders than reliance on notions of 'the general welfare' and the public, or even national, interest. The Administration's spokespeople only had to move business a half step away from its traditional ideology. Having proclaimed its acceptance of all the prerogatives of private property and demonstrated this with the granting of self-regulation under the National Recovery Act (NRA) codes during the First New Deal, all that the Administration needed to do in the defence of the Second New Deal was to convince business of the responsibilities entailed by such untrammelled freedom. Hence the main argument that the Administration employed in seeking to win support for its proposals was that it was only asking that contractual rights embedded in the employment relationship under monopolistic conditions, but not previously recognized, should now be honoured. Thus it argued that, where it is typically beyond the resources of even the most thrifty worker to possess means of production, the employer is subject to an obligation to provide not only employment, but also compensation to what might be called the 'deserving' unemployed. The latter point was underlined by the bill's exclusion of striking workers and those dismissed for industrial misconduct from receipt of any benefits.

A more material incentive to support the bill was provided by the fact that the administration of the unemployment scheme was to be left to the states, which not only allowed the adjustment of benefits to suit local labour market conditions, but also allowed the possibility that the states might further enhance the tax-saving possibilities of participation in the scheme. The bill stated that employers were entitled to a 90 per cent offset against federal taxes, but it did not say that the unemployment tax had to be levied from all employers at a uniform level. In fact, following the Wisconsin example, many states introduced what was called a 'merit-rating' system, whereby the tax level could be adjusted downwards to favour companies with good employment records. Such companies could still, however, claim federal tax relief as if they had been paying the full rate, and it was therefore possible that participation in the scheme could prove to be not simply cheap but positively advantageous.

Old age insurance, which Congressional Republicans condemned for imposing 'a crushing burden upon industry and upon labour', was the single element of the original Wisconsin Plan to escape more or less unscathed. The Administration had to balance against business opposition the fact that old age pensions had inspired a highly organized and effective social movement, with a large constituency amongst the self-employed and the new salariat. Moreover, this movement on behalf of what was called 'The Townsend Plan' was a radically redistributive one. The Townsend Plan proposed pensions of $200 per month, which, although they were to be financed through a 2 per cent sales tax, would have been highly redistributive, since they amounted to more than double the average earnings of the white, and more than four times those of the African-American population. The Plan had considerable support in Congress, where indeed it was the most popular of a whole series of radical welfare proposals that were being incorporated into formal legislative proposals, such as the Lundeen Bill (Douglas, 1936).

Because of the intensity of the pressure for substantial and uniform pensions, the provisions relating to the aged contained in the Social Security Act were the one section of it that replicated those to be found in the Western European schemes, and were therefore the last remaining source of any social democratic tinge the Act might still have had. In order to safeguard uniformity, old age pensions were to be financed and administered on a federal basis; and in order to ensure that they would be of a reasonable level, they were to be paid for by insurance contributions from employees as well as employers. This last point caused the Administration some trouble, since its purpose was to minimize the cost to employers of what in the long term was expected to be the most expensive scheme in the Act. Notwithstanding some retrospective comments to the contrary by the President, rather than give expression to any, even implicitly, social democratic notion of shared responsibilities and therefore rights in a social commonwealth, it was justified at the time as a low-cost way of stilling the popular clamour. In the short term, however, it made it more difficult than it might have been for the Administration to gain support for the otherwise uncompromisingly paternalist ideological reasoning it had developed to justify the ostensibly employer-only contributions to the unemployment insurance scheme. In the long term, it was this last and faintest of social democratic tinges which secured the loyalty of the working population, as part of an overall strategy which gave away very little in terms of rights against capital that were either contractually, politically or ideologically enforceable. As was to become very clear in the 1980s, what has been obtained on a more egalitarian basis is much harder to take away than what has been paternalistically given.

Ideology and the Structure of the Corporate Liberal State

The chief purpose of the discussion of the Social Security Act so far has been to illustrate how a reluctantly paternalistic welfare system re-established 'self-reliance' as a key sign in the newly emerging hegemonic discourse. In addition some evidence has been presented for the affinity I have claimed elsewhere (Woodiwiss, 1990b: 132) between administrative centralism and the emerging corporate liberalism. The latter has been illustrated in general terms by the fact that the Act originated in the Executive Branch and was 'sold', almost literally, to the federal and state legislatures and to the business community. Also, it has been exemplified more specifically by the Administration's insistence on a federal programme of old age insurance. The reasons for this insistence, as well as for the compromise arrangements arrived at for the rest of the Act, suggest, however, that this was not an especially assertive centralism. Rather, it was more of a reserve one, resorted to only where there was

no other way of securing what was considered to be a 'must' programme. In this respect, the Administration's attitude to centralism
paralleled its hesitant adoption of what was then becoming known as
Keynesianism.

That it should move in this direction at all is, of course, not surprising, since there is an explicit and generally recognized mutual entailment
relationship between a relatively centralized state structure and the
possibility of the adoption of Keynesian policies. The fiscal instruments
used to give effect to such policies involve the state in a more intrusive
mode of socio-economic intervention than do the interest rate adjust-
ments emphasized by those who take their lead from neo-classical
economics. So long as there is a low level of indebtedness, such fiscal
instruments as changes in taxation levels affect the economic activities of
a far larger section of the community than do changes in interest rates.
Keynesian policies are based upon the assumption that investment is a
response to demand, to the possibilities of realizing productive investment through sales, and that therefore investment is a function of
income. Thus the basic theory, as applied under depression conditions,
is that if incomes are raised, demand will rise, investment will rise, the
number in employment will increase, and therefore a self-sustaining cycle
will be initiated. Within this framework, budgetary deficits incurred with
the aim of increasing aggregate demand may be relatively easily justified
as temporarily expedient in the interests of general economic well-being.

By contrast, budgetary deficits of any kind are anathema from the
point of view of neo-classical theory since, apart from the more intrusive
state intervention in the economy that they imply, they also put a further
strain on society's investment resources, whose periodic insufficiency is
regarded as the root cause of recessionary phenomena. According to neo-
classicism, investment will only rise if people, and especially the better
off, save rather than consume, which means that interest rates have to
rise to attract savings. Under these circumstances government borrowing
and spending are regarded as unsound, not only because the former is
likely to increase still further the cost of private borrowing but also
because the latter supposedly pre-empts private investment.

During the 1930s, various political and economic factors combined to
force the Administration to switch to and fro between these two
contrasting, but then seldom clearly distinguished, recipes for recovery:
sometimes it tried to spend its way out of depression and sometimes it
tried to save its way to recovery. There is no reason for me to detail
these switches here, since this has already been done very comprehen-
sively by Lewis Kimmel (1959: 190ff.). It is more important here to stress
that, whilst the necessity for state centralization may have been strongly
implied by some of the policies adopted in both the welfare and
economic spheres, the Administration moved in this direction only
hesitantly and on a strictly pragmatic basis. Not only was Roosevelt's
Administration in no way committed to a crypto-fascist belief in any sort

of 'leader principle', despite what some critics to the left and right of it said at the time and even repeat today, but it was also in no way consciously Keynesian.

In the United States, then, a more centralized state emerged slowly and organically, and the structure that eventually crystallized was far less centralized than, and focused very differently from, the more social democratic apparatuses of Western Europe (cp. Waldo, 1948). The absence of a strong political challenge from labour allowed a significant amount of state power to devolve upon joint government/business agencies and committees, and this in turn allowed a rapid reversal of the constitutionally sanctioned asymmetry between the executive and legislative branches of government. Once large-scale industry had become the state's most important constituency, it gradually became self-evident to its embodiments that they should seek direct links with the executive in order to institutionalize their political interests. Even if they had not been encouraged in such a strategy by the Roosevelt Administration, they would have been forced to take it up on account of Congress' domination by other interest groups – southern conservatives, farmers, smaller businessmen and labour – all of whom were deeply suspicious of large-scale capital.

The Administration discovered early on that, as things stood, the passage of desired legislation was something of a lottery, where the most important determinant of success was the often totally unpredictable process whereby bills were initially assigned to committees for consideration and amendment. As a result it gradually moved towards seeking enabling legislation which would permit it to take action and advice on the issues of most vital concern to it without always having to go through Congress. It also realized that it could use its own taxing power rather than continue to have to attempt to cajole Congress into using its spending power for the financing of its programmes. Finally, the Administration even more slowly discovered and used what Louis Fischer has called 'the presidential spending power', that is, the capacity that the executive has to spend Congressionally approved funds in ways other than intended, through such ruses as: saving on lump-sum appropriations, reprogramming within accounts, transfers between accounts, retiming programme timetables, proclaiming impoundments, and, finally, claiming that the national security is at stake (cp. Karl, 1963: 197).

The major piece of Administration-sponsored legislation which exemplified and gave institutional form to this centralizing movement was the Reorganization Act of 1939 (Karl, 1963; Polenberg, 1966). The most important result of the passage of this Act was the provision of full legal recognition for the existence of a presidential staff, henceforth known as the Executive Office, and the confirmation of the extraction of its most potent element, the Bureau of the Budget, from the Treasury. However, instead of repeating the excellent accounts of this Act and their significance which already exist, I intend to return to my discussion of the Social Security Act.

A consideration of the Administration's activities in connection with its passage through Congress will enable me to make three further points about the centralizing process during its embryonic stage – each of which tends to support my stress on the 'organic', figuratively corporate liberal, nature of New Deal policies, rather than the teleological instrumentalism implicit in the analyses of those (Fraser and Gerstle, 1989: *passim*; Weir and Skocpol, 1985, for example) who would prefer to refer to them as in some sense 'Keynesian'. Firstly, it was the practical, executive-centred arrangements made to administer the relief programme and draw up the Social Security Bill that first suggested to the New Dealers the advantages of centralized policy formation and implementation (Perkins, 1946: 286). Secondly, it was again a practical issue, namely anxiety over the constitutionality of the bill, which led them to understand the possibilities inherent in the President's taxing power. Secretary Perkins described the circumstances of this realization most vividly:

> I drew courage from a bit of advice I got accidentally from Supreme Court Justice Stone, I had said to him in the course of a social occasion a few months earlier, that I had great hope of developing a social insurance system for the country, but that I was deeply uncertain of the method since, as I said laughingly, 'Your Court tells us what the Constitution permits.' Stone had whispered, 'The taxing power of the Federal Government, my dear; the taxing power is sufficient for everything you want and need.' This was a windfall. I told the President but bound him to secrecy as to the source of my sudden superior legal knowledge. I insisted in Committee on the taxing power as the method for building up the fund and determining its expenditure for unemployment and old-age benefits to be paid in the future. (Perkins, 1946: 286)

Thirdly, one of the earliest instances of the employment of 'presidential spending power' was the use made of what Perkins called 'risky techniques' of financing to get the social security apparatus established. Huey Long had successfully delayed the bill's passage, so that the Congressional session ended in the summer of 1935 without having authorized the necessary monies. Roosevelt's response to this was to say that same summer:

> 'Well, the NRA [National Recovery Administration] is being liquidated. There has been an appropriation from Congress to enable them to liquidate. You can take the people laid off there.' (Perkins, 1946: 299–300)

These activities in and around the struggle to create a social security system all, then, support my suggestion as to the practical sources of the realization of the emerging affinity between corporate liberalism and the centralization of the state. However, both this affinity and the distinctively limited nature of the centralization involved become still clearer, if one looks at the broader Administration strategy represented by the Reorganization Act and the establishment of the various advisory committees and Regulatory Commissions that these and other Acts either required or encouraged. Further, the spontaneous character of the realization of this affinity also becomes still clearer once it is appreciated that these measures were introduced long after the avowed centralizers, such as Tugwell, had lost their influence and had been replaced by the 'small is beautiful' lawyers, who drew their inspiration from Louis Brandeis, and whose chief spokesman was Felix Frankfurter. It is perhaps surprising that Roosevelt's Administration, which latterly became dominated by such champions of smallness and decentralization, should formulate the measures that established the corporate liberal state – the Brandeisians did after all simultaneously mount a double-pronged attack on bigness, one part of which was carried into law, namely the Public Utilities Holding Company Act (Leuchtenburg, 1963: 152ff.). Put more specifically, the surprise is caused by the contrast between the avowed individualism of these lawyers and Roosevelt's declaration in the course of his 1936 Inaugural Address: '[democracy does not depend] upon the absence of power . . . the Constitution of 1787 did not make our democracy impotent.'

There is no need to suppose hypocrisy or corruption in order to explain what appears to have been such a striking about-face on the part of the Brandeisian lawyers. The American Bar Association had indeed denounced what it called 'a flood of administrative legislation', which had upset the 'balanced order' of the separation of powers and threatened the judiciary, and they had blamed all this on a 'fifth column' of professors infatuated with 'continental ideas' (Auerbach, 1976: 191). However, as Jerold Auerbach has persuasively argued, there was an important and increasingly influential current within indigenous jurisprudence, namely Legal Realism (Hunt, 1977; Woodiwiss, 1990b: 148ff.), which supported just such legislative ideas and made any talk of external inspiration, whether continental or Keynesian, totally redundant. This current claimed to be non-political in contrast to the *laissez-faire*-inspired ideologues who dominated the American Bar Association (ABA). The guiding idea of the Realists as regards public law was that politics should be left to the executive and legislative branches of government, and that the judiciary should restrict itself to ensuring the clarity and fairness of legislation once it had been passed. It was not surprising, therefore, that lawyers identifying with this current should 'flock' to Washington during the New Deal to fill the legal vacuum left by the non-cooperation of their more traditional colleagues (Leuchtenburg, 1963: 164).

The influence of these lawyers was so great that Auerbach (1976) quite justifiably entitles the chapter in which he discusses it, 'The New Deal: A Lawyer's Deal'. However, the general circumstances within which this influence was obtained ensured that it was in fact far from non-political in its consequences. The Realists' underlying lawyerly commitment to the universal advisability of negotiation and compromise caused them to blunt the sharper edges of many proposals. Thus it was on the basis of Realist advice, rather than in direct response to any pressure from capital, that the Administration opted for the joint federal/state administration and financing of the unemployment provisions of the Social Security Act. Auerbach has summed up this aspect of the Brandeisian influence as follows:

> Lawyers guided New Deal solutions between bargaining extremes but invariably toward the existing balance of power between competing interest groups. Lawyers' skills (drafting, negotiation, compromise) and lawyers' values (process divorced from substance, means over ends) permitted New Deal achievements yet set New Deal boundaries. No substantive result was permitted to assume such transcendent importance as to rule out compromise, a value commitment that gave the New Deal its opportunistic, shallow side and made it all too willing to capitulate to private power-holders. . . Lawyers all too easily assumed that any social problem was amenable to resolution by enacting a statute, creating an administrative agency, and staffing it with law review editors. (1976: 227)

In sum, the Realists' belief in the political neutrality of their legal skills, plus their support for the notion of a public interest (Woodiwiss, 1990b: 154–6), fused with and greatly strengthened the belief in executive neutrality which by the late 1930s, was emerging as the chief justification for executive-focused, state centralization even amongst the more ideologically committed members of the Administration.

The Figurative Significance of the Social Security Act

Although the Social Security Act was consciously and manifestly, even if modestly, an instance of social engineering, I must make clear that when I speak of it as a figuration I am not saying that either its authors or its critics knew what the consequences of its promulgation would be. Quite the contrary, I use the postmodernist term 'figuration' rather than 'prefiguration' in this context because it suggests that the Act was but one aspect of a wider set of changes, of whose existence, let alone significance, contemporaries were profoundly unaware. Hence, perhaps, the absence of an at all developed interpretative preamble to the Act, like that which prefaced the Wagner Act.

In any event, the set of changes of which I am thinking were occurring at the level of what, in Foucauldian terminology, is called the 'discursive formation' (that is, at the level of the conditions of discursive possibility), and so were unlikely to be consciously apprehendable at the time. As a figuration, the Social Security Act, especially in its provisions as regards old age, confirmed what the more or less simultaneous passage of the Wagner Act also declared, namely that there was to be an enhanced respect for labour in the new America, provided that it was 'responsible' in the sense that it either paid its insurance contributions or could not do so for reasons totally beyond its control. It also confirmed, by the minimalist nature of the qualification to 'self-reliance' that it represented, as well as by the actuarial assumptions upon which its financing was based, that America would continue to be a society that aspired to provide 'opportunity' rather than 'equality' for its citizens. In addition, its administration, by requiring that every citizen or bona fide resident be issued with a social security number, created a basis upon which a distinction could be drawn between licit and illicit presences within the population, a distinction that was later to be repeated on a different basis as that between the loyal and the disloyal. Finally, the Act was figurative in negative as well as positive terms in that it confirmed that this new America would not necessarily be characterized by any enhanced respect for African-Americans, since the sectors of the economy – agriculture and domestic labour – in which the vast majority of the latter were to be found were not covered by it.

The Social Security Act, then, both exemplified and figuratively represented a rather particular set of changes to the objects of concern, to what sort of people were to be allowed a voice in determining these objects, and to the ways of delimiting them, as well as to the ways of talking and thinking about them. This set of changes pertained to the relations that either existed or, it was thought, should exist between the state and the citizenry, and was subsequently to become manifest in the discourse of corporate liberalism.

Elsewhere (Woodiwiss, 1990b: ch. 7), I have outlined these changes in more detail than is appropriate here. In the present context, it is sufficient to repeat that, apart from those associated with and directly embodied in the Social Security Act, the most important of these changes at the level of the discursive formation were: (1) those which were associated with the industrial relations system and partially embodied in the Taft–Hartley amendments to the Wagner Act, and which together rather narrowly defined and confined 'responsible unionism'; (2) those associated with and embodied in the class-structural changes that created millions of new 'opportunities' for those who were to become 'middle-class' Americans; and, finally, (3) those associated with and embodied in the requirement that anyone aspiring to, or enjoying, such 'opportunities', whether as individuals or members of trade unions, should be 'loyal' to both the companies and the state that provided them.

The Crystallization of Corporate Liberalism

As with any hegemonic regime, corporate liberalism, even in its more narrowly ideological sense, did not emerge out of nowhere, as a piece. Rather, it crystallized out of a complex of sets of ideological oppositions, whose last hurrah was the antagonism between the Republicans and the Wallace Progressives in the 1948 election (see Brick, 1986; Hamby, 1973; Lichtenstein, 1989; Pells, 1985). This antagonism may be summarized as one between *laissez-faire* liberalism and a very moderate variety of social democracy. The former insisted on a reassertion of absolute self-reliance, the crippling of trade unions, the limiting of opportunities to those who were self-reliant, and the identification of loyalty with anti-communism. By contrast, the latter wished to see an expansion of the welfare state, the further strengthening of responsible trade unions, the socializing or collectivizing of opportunities and a rapprochement with the Soviet Union. As the domestic and geo-political conditions of existence of this set of antagonisms crumbled, a version of the New Deal synthesis, whose enunciator in 1948 was President Truman, triumphed and was left in more or less sole control of the ideological field. Perhaps the most succinct summary of this synthesis is contained in the section of Truman's 1949 'Fair Deal' speech, in which he simultaneously debunks the 'scare word' tactics of the Republicans and distances his position from that of those to his left:

So the selfish interests. . . came up with a new set of scare words. Now they're talking about 'collectivism,' and 'statism,' and 'the welfare state.'
    The selfish interests don't know – in fact they don't care – what those words mean. They are using those words only because they want to turn the American people against the programs which the people want, and need, and for which the people voted last fall. . .
    The people want fair laws for labor. The selfish interests are against these laws because they mistakenly fear that their profits will be reduced; so they call that 'statism'.
    Well, we don't care what they call it.
    We believe that the workers in this country have a fundamental right to square treatment from employers. . .
    The people want a better social security system, improved education, and a national health program. The selfish interests are trying to sabotage these programs because they have no concern about helping the little fellow; and so they call this 'the welfare state.'
    Well, we don't care what they call it.
    We know that the little fellow is the backbone of this country, and we are dedicated to the principle that the government should promote the welfare of all the people.
    The spokesmen of these special interests say that these programs make the government too powerful and cause the people to lose their freedom. Well now, that is just not so. Programs like these make the people more independent – independent of the government of big business and corporate power.
    People who have opportunity to work and earn, and who have an assured income in their old age, are free. . .

Because of the ideological assymetry of American politics what Laclau and Mouffe (1985: 127–34) have termed Truman's set of equivalencies was considerably to the 'right' of the Western European norm. Corporate liberalism's hegemony was confirmed by the ideological torpor that descended upon the society after Truman's 1948 victory – a torpor which neither Eisenhower's promises to overturn the New Deal, nor McCarthy's attempt to make 'loyalty' the ideological touchstone, were able to lift (Woodiwiss, 1990b: 206ff.).
    To many, including most famously Bell (1960), the 1950s witnessed 'the end of ideology', or, to use Bell's subtitle, 'the exhaustion of political

ideas' – a diagnosis that in many ways prefigured, and indeed prepared the way for, the postmodernists' 'incredulity towards metanarratives'. As should be clear, I do not share Bell's view. On the contrary, my argument is that the 1950s saw the final crystallization of a new hegemonic project – that is, the 1950s saw an extremely energetic effort at the absorption of ideologies, led as it happens by Bell amongst others (Pells, 1985), rather than their simple exhaustion. Thereafter, only arguments couched in terms of the component signs of the social modernism that they were to make out of corporate liberalism – the new 'secular religion', it seems to me – could expect to be heard, let alone acted upon. And this was in no small measure thanks to a stoical, world-weary reading of the social diagnosis implicit in aesthetic modernism (to the effect that self-reflexiveness, fragmentariness, imperfection, etc. are *all* one can expect or indeed need in the modern world). This reading provided a convenient resting place in the course of a very uncomfortable journey on the part of Bell and many of his generation – a journey which began with socialist 'estrangement', ended in 'reconciliation' with the status quo, and was explicitly justified by American socialism's failure to measure up to the demands of 'modernity' (Bell, 1967: 5; Brick, 1986; *passim*; Wolfe, 1988: 66–8).

The result was that when, after 1952, the major political parties put forward programmes which were based simply on competing readings of corporate liberalism rather than on alternatives to it, they heard few intellectual demurrals and instead heard themselves being praised for their modernity. Thus the incumbent Republicans emphasized that the rapidly growing number of opportunities were a reward for self-reliance, responsible unionism and loyalty, and that the state should not interfere with this process; their Democratic challengers, by contrast, stressed that the availability of opportunity should be broadened somewhat; that ways should be found to help those who, through no fault of their own, had difficulty being self-reliant; that responsible unions had a role to play in the broadening of opportunity; that there was nothing in any way unpatriotic or disloyal about espousing such ideas; and, finally, that the national interest required the state to intervene in order to encourage such developments.

A Special Kind of Hope

For reasons that will be spelt out in some detail in the following chapter, by the end of the 1950s the hegemony of corporate liberalism, become social modernism, appeared to be very secure. Thanks to a Congressionally voted change to the Pledge of Allegiance, the United States even became 'One nation *under God*, indivisible, with liberty and justice for all' (the italicized words were inserted in 1954). All this occurred despite the voicing of some concerns as regards the state of some of its principal conditions of existence – economic growth had slowed down, technological unemployment was increasing, and African-Americans were becoming increasingly militant in their rejection of their exclusion from 'the good life' vouchsafed by social modernism. In promising to attend to these concerns and, particularly, in refusing to accept that there were ultimately any limits on what America might achieve for its citizenry, the incoming President Kennedy implicitly declared his allegiance to the modernist gloss on corporate liberalism and to what David Apter was later to call 'its special kind of hope'.

This was the same kind of hope that David Riesman had presciently expressed at the beginning of the 1950s when, in his sociological bestseller *The Lonely Crowd*, he spoke of:

> The new possibilities opening up for the individual [which] are possibilities not so much of entering a new class but rather for changing life style and changing character within the middle class. (1950: 293)

As he explained further, drawing on a 1949 essay published in a collection aptly entitled *Years of the Modern*, these were possibilities for what he called 'autonomy' and were now available to a far larger group than ever before:

> For, as the inner-directed man is more self-conscious than his tradition-directed predecessor and as the other-directed man is more self-conscious still, the autonomous man growing up under conditions that encourage self-consciousness can disentangle himself from the adjusted others only by a further move toward even greater self-consciousness. His autonomy depends not upon the ease with which he may deny or disguise his emotions but, on the contrary, upon the success of his effort to recognize and respect his own feelings, his own potentialities, his own limitations. This is not a quantitative matter, but in part an awareness of the problem of self-consciousness itself, an achievement of a higher order of abstraction. (Riesman, 1950: 305)

Interestingly, as Riesman himself was later to acknowledge with some bewilderment, few of his readers in the early 1950s paid much attention to the possibility of 'autonomy'. They preferred instead to join with such as C.W. Mills (1951), and later William H. Whyte (1963), in regretting the passing of the 'inner-directed' type and fulminating against the arrival of the 'other-directed'. The result was paradoxical. The promise of modernism only became widely known just as the conditions which gave it plausibility were beginning to crumble (that is in the late 1960s); and some of those who, ostensibly at least, refused to believe it (the hippies, for example) did so because of a preference for a culture based on the very 'play' which Riesman had suggested was essential to the growth of individual 'autonomy'.

Despite the contemporary tendency to look back on the 1950s and the early 1960s as yet another American 'golden age', the robustness of the economy and therefore the solidity of the grounds for the optimism of the period should not be exaggerated. Chapter 4 will provide a review of the condition of American capitalism at the four points of tension identified in the Introduction, a review which will emphasize the increasing softness of any grounds for optimism.

2
THE SOCIETY THAT WOULD BE MODERN

By the late 1960s, the proportion of the labour force which was to some degree contradictorily positioned, and was supposedly therefore enjoying 'the possibilities' to which Riesman had looked forward, stood at between 37 and 59 per cent, depending upon whether a high or low estimate is adopted (Wright, 1978). Between 1950 and 1960, the number of such positionings rose by roughly 30 per cent for each of the pertinent occupational categories, except for that of 'foremen and craftsmen', which remained constant. This rate of increase was some 20 per cent faster than it had been in the ten years before 1950 (R. Edwards et al., 1972: 178). Thus, in discussing what happened under the Eisenhower Administrations, one is concerned not only with a substantial increase in the number of persons who were contradictorily positioned, but also with a significant increase in the rate at which such positionings were appearing. In sum, one is concerned with a significant blurring of the boundary between the embodiments of the capitalist and working classes in many workplaces. Before I attempt to specify the consequences of this blurring for the balance of forces between the two classes, I will outline the state's role in facilitating and giving a particular form and significance to it. To this end, I will begin by outlining the Eisenhower Administration's expansionist economic policy, especially its monetary aspect, and more specifically still its consumer credit, transportation, housing and education policies.

The Making of a Modernist Utopia

The 1950s was a period of more or less continuous prosperity, during which high levels of profitability were maintained and any downturn in the economy was more or less successfully corrected by reasonably prompt state action. The basis of this prosperity was the rising productivity of labour, which rose by 33 per cent over the decade. This was made possible by the settlement made with organized labour alluded to earlier and discussed at some length elsewhere (Woodiwiss, 1990b: 194–206), whereby any control that labour had over the process of production was progressively surrendered in exchange for 'high wages', seniority systems, grievance procedures, etc.

Once the new and initially somewhat narrowed system of differentials had been established, as it had been by the end of the 1940s, capital once again obtained more or less unqualified control over the wage system. The net effect of this was a substantial widening of differentials by the end of the 1950s, especially between those positioned solely by the working class and those positioned contradictorily. In other words, the contradictorily positioned shared disproportionately in the prosperity, in that their incomes rose by more than would have been allowed by any productivity increases they may have contributed to. The 40 per cent increase in money earnings received by those positioned as proletarian 'service and non-farm labourers' represented a 15 per cent increase in real earnings over the decade. The 50 per cent increase in money earnings received by those positioned as proletarian 'salesmen and operatives' represented an increase in real earnings of 19 per cent. The 60 per cent increase in money earnings received by the sometimes contradictorily positioned 'craftsmen and clerical workers' represented a 23 per cent increase in real earnings. Finally, the 65 per cent increase in money earnings received by the always contradictorily positioned 'professionals and managers' represented a 25 per cent increase in real earnings.

Thus the income differentials between those solely positioned by the working class and those positioned contradictorily increased consistently and substantially throughout the 1950s. Indeed, the statistics on which the above percentages are based, being for 'money earnings' rather than 'money income', give an underestimate of the growth in differentials, since those who embody contradictory positionings are more likely both to be in receipt of fringe benefits and to under-report their incomes than those who embody solely working class positionings (H. Miller, 1966: 80ff.; Perlo, 1973: 228ff.).

The increasing relative 'affluence' or 'disposable income' of the contradictorily positioned permitted a dramatic widening of credit availability to people who, possessing no 'wealth' or collateral to speak of, would not otherwise have qualified for it. This development, in addition to state roadbuilding and housing policies, enabled those who were contradictorily positioned to acquire consumer durables such as automobiles and suburban houses, which made their relatively high positions in the occupational hierarchy very visible. Thus the use that the 'middle classes' made, and indeed continue to make, of credit may be distinguished from that made by the embodiments of the working class. The 'middle classes' tend to use credit in order to acquire 'status goods', whilst those positioned solely by the working class resort to it in order to acquire 'material goods': that is, those that have become part of Marx's 'traditional standard of life', such as refrigerators, washing machines, cheap or secondhand cars and 'tract' housing (Caplowitz, 1963).

The 1950s, then, saw a marked differentiation of 'lifestyles' and rapid residential segregation as between those who were positioned contradictorily and those who were positioned by the working class alone. The bases of solidarity among the embodiments of the working class were already attenuated by gender, ethnic and racialized divisions, and, not surprisingly, all the individualized consumer activity and its visibly divergent outcomes further undermined them. Those whose lives were changed by the developments gradually came to understand what was happening to them in social modernist terms, and what C.W. Mills (1956) called a 'conservative mood' began to suffuse American society. The result was that the Republicans dominated politics, and the social critics who received by far the most attention were representatives of a 'radical right' (Bell, 1955) which spoke for those who found the ongoing reconstruction of the status system confusing and even threatening.

As was indicated at the beginning of this chapter, the focus of this account of the Eisenhower Administration's economic policy will be on its monetary and non-defence fiscal policies, since they were the most important instruments of economic management at the time. Defence expenditure will be discussed at some length in Chapter 4. For now, it is sufficient simply to note that it affected incomes as a whole through its 'priming' function – that is, by putting 'surplus' capital to work and in this way sustaining the level of aggregate demand – and, because defence-related industries were becoming ever more capital-intensive, it contributed to the increase in the number of contradictory class positionings.

The State's Management of the Economy

In order to understand how monetary policy in general, and interest rate policy in particular, may affect the growth of contradictory class positionings, one has simply to realize that changing interest rates changes capital's costs and so changes the amount available for paying wages, especially that available for paying the discretionary, revenue element in the incomes of the contradictorily positioned. Thus differentials tend to rise under 'easy' money conditions and fall when they become tighter. In sum, the state may make it easier or harder for capital to expand and to meet whatever exigencies arise as the process whereby surplus labour is appropriated becomes either more complex or simply different (Woodiwiss, 1990a: 180–1). If it lowers interest rates, both of these activities become easier. If it raises them, both become harder. In the former situation, the focus of the struggle between the embodiments of the classes, and presumably also capital's best hopes of advancing its position, will tend to be inside the individual production units, whilst in the latter they will tend to be at the level of the whole society or the polity. Given that interest rates were generally low during the 1950s, it is possible to understand why – ideological resistance aside – state intervention in the economy took, if not a *laissez-faire* form, then an enabling rather than an activist one; *ceteris paribus*, the former stance allows individual capitals the maximum freedom as to how best to pursue their efforts to appropriate surplus labour.

In his State of the Union Message of 1953, Eisenhower summed up his Administration's economic policy in the following terms: having mentioned balanced budgets, debt and tax reduction, fiscal and monetary checks on inflation, he described them as 'incentives that inspire creative initiative'. The 'hands off' rhetoric that Eisenhower employed on such occasions, should not, however, deflect attention from the fact that the one area of the state structure that he was reorganizing even then was the section of the executive concerned with economic affairs. He appointed a special presidential assistant on economic matters, Hauge, and he revivified the Council of Economic Advisers (CEA), which had been the object of such sustained hostility from the Republican Congress that it had only been voted nine months' funds in 1953. The Council was restructured and centralized with most of its power vested in the chair, which was taken by Arthur Burns, a man attracted by the practical promise, if not by the theoretical underpinnings, of Keynesianism.

In addition, Eisenhower created the Advisory Board on Economic Growth and Stability, whereon sat the heads, or representatives, of the Treasury, the Departments of Agriculture, Commerce and Labor, the Federal Reserve, the Budget Bureau and the Executive Office, and which was chaired by the chair of the CEA (Flash, 1965: 101ff.). In so doing, Eisenhower created a mechanism whereby all the abovementioned economic measures, including balancing the budget, could be coordinated in relation to a closely monitored economy so as to 'inspire creative initiative'. He undoubtedly hoped that this 'initiative' would prove to be self-sustaining, but he had constructed a mechanism whereby any faltering could be picked up quickly and corrective action undertaken. In the event, the CEA and the Advisory Committee did indeed become the principal means by which the state's capacity for economic intervention was coordinated.

It was very quickly impressed upon the Administration, in a somewhat galling way, that such intervention was unavoidable. In order to finance the Korean War, Truman had enacted an excess profits tax and increased income tax rates. The first was due to be removed automatically in June, and the increase in tax rates to be reversed in December, 1953. However, such were the fears concerning the inflationary impact of any tax cuts at a time of high, albeit decreasing, state expenditure that the Administration was forced to ask Congress to extend the excess profits tax for a further six months, even though it must have regarded it as cramping initiative. On the other hand, the Administration must have been impressed and pleased by the fact that, when the tax finally was removed at the end of 1953, much of the profit loss caused by the recession consequent upon the ending of the war was recouped (Stein, 1969: 95). No doubt this was remembered as the recession deepened in 1958 and Eisenhower came close to endorsing the real tax cut of his own making which he had always hoped would be possible. In the end, however, what is most significant about Eisenhower's general fiscal policy is that it never in fact took the form of the tax cuts that Republican ideology would have led one to expect. Instead, it took the form of increasing, decreasing and retiming state expenditures, especially on armaments (see below, p. 68ff.) and with but little concern for budgetary deficits (Flash, 1965: 151). In other words, general fiscal policy evolved in response to the demands of an economy of which the state had become an integral part and which, as a critical part of the 'affluent', 'middle class', or 'modern' society, was gradually becoming understood to possess a different and more compelling intrinsic ideological significance as compared to that of the party's formal ideology.

The Economy's Management of the State

In order to understand how this happened, it is necessary to consider the state's monetary policy under Eisenhower. Milton Friedman and his collaborators (1963) entitle the chapter in which they discuss monetary policy under Eisenhower 'The Revival of Monetary Policy'. Flash concludes his discussion of the interest rate changes of 1953–4 as follows: 'The Federal Reserve's steps to ease credit appear to have constituted the most important series of measures adopted consciously for counter-cyclical purposes' (1965: 151).

He estimates that the ½ per cent lowering of the rediscount rate and the 1 or 2 per cent lowering of reserve requirements released $1.5 billion of reserves and created a potential expansion of $9 billion. A period of monetary restraint followed in 1955, and another period of easing in 1958. However, Friedman et al. argue that the state's capacity to increase the money supply was more important and more widely influential than direct state action to raise or lower interest rates, a conclusion shared by Cornard (1966). Despite the ups and downs of interest rates, Friedman et al. (1963: 592) conclude that 'the outstanding monetary feature (of the period 1948–60) was the unusually steady growth of the money stock'. Elsewhere they describe this as 'a near revolutionary change'. By this they mean that for the first time it was realized that changes in the money supply could have an independent effect on the economic climate (cp. Cornard, 1966: 64–6). An important contributory factor to the increasing effectivity of monetary policy was the 45 per cent increase in the velocity of money, which was itself the consequence of the build-up in demand over the war years, the generally higher level of interest rates in the postwar years as compared to the 1930s, the rise of 'near money', and the expectation of economic stability (M. Friedman et al., 1963: 641).

Before moving on to examine the more specific effects of these policies and developments, I should make the point that this important change had required, and was confirmed by, a significant reordering of the internal relationships of the state apparatuses concerned with economic management. Specifically, after a long struggle, the Federal Reserve was freed from the tutelage of the Treasury. In 1951, an 'Accord' was formulated between the two institutions which allowed 'the Fed' to develop its own monetary policy (Stein, 1969: ch. 10). The first serious test of this new freedom occurred during the recession of 1953, when the Federal Reserve directly countered the Treasury's efforts to raise interest rates, and won (Vatter, 1963: 91–2). The Federal Reserve is a regulatory agency and not a department of state like the Treasury. For this reason, it is even more likely to give priority to the needs of the regulated (that is, money capital) than the Treasury, which always has to square any favouring of 'special' interests with the interests of the President's party.

To similar effect, federal agencies: (1) encouraged the growth of consumer credit and refrained from instituting direct controls over the level of credit or purposes for which credit could be granted; (2) developed a massive programme of highway construction at the behest of a 'highway lobby' which was dominated by the auto industry, and then left its administration to the states, at which level small and medium-size capital still had considerable political clout; (3) encouraged residential construction, but primarily by guaranteeing mortgages for private housing rather than by offering grants for public housing; and (4) supported educational expansion at all levels, but allowed the prevailing hierarchical pattern of state, local and private provision to continue.

According to Vatter (1963: 99), it was the steady growth of consumer spending that ensured the continuance of economic growth after the ending of the Korean War. Although this growth was largely the product of the general increase in incomes, it is easy to see that the greater freedom allowed to financial institutions also contributed significantly to this result. At the end of World War II, Americans as individuals were virtually debt-free, but by 1950 they were buying 69 per cent, and by 1960 88 per cent, of their consumer durables on instalment credit (Sweezy and Magdorf, 1972: 16). The only means by which the magnitude of consumer credit could be controlled was changes in the prime rate and bank loan–deposit ratios, both of which were the preserve of the Federal Reserve. In other words, although the state had become an integral part of the economy, the government had virtually no control over the economy, which consequently developed more or less just as capital desired. Furthermore, although the Federal Reserve may increase or restrict the amount and cost of money available, it remains up to the individual institutions how they use the resources they have available. And, in the end, the high profitability of the consumer credit industry ensured a more or less continuous increase in credit extensions.

By 1963, 32 per cent of those with incomes of $3,000 and below had incurred some instalment debt, but only 9 per cent of them had incurred a debt of more than $500; that is, had used it to purchase items typically regarded as 'status goods' such as new cars, expensive furnishings, etc. By contrast, more than 53 per cent of those in the income range $3,000–$5,000 (that is, the best paid operatives and clerical workers) had some instalment debt and 28 per cent of them owed more than $500. These percentages rose through the occupations that I have termed 'contradictorily positioned', reaching their peak in the $7,500–

$10,000 range at 63 per cent and 41 per cent, respectively.

Another credit development, which was to become much more important in the 1970s and 1980s, was the appearance of the credit card. Diners Club cards were first issued in 1950, but they were then and for most of the following decade only available to the very highest income groups. Their dispersion through all the middle-income groups, along with the appearance of American Express, Visa and Mastercharge cards, documents an important change in the use of credit. In the first half of the 1950s, as consumer durables became easier and easier to obtain, their ever wider dispersion created a strong demand for related services. The provision of these was very underdeveloped at both the product and the labour market levels and therefore latterly came to offer superior opportunities for profit-making as compared to the manufacture of durables. Thus, once the dispersion of durables and especially 'status goods' reached a particular point, defined by a certain level of disposable income and represented by the $3,000 line in 1963, the dictates of profitability shifted both investment and the provision of credit towards the service area, with the result that, by 1960, fully 40 per cent of all consumer spending was on services. This slowed the consumption of durables and so froze their dispersion in a pattern of particular significatory import. In this way, then, participation in the modern, middle-American lifestyle was restricted to the contradictorily positioned plus the best paid and usually unionized embodiments of the working class (Vatter, 1963: 104ff.).

The conclusions that may be drawn from the above are that the profit-centred dynamics of American society dispersed the possession of 'status goods' differentially through the occupational structure, and also froze their dispersion in such a way as to reinforce a particular motivational strategy and a particular distribution of power within the corporations and therefore the wider society. And the latter both served in their turn to ensure the embourgeoisement and therefore the continuing complicity of the contradictorily positioned in the process whereby a difference between necessary and surplus labour is maintained. Thus a new and social-structural dimension should be added to Robert Lynd's insightful comment:

> The business of selling commercial products as substitutive reactions for more subtle forms of adjustment to job insecurity, social insecurity, monotony, loneliness, failure to marry and other *situations of tension* has advanced to an effective fine art. The tendency of contemporary merchandising is to elevate more and more commodities to the class of personality buffers. At each exposed point the alert merchandiser is ready with a panacea. (1933: 867; emphasis added)

In 1953, Arthur Burns concisely summarized the social significance of highway construction, and even pointed to its role in increasing the fractionalization of those who had previously been positioned solely by the working class, when he specified the nature of its multiplier effects as:

'those of encouraging community subdivisions, of creating suburbs, of developing stores and shopping areas' (Flash, 1965: 145; see also Fellman and Brandt, 1973). At that time federal highway expenditure was already running at $5 billion per annum and Burns underlined his appreciation of such effects by supporting the passage of the Federal Aid to Highways Act of 1954, which was described as the 'largest highway bill ever passed', and which added some $2 billion to highway expenditures for each of the years 1956 and 1957. Finally, he formed the President's Advisory Committee on a National Highway Program, thus formalizing the 'Highway Lobby'. This body produced proposals for an Interstate Highway System of some 35,000 miles of rural highways and some 6,000 miles of urban superhighways and received $4.1 billion of Federal funds under the provisions of the Highway Revenue Act of 1956 (Gelfand, 1975; R. Davies, 1966).

Such expenditure did indeed create 'community subdivisions', though perhaps not of the kind that Burns had in mind. This was because federal aid to housing took the form of mortgage guarantees by the Federal Housing Association (FHA) and the Veterans' Administration, rather than the financing of public housing. As Flash has pointed out, the Eisenhower Administration's housing policies:

> were directed less toward realizing 'decent homes and suitable living environment for every American family' and encouraging 'a high annual volume of residential construction' as specified in the Housing Act of 1949 than toward, in the words of the [President's Advisory Committee on Government Housing Policies and Programs] report, 'facilitating the operation of [a strong, free, competitive economy in order] to provide adequate housing for all people'. (1965: 145; see also, Wolfe, 1981b: 82–8)

As a consequence, the suburbs that grew in the interstices of the highway system were left to develop, like the consumer credit industry that they helped to spawn, solely under the influence of 'market forces', which were as often shaped by class-divisive and racist discourses as by more narrowly economic factors. Any hope there might have been that residential segregation would decrease in a more affluent and modern America disappeared with the Administration's refusal to embark on a massive public housing programme informed by some sort of communitarian discourse. Indeed, the growth of the suburbs and the effects of highway construction in urban areas seem to have radically increased both this segregation and its baleful social consequences (cp. Sennett, 1973).

This, of course, was not at all surprising, given that houses and their location are the most important of 'status goods'. By 1965, the percentages of particular income groups owning their own homes were as follows: for the under $3,000 group, 40 per cent; for the $3,000–$5,000 group, 45 per cent; for the $5,000–$7,500 group, 60 per cent; and for the $15,000 and up group, 90 per cent (Flash, 1965: 127; Parker, 1973: 157). In other words, the distribution of houses as 'status goods' was even more skewed towards the contradictorily positioned than was that of the more expensive consumer durables. Finally, because housing had become the principal form of wealth, its unequal distribution made the difference between the modern 'lifestyle' of those positioned contradictorily and that of those positioned solely by the working class transferable to other generations.

The last of the more specific effects of the Administration's expansionist and interventionist economic policies to be referred to here is that produced by the hierarchist education and especially higher education policy. This effect was to make the intergenerationally transferable nature of the difference between the contradictorily positioned and those positioned solely by the working class appear to rest upon meritocratic grounds (that is, to rest upon supposedly superior intelligence and effort rather than unequal access to educational opportunities) (Bowles and Gintis, 1976).

Conclusion

In sum, then, given the absence of a politically powerful, European-style, social democratic labour movement, the most important social consequence of the 'affluence' of the 1950s was a striking expansion of the number of contradictory positionings or 'opportunities' in the class structure, a radical enhancement of the social distance between their embodiments and those who embodied only the working class, a shift in the balance of class forces which was very favourable to capital, and a marked strengthening of the hegemonic position of the emerging social modernism.

3

A MODERNIZING DISCOURSE

Riesman and the later modernization theorists, whose more direct source of inspiration was Talcott Parsons, were moved by a sometimes explicit but usually implicit desire to formulate an alternative to 'soviet communism' that could give some ideological coherence to the cause of a 'West' which included the four principal antagonists of the Second World War (Dower, 1975: intro.). As Riesman saw it: '(For) . . . men standing on the threshold of new possibilities of being and becoming . . . the Communists . . . have become perhaps the most *reactionary* and most menacing force in world politics . . .' (1950: 248; emphasis added).

Modernization theory itself arose in the course of a more direct confrontation with 'communism', one which took place in what was later to be called the 'Third World'. Thus, as David Harrison (1988) has recently reminded us, the first major postwar collection of American discussions of the development prospects for such countries, *The Progress of Underdeveloped Areas*, edited by Bert Hoselitz (1952), was in part a response to the Point Four aid programme which had been launched by President Truman in the same 'Fair Deal' speech that saw the first ceremonial crystallization of corporate liberalism (see above, p. 27). The ideological pluralism still evident in this volume rapidly disappeared as the 'pattern variable' schema developed by Parsons came to determine the dominant conceptions of both the ends of, and the obstacles to, modernization. If one opts for what were quickly defined as the 'modern' rather than 'traditional' choices presented by the schema – that is, if one opts for 'affective neutrality' (self-discipline), 'self-orientation' (the privileging of individual interests), 'universalism' (the application of universal standards) and 'achievement' (judging people by their achievements) – one opts for a set of social goals derived from the aforementioned world-weary reading of aesthetic modernism (see above, p. 28) and an idealized conception of the United States (D. Harrison, 1988: chs. 1, 2; Robertson and Turner, 1991: *passim*; Taylor, 1979: ch. 1).

In this way, then, and in a move which seems more and more bizarre the longer one thinks about it, an aestheticized version of the United States' hegemonic ideology was transmuted into social scientific terms, so that ideological pluralism disappeared from the mainstream of American development studies, along with any awareness that such studies were in the thrall of any sort of ideology. Moreover, this lack of awareness deepened as social scientists began to acknowledge the idealized character of their vision of modernity and so make it into a goal for Americans as well as others to pursue; the meaning of the very term 'ideology' changed and shrank as the *way* in which things were believed came to be regarded as more indicative of an ideology than what was believed (see Hoffer, 1989).

Modernization on the Home Front

During the latter part of Eisenhower's second term there was increasing dissatisfaction with both the economy and the state's supposed management of it. Industrial capacity was underutilized, unemployment was refusing to fall, productivity was lagging, profitability was erratic and, contradictorily, the rate of inflation was rising. Nevertheless, no one appears to have been seriously worried by any of this: the term 'stagflation' had not yet been invented. Also, none of the indicators commonly depended upon by social analysts suggested that anything untoward was happening. Union growth had stagnated, but the rank and file appeared to be more concerned by the corruption of their leaders, as exposed in the course of the Congressional hearings associated with the formulation and passage of the Landrum Griffin Act of 1959, than by their own as well as their leaders' complacency. African-Americans were disappointed by the slow rate at which the restoration of their civil rights was proceeding, but they still evinced tremendous faith in constitutional procedures. There was some concern amongst the 'middle classes' about the materialism of their culture, but there was little evidence that any of those so positioned intended to enhance the meaningfulness of their lives through any kind of action. In short everything appeared 'cool'. And, as Erving Goffman (1959) was already and appropriately saying, 'coolness' was simply (complexly?) a product of 'impression management' on the part of the masses of the 'other-directeds'. Out of sight of the practitioners of the new social science orthodoxies, things were warming up, however. Industrial workers were losing faith in their leaders and the deal the latter had made with the corporations. The seeds of the rank and file movement of the 1960s were germinating (Peck, 1963; Swados, 1973; Weir, 1973). The techniques of non-violent resistance advocated principally by Martin Luther King had already proved their effectiveness in the Montgomery bus boycott of 1955, and African-American people were increasingly impressed by the relevance of these techniques to the conditions they faced. They were about to take 'direct action' in pursuit of the constitutional rights that they had for so long been unable to exercise. The 'middle classes' were beginning to shrug off the inhibitions that McCarthyism had made so advisable. Acute social commentators such as Jules Fieffer were satirizing various aspects of 'middle class life' and the Beats were trying very hard (too hard?) not to be part of it. Discussions of 'something else' began again as socialist clubs reappeared on the campuses of Berkeley, Chicago and Madison in the course of 1958. Clark Kerr was about to have his famous judgement as to the passivity of American students proved very badly wrong, and David Riesman was about to have his advice accepted:

> . . . hearing undergraduate complaints in the late fifties [he] wrote, 'when I
> ask such students what they have done about these things, they are surprised
> at the very thought they could do anything. They think that I am joking when
> I suggest that, *if things came to the worst,* they could picket. . . It seems to
> me that students don't want to believe that their activities might make a
> difference, because in a way, they profit from their lack of commitment to
> what they are doing. (Schlesinger, 1965: 739; emphasis added)

Little did he know that the worst was just around the corner, especially
because many students were about to feel that they had been already, or
were about to be, deprived of the very expectation of profit that he
correctly regarded as a central reason for their passivity.

A Thoroughly Modern President

However, shortly before the worst occurred, there arrived in the White
House a President whom many were soon to regard as the best. Moved
by the same ideological imperative as Riesman and the modernizationists,
but even less diffident about emphasizing his anti-communism, President
Kennedy adopted a remarkably similar tone and language as he formally
converted the scholars' goal of modernization into a national one. Thus
fragments of the discourses of modernization and anti-communism may
be found sitting comfortably alongside one another in the 'New Frontier'
speech he made in 1960 when accepting his party's nomination to be its
Presidential candidate:

> The times are too grave, the challenge too urgent, and the stakes too high –
> to permit the customary passions of political debate . . . if we open a quarrel
> between the present and the past, we shall be in danger of losing the future.
>   Today our concern must be with that future. For the world is changing. The
> old era is ending. The old ways will not do . . . [because] communist influence
> has penetrated further into Asia, stood astride the Middle East and now festers
> some ninety miles off the coast of Florida. . .
>   Here at home the changing face of the future is equally revolutionary. The
> New Deal and the Fair Deal were bold measures for their generations – but this
> is a new generation. . .
>   All over the world . . . young men are coming to power . . . young men who
> can cast off the old slogans and delusions and suspicions. . .
>   . . . the problems are not all solved and the battles are not all won – and we
> stand today on the edge of a New Frontier – the frontier of the 1960s – a fron-
> tier of unknown opportunities and perils – a frontier of unfulfilled hopes and
> threats. . .
>   [And] I tell you the New Frontier is here, whether we seek it or not. Beyond
> that frontier are uncharted areas of science and space, unsolved problems of
> peace and war, unconquered pockets of ignorance and prejudice, unanswered
> questions of poverty and surplus. . .

Kennedy deployed the same technocratic and modernizationist rhetoric
during the succeeding campaign, thereby echoing Bell, who, like Riesman,
was a highly energetic, proto-modernizationist:

There is now, more than ever, some need for utopia, in the sense that men need – as they have always needed – some vision of their potential, some manner of fusing passion with intelligence. Yet the ladder to the City of Heaven can no longer be a 'faith ladder,' but an empirical one: a utopia has to specify *where* one wants to go, *how* to get there, the costs of the enterprise, and some realization of and justification for the determination of *who* is to pay. (Bell, 1960: 405; emphasis in the original)

It was upon such bases, then, that Kennedy lambasted the Republicans for allowing the occurrence of a 'missile gap' between the United States and the Soviet Union, as well as for allowing the persistence of 'islands of poverty' (see, for example, the texts of his debates with Nixon in S. Kraus, 1962). He then proceeded to embark upon the 'conversion of ideas into social levers', something Bell had (1960: 400) suggested in the very same paper is only possible with respect to just the kind of 'total ideology' that no longer existed in the United States.

The Need for a 'Social Lever'

The fact that Kennedy's famous Inaugural prescription – 'ask not what your country can do for you, ask what you can do for your country' – was totally inadequate as a guide to policy making and the speed with which he realized this, may best be demonstrated by considering the very rapid evolution of his economic policy. It has often been said that Kennedy lacked interest in domestic as compared to foreign affairs and that this indicated a certain weakness on his part in terms of both character and political will. The suggestion is that achievements in foreign affairs gain easier recognition amongst historians and so appeal to those more vainglorious Presidents who are preoccupied with how history will judge them. Also foreign affairs are generally recognized as being within the prerogative of the executive branch and so appeal to Presidents who lack the stomach to embroil themselves with Congress. However, I will argue that President Kennedy embroiled himself deeply in domestic, if not Congressional, politics, and by so doing displayed an unusual degree of awareness of that interdependence of foreign and domestic policy of which another Kennedy (1987) has recently reminded us.

The significance of domestic policy to a particular Administration cannot be gauged simply by reference to the number of directly interventionist measures it introduces. Rather, it may be judged best by reference to the appropriateness and effectiveness of whatever policy or even non-policy it adopts. On this basis I would argue that, as many have noted, Kennedy did indeed learn a lot from Neustadt's *Presidential Power: The Politics of Leadership* (1960), but not so much because he wished to be counted a hero as because he wanted to be effective. Thus what he learnt from Neustadt was that:

'The essence of a President's persuasive task with congressmen and everybody else is to induce them to believe that what he wants of them is what their own appraisal of their own responsibilities requires them to do in their own interest, not his . . .'. (Cater, 1972: 14)

Bruce Miroff, summarizing the conclusions reached in his exhaustive review of Kennedy's presidency, shows how well Kennedy learnt this lesson: 'he calculated carefully the effect of supporting unsuccessful measures in Congress, sensitive to a possible decline in prestige which would diminish his store of power' (1976: 29).

It may not have been what he had initially intended, but Kennedy in fact expended by far the greatest proportion of his patiently amassed store of political capital on a very substantial modernizationist intervention in the economy on behalf of capital. This task was given priority over all others, whether they were the alleviation of poverty, the dismantling of southern racism or the quietening of the growing youthful unrest. As Wolfe (1981b) has emphasized, the hope was that quickened economic 'growth' would dissolve all of these problems more or less automatically. As Walter Heller was later to put it in a way which nicely illustrates social modernism's obeisance to 'the myth of deliverance':

policies that enable an economy to grow and prosper give substance to Presidential pledges to 'get the country moving again' or to move toward a great and good society. That society takes root far more readily in the garden of growth than in the desert of stagnation. When the cost of fulfilling a people's aspirations can be met out of a growing horn of plenty – instead of robbing Peter to pay Paul – ideological roadblocks melt away, and consensus replaces conflict. (1966: 11–12)

President Kennedy himself summarized the situation which he faced and outlined his aims in the following words:

In the past seven years, our rate of growth has slowed disturbingly. In the past three and one-half years, the gap between what we can produce and what we do produce has threatened to become chronic . . . Realistic aims for 1961 are to reverse the downward trend in our economy, to narrow the gap of unused potential, to abate the waste and misery of unemployment. . . For 1962 and 1963 our program must aim at expanding American productive capacity at a rate that shows the world the vigor and vitality of a free economy. (quoted in Lekachman, 1969: 176)

His problems were: an unemployment rate of 7 per cent; a growth rate of 3 per cent; an inflation rate of 3 per cent; a productivity rate of 1.9 per cent; an unused capacity rate of 20 per cent. And his goals were: to reduce unemployment to 4 per cent; to increase growth to 5 per cent; to hold inflation more or less steady; to restore productivity to at least its postwar average of 2.5 per cent; to reduce unused capacity as much as possible. By the mid-1960s virtually all of these goals had been achieved. One must conclude therefore that, on the surface at least, Kennedy's economic policy was a great success.

In spite of the impressiveness of this achievement, subsequent commentators have been singularly unwilling to grant the Administration credit for it. On the one hand, economic historians have tended to point instead to the intrinsic strength of the economy and the advances made in economic science. On the other hand, politically oriented historians have refused to be at all impressed by the Kennedy Administration's economic record. They have preferred to emphasize Johnson's political acumen and post-assassination guilt for any retrospective lustre it may have gained. To my mind, both sets of judgements point up the artificiality and dangers of such disciplinary boundaries (cp. S. Harris, 1964: ch. 5).

Economic historians, or rather in this case economists turned historians, do not of course neglect political factors when making their analyses. However, even when they have as acute an understanding of them as Kennedy-insider James Tobin, they seldom seem to appreciate either their intractability or the methods necessary to neutralize them. Thus Tobin concludes his discussion of the political obstacles to economic policy innovation as follows: 'Gradually, but only gradually, the political constraints relaxed' (1974: 23). Such a conclusion is unsatisfactory on two counts. First, given the profundity of the constraints, their relaxation over two or three years would have been better described as rapid rather than gradual. A week may be a long time in politics, but it depends upon what is being attempted. Second, simply saying that 'the political constraints relaxed' begs the questions as to how and why they relaxed. These are questions that I will now attempt to answer, but first I will outline the political constraints and the principal ideas of the highly modernistic New Economics which underpinned the innovations that Kennedy sought to sponsor.

On assuming office, the President himself was, if anything, a fiscal conservative, suspicious of budgetary deficits as instruments of economic management. However, he had made clear to his aides that his Administration's economic policy should be mindful of the needs of the poor and the unemployed. This had aroused some suspicions of him within the business community. At the beginning of his Presidency, his political position was rather weak, because of the narrowness of his victory, the small majorities held by his party in Congress and his dependence for even these on Southern conservatives. Within this context, any departures from economic orthodoxy were likely to be very difficult to achieve. Not the least of the reasons for this were the rules of political calculus then in force. More specifically, a reduction in general unemployment has less Congressional impact than more precisely targeted reductions in local and/or regional unemployment. Also, stimulative policies are less likely to get a favourable hearing when the economy is considered to be healthy than when it is thought to be in trouble. Besides, even the Congress' economically more open-minded members, such as Senator Proxmire, were fundamentally neo-classicists who, although they may have favoured some loosening of monetary constraints, were very definitely not advocates of any of the 'new-fangled' ideas of the New Economists.

Even within the White House itself there were those who would resist any innovative course in economic policy. As President-elect, Kennedy had established two task forces to consider economic policy, one headed by Paul Samuelson and the other by George Ball. Both were considered to be Keynesian. He had also appointed Douglas Dillon and Robert Roosa as Secretary and Under-Secretary to the Treasury. Dillon had been an investment banker as well as Eisenhower's Under-secretary. Roosa had been Vice President of the Federal Reserve Bank of New York. In other words, they were more conservative than Samuelson et al., and they prevailed upon the President to set up a third task force under Allen Sproul, a former President of the Federal Reserve Bank of New York. The report produced by this task force emphasized the factors in the inherited situation, especially the balance of payments problems, which indicated that a restrained economic policy would be the most appropriate for the Administration to follow. Chief aide Theodore Sorenson, and presumably the President-elect too, 'felt boxed in' by the budget for fiscal 1962 which the outgoing Administration had bequeathed to them. They felt that their initial credibility as economic managers in the eyes of Congress and business required that their budget proposals should not involve a deficit larger than Eisenhower's unless the latter could be shown to have been erroneous in either its revenue or outlay estimates.

Modernizing Economic Policy and the Management of the State

This cluster of constraints might seem to have predetermined an inertia in economic policy. As it happens, the principal counter to this inertia was also located in the Executive, namely the Council of Economic Advisors (CEA). Its chair was Walter Heller and its other two members were Kermit Gordon and James Tobin, who was replaced by Gardner Ackley in August 1962. These men represented and argued for what only later became known as the New Economics. According to Tobin (1974), their approach rested on five main ideas. First, they believed that business cycles were not inevitable, and could be flattened out rather than merely qualified by state-sponsored measures. Second, they were convinced that fiscal stimulants should be used boldly, not just to coax the economy out of recession but also, notwithstanding any deficits, to force it up to full-employment performance (that is, to a growth rate of 5 per cent). This would overcome the 'fiscal drag' which they believed occurred when such stimulants were withdrawn too quickly, as they believed they had been throughout the 1950s.

Third, they believed that monetary policy, and in particular the lowering of interest rates, had an important part to play in the pursuit of full-employment growth. Fourth, they felt that fiscal and monetary policies should foster the kind of economic activity that encouraged long-term growth of both actual and potential GNP:

> True to the neo-classical synthesis, we pointed out that some ways of restoring employment are more favorable to growth of capacity than others. Growth would be fostered by mixtures of policy that would leave plenty of room in a full employment economy for accumulation of public and private capital and at the same time would stimulate enough investment demand to fill the space. (Tobin, 1974: 14)

Finally, they believed that the principal cause of unemployment was insufficient demand, and not technological progress or so-called automation, as many other prominent economists believed (Bowen and Mangum, 1966; Leckachman, 1969: ch. 9). In sum, then, the intent of the New Economists was to create an economic climate within which the economy could expand, rather than resort to direct state intervention of the kind that Galbraith (1958), for example, had advocated when he had spoken of the need to reduce the contrast between America's 'private affluence' and its 'public squalor'.

Even before Kennedy had finally decided upon the form that his Administration's economic policy should take, and because of his modernistic insistence on effectiveness, he clearly understood that if he wanted to achieve anything at all he had to be in control of the executive branch. For this reason, he took as much care over selecting people to fill the second and third order positions within his gift as over that of his Department heads. In addition, he developed the habit of directly communicating with such appointees and also with career civil servants of equivalent rank in order to request policy advice and progress information. He replaced the pre-existing interdepartmental committees with personally chosen 'task forces', which included White House staffers as well as departmental representatives. The general brief given to his personal staff, who included Kenneth O'Donnel, Theodore Sorenson, McGeorge Bundy, Lawrence O'Brian, Pierre Salinger, Ralph Dungan and Arthur Schlesinger, emphasized that they should feel free to be critical of the various departments of state and be willing to engage in trouble-shooting when problems were discovered. Finally, as illustrated by his appointment of three economic policy task forces before he was even inaugurated, the President always tried to ensure that he could draw on advice from divergent points of view (Koenig, 1972).

In the more general interest of expediting decision-making, Kennedy radically reduced the frequency of full cabinet meetings, reasoning that Secretaries could spend their time more profitably minding their own business rather than that of departments of whose problems they had little knowledge (Graham, 1976: 135; Thomas and Baade, 1972). Coordination was left to the Bureau of the Budget, although its role was reduced to the performance of an accounting function divorced from the function of overall policy planning which it had gained under Truman and Eisenhower (see above p. 22; and also Graham, 1976: 136; Schick, 1972). Although, on Neustadtian grounds, the President decided against supporting the most important of James Landis' recent proposals for reforming the Regulatory Commissions, specifically the establishment of a White House 'oversight' office, he nevertheless recommended the reform of the Commissions in a centralized direction for reasons of speed and efficiency (Graham, 1976: 132ff.; Mansfield, 1972). More decisively, he abolished the central organs of the National Security Council – the Planning Board and the Operations Coordinating Board – and filled the vacuum occupied by the now vestigial Council by appointing *ad hoc* advisory groups to deal with major foreign policy crises. Although the direct effect of these measures did not last much beyond the first year, it was enough to engender criticisms of 'White House despotism', and it prepared the body politic for the more substantial but rather less obvious centralization which was to come (Cronin, 1972).

The clearest indications at the administrative level of this new centralism and its modernist animus were the reforms of departmental decision-making processes which Kennedy initiated. Soon after the President arrived in the White House, the Office of Management and Organization within the Bureau of the Budget commenced a programme of studies focused on automatic data processing, work measurement, cost reduction and manpower utilization within the civil service. These studies had as their aim a radical improvement in the productivity of the civil service (N. Bernstein, 1972). More specifically, Secretary McNamara in the Department of Defense introduced, for the first time in the Federal Government, the decision-making strategy known as the Performance–Planning–Budgeting System (PPBS). Since this reform illustrates so clearly the White House's determination to take control of the Executive and thereby improve its effectivity as well as strengthen its hand vis-à-vis the Congress and its own civil service, it will be discussed in some detail.

The central concepts of PPBS have been defined by David Novick as follows:

> *Planning* is the production of a range of meaningful potentials for selection of courses of action through a systematic consideration of alternatives. *Programing* is the more specific determination of the manpower, material, and facilities necessary for accomplishing a program. In addition, except in the very short term where dollars are in effect 'given,' programing entails interest in the dollar requirements for meeting the manpower, material, and facility needs. (Novick, 1965: 91)

The substantive meaning of these terms and the significance of their adoption as the basis for the reform of the federal government may be best understood through a consideration of what happened in the Department of Defense (DOD) under McNamara. The Secretary of State, who had earlier overseen the introduction of PPBS at Ford, described the situation that confronted him at Defense thus:

> From the beginning in January 1961, it seemed to me that the principal problem in efficient management of the Department's resources was not the lack of management authority. The problem was rather the absence of the essential

managerial tools needed to make sound decisions on the really crucial issues
of national security. (Enthoven and Smith, 1971: 32–3)

There was no clear statement of security goals underlying the pre-
McNamara budget of the DOD, hence there was no basis upon which
to construct criteria for judging in any at all 'objective' way either the
effectiveness of the measures undertaken by the three services, or their
value for money. All there was were figures describing the past
distribution of resources. The budgetary system was therefore in no
way a mechanism which could be used to control the services. It
provided merely a means of recording previous service requests and
comparing them with the current ones. In the absence of judgemental
criteria of its own, the DOD had become largely a spectator and at
best a referee in the perennial struggles between the groups of
Congressmen, service representatives and suppliers who supported
particular projects. In sum, the situation in the DOD provided a prime
example of what Wildavsky (1964) was soon to term 'incremental
budgeting'; that is, its programmes too often remained in existence
because they had the support of vested interests rather than because
they had proved their effectiveness.

In an effort to change this state of affairs, McNamara decided to
reorganize the DOD's budgetary process on PPBS lines and, on
Enthoven and Smith's analysis, he sought to 'plan' and 'programme'
by the introduction of the following management tools: 'the Five Year
Defense Plan (FYDP), the Draft Presidential Memorandum (DPM), the
Systems Analysis Office and the active use of the technique of systems
analysis' (Enthoven and Smith, 1971: 48). The FYDP was a series of
tables set out according to specific strategic missions, which contained
information projected eight years into the future on force levels, and
five years into the future on costs and manpower requirements. As
such it stated the Department's goals and estimated resource needs, as
well as providing, with the passage of time, a basis upon which to
judge the degree to which the former had been reached and the
accuracy with which the latter had been estimated.

The purpose of the DPM was to order, on the Secretary of State's
terms, the process by which strategic missions were developed, had
their weightings altered and were added to or deleted from the FYDP.
DPMs emanated from the Secretary's Office and consisted of costed
comparisons of his draft proposals with those of the separate services
and the Joint Chiefs of Staff, plus arguments for and against the
various proposals. They were circulated to all interested parties, who
were obliged to respond and, because the DPMs had been prepared by
the Systems Analysis Office, the responses had to be in the language
of systems analysis, thus ensuring that everyone was talking the
Secretary's language – the archetypal language of the modern world.

The Politics of Economic Modernization

So much for the modernizing and centralizing animus of the Kennedy Administration as illustrated by its style of working and its efforts to centralize policy-making in the Executive and especially the White House. I will now move to outline what, according to one authority (A.S. Miller, 1968: 93), represented 'one of the quietest pragmatic innovations in our constitutional history', the growth of presidential initiative in legislation which Kennedy pioneered and which was an instance of the same animus. The account of Kennedy's economic policy and the struggle over its implementation which I will now present will provide further evidence that Kennedy's attempt to confirm capital accumulation as the nation's number one priority depended upon the same equation of 'management' with science and hence with modernism, the same almost literal 'use of ideas as social levers', which was apparent in the introduction of PPBS at the Department of Defense.

To begin with, I will explain how Kennedy sought to overcome the obstacles in the way of economic innovation which were outlined above (pp. 44–5). The first problem to be addressed was the Southern conservatives' pre-eminence in the Congressional committee structure and especially on the crucial House Rules Committee. This committee decides which of all the bills introduced each session should actually be voted upon in the House. Kennedy's solution was to 'pack' the committee by increasing its membership by three, at least two of whom would be loyal to the party leadership. As a result of intense lobbying by the Administration and its supporters the proposal was passed by just five votes out of 429 (Heath, 1975: 63).

The second obstacle was referred to earlier as 'the rules of the political calculus'. Kennedy's initial anti-recession programme consisted entirely of measures that had the kind of tangible effects on voters that members of Congress appreciated: a thirteen week extension of the maximum period for which federal unemployment benefits could be drawn; increases in the funds available for public housing, depressed areas, the children of the unemployed and feed grain farmers. Similarly, for two years he consistently refused, often against the advice of his economic councillors, to recommend any of the bolder suggestions derived from the New Economics unless conditions were visibly worsening. Such careful attention to the rules of the game greatly improved the President's stock in the eyes of Congress, and also created conditions within the White House wherein the New Economists of the CEA were gradually able to out-manoeuvre the neo-classicists of the Treasury.

Kennedy contributed to this latter development in more direct ways too. In 1961, at the same time as he was resisting the CEA's growth proposals, he told its chair, Heller, to 'use the White House as a pulpit for public education in economics' (Heath, 1975: 65). Moreover, also in the same year, he demonstrated early and clearly that he understood and was prepared to put into practice the ideas of the New Economics, provided only that the political conditions were right: despite an improving economy, he made only three requests to Congress and these were for increases in defence spending. These added up to an increase of $6 billion in the military budget, none of which was to be financed by increased taxes despite strong arguments from the Treasury. However, at the same time, by making the Trade Expansion Bill, whose object was the improvement of the United States' international trade balances, the centrepiece of his 1962 legislative programme, Kennedy demonstrated to both the Treasury and the Congress that he appreciated the problem represented by the $2–$3 billion annual trade deficit – the economic fact which underpinned most of the economically conservative positions.

Although the actions just outlined illustrate how acutely the President appreciated the interdependence of politics and economic policy making, perhaps the most dramatic illustration of this appreciation was his decision to campaign actively for Democratic candidates in the mid-term elections of 1962. Such elections typically go rather badly for the majority party for reasons often thought to have more to do with the mysteries of voter psychology than with any 'objective' assessments of Administration policy. As a result, Presidents from the majority party are normally unwilling to risk their prestige in the face of such an unknown and unknowable force. Kennedy's decision was therefore a bold one. Moreover, since his own rating with the voters was anyway very high, the candidates who stood to benefit from his decision could readily interpret it as an altruistic one. Fortunately for the President, and helped no doubt by the way in which he had conducted himself in the course of the Cuban missile crisis, the gamble paid off. The Democrats gained four seats in the Senate and only lost two in the House with the result that the President had the majorities he needed to give his preferred items of legislation a good chance of being passed.

The business community is 'naturally' suspicious of a Democratic President but, as Jim Heath (1975) has made very clear, this community was far from monolithic politically and had varying degrees of influence. As was suggested above (see p. 22), one of the less obvious consequences of the increased centralization of the economy and of the federal government following the New Deal were changes to the objects and techniques of influence which had meant that the larger corporations had become even more influential than they had been before. The increased economic weight of the larger firms had given many of their representatives at least as much, and often more, interest in the macro-economic management role of the executive as in the rule-making role of the legislature. This change was reflected in an alteration in the methods of influence deployed by business. The lobby and the campaign contribution were supplemented by far more modernistic devices, such as the seminar, the research report and the 'think tank'. Although large capital predominates within such traditional instruments of influence as the National

Association of Manufacturers (NAM), its freedom of expression is often significantly qualified by the necessity of taking into account the often rather different views of small and medium capital. By contrast, large capital is much freer to express its views in such more exclusive and largely executive-focused organizations as the Committee for Economic Development (CED), the Business Council (BC, earlier the Business Advisory Council), the Rand Corporation and the great foundations (Domhoff, 1970, 1972; Eakins, 1969).

The business community in general took Kennedy's election victory very calmly. It was, however, somewhat disturbed by the lack of businessmen in the Administration, as well as by the presence of a large number of 'pointy heads' (intellectuals), some of whom were considered dangerous (Galbraith and Schlesinger, for example). However, it was reassured by the assignation of such people to marginal posts and by the President's early speeches on the economy. Addressing the National Industrial Conference Board in February 1961 the President said:

> I feel . . . that I can claim kinship here. . . Our revenues and thus our success are dependent upon your profits and your success. Far from being natural enemies, Government and business are necessary allies. . . We know that your success and ours are intertwined – that you have the *facts and knowledge* that we need. Whatever past differences have existed, we seek more than an attitude of truce, more than a treaty – we seek the spirit of a full-fledged alliance. (Heath, 1969: 28; emphasis added)

The obstacles in the way of any such alliance became clear with discomforting rapidity. The Administration's initial anti-recession package, which had generally pleased the Congress, found favour only with the small businesspeople and some of the more economically modernistic corporate leaders who had embraced a 'public interest' conception of their organizations' social roles. The NAM and the national Chamber of Commerce spoke for the majority when they criticized the extension of unemployment benefit and the aid to depressed areas as dangerous governmental incursions on, respectively, the autonomy of state governments and the market system (Heath, 1969: 17ff.). The weakness of the more modernistic businesspeople was more dramatically illustrated by the breakdown in relations between the Administration and the Business Advisory Council, long the principal voice of large capital. Even the new Commerce Secretary, Luther Hodges, who described himself as the Administration's 'only tie with the nineteenth century', felt it necessary to make two major criticisms of the BAC. Firstly, it had not done enough for, or been sufficiently representative of, the spectrum of business opinion to justify what Schlesinger called its 'cosy' relationship with government. Secondly, Hodges thought it inappropriate that the BAC should retain as chairman the chairman of General Electric, since the latter corporation had been found guilty of price-fixing in January 1961. The BAC's response to these criticisms was to add five representatives of small business to its sixty existing active members, appoint a new chairman in the person of Roger Blough of United States Steel, and declare its total independence of government (Heath, 1969: 42ff.). The modernistic notion of 'business responsibility' clearly had few supporters in the Business Council, as the 'steel crisis' was soon to underline.

A Programme for Economic Modernization

In April 1961, whilst the row with the BAC was still in progress, the Administration unveiled its proposals for encouraging investment as the first stage of its growth plan. The proposals featured a tax credit for new investment, the size of which would be determined by a sliding scale related to the size of the investment, and tax reforms which would close some of the more indefensible tax-avoidance loopholes. In addition, a promise was made that the existing depreciation schedules would be revised and made more generous. Although Kennedy was offering business more than Eisenhower ever had, he received singularly little thanks for his pains. Most of the leading organs of business opinion condemned the tax credit suggestion as either a gimmick or a subsidy to large firms. Their preference was for a general upward revision of the depreciation schedules or, if the tax credit idea had to be accepted, a flat-rate formula. Rejection of the tax reform proposals was virtually unanimous. Every section of business opinion disliked one or other aspect of the reforms: they did not want their expense accounts reduced, the taxes due on interest and dividends withheld at source, or the profits on their foreign subsidiaries taxed. Even the relatively liberal CED, which had recommended similar reforms in its policy statement, 'Growth and Taxes: Steps for 1961', played down its support for them and emphasized its rejection of the tax credit idea (Schriftgeisser, 1967). The virulence of the CED's rejection of the tax credit idea was a surprise to Kennedy, since not only had he been an appreciative reader of its reports and statements since 1953, but Walter Heller had been a respected if somewhat radical consultant to it.

The Administration had hoped for a more considered and favourable response when it announced its Wage–Price Guideposts in January 1962, especially since, on Karl Schriftgeisser's analysis, even the wording used could have been taken from an earlier CED statement 'Defense Against Inflation' (see also Sheahan, 1967). The one notable difference between the two proposals was that the Administration specified a guide for prices instead of assuming, as the CED had done, that prices would follow wages. In essence the Guideposts suggested that, in order to avoid the inflation potential intrinsic to an oligopolistic economy, wages should rise only with productivity and prices should rise only if costs other than those for labour had also risen.

Although the Guideposts lacked the force of law, they were ultimately successful. Their enunciation was a bold move in the direction of the aforementioned more economically modernistic business leaders, since the large multinational corporations which they headed were the only economic actors who were likely to welcome them. The reasons for labour's hostility have been well put by Miroff, who, after pointing out that the Guideposts for wages were much more precise than those for prices, goes on to argue that:

> Nor was it only that labor was governed by more precise standards than management. More important, those standards precluded some traditional labor concerns. They ruled out the possibility that wage increases might come out of corporations' expanding profits, or that wages might claim a larger percentage of corporate income. Improved productivity was the sole legitimation for higher wages; the symbolic, if not the economic, meaning was that workers should get better pay only to the extent that they did better work. For a union to argue on grounds other than productivity, to question, for example, the equity of the prevailing distribution of income between management and labor in its industry, was now illicit. The guideposts, Nossiter pointed out, clearly implied that there was to be 'no change in the relative shares of labor and the other claimants for the economic pie'. (1976: 176–7)

As is indicated by the economic implications of Miroff and Nossiter's argument, the CED's espousal of the idea and the evidence relating to specific supporters collected by Heath (1969), the Guideposts represented a significant move in the direction of state-sponsored, pre-planned economic management and as such a very specifically modernistic idea. This specificity was well illustrated some years later when Heller said of the still existing Guideposts:

> They pit the power of public opinion and Presidential persuasion against the market power of strong unions and strong businesses. They try to bring to the bargaining tables and board rooms where wage and price decisions are made a sense of the public interest in non-inflationary wage and price behavior. Indeed they try to appeal also to labor and management's broad self-defeating price–wage spiral. Their major thrust, then, has been through the process of informing labor, management, and the public of the explicit ways in which wage and price decisions should be geared to productivity advances if they are to be noninflationary. Under the guideposts, wage rate increases averaging no more than the average national increase in productivity . . . are seen as noninflationary. (Miroff, 1976: 175–6)

The Steel Crisis

At the time the Guideposts were announced, an economic storm was brewing which would severely test Kennedy's determination to pursue such ideas. This storm soon became known as the 'Steel Crisis'. In line with the Guideposts, the Administration had let it be known that it did not want to see an inflationary price rise in what it called the 'bell-weather' industry of steel. To underline how seriously it viewed the matter, it had promised to use its influence with the Steelworkers' Union in an effort to get it to settle for a wage rise based on productivity increases. It was successful and the industry appeared grateful. All the same, on 10 April, US Steel and CED chairman Blough called at the

White House to announce a $6 per ton price increase. The President was furious and publicly attacked the steel industry at a press conference on the following day. In addition, he instructed the Defense Department to tell its contractors to buy steel only from companies who had not raised their prices, and he told the Justice Department to investigate possible price-fixing in the steel industry.

Within 24 hours of Blough's announcement, so many companies had followed suit that 80 per cent of the industry's capacity was working to the new price levels. However, three of the top twelve companies did not immediately raise their prices. Of these, one, Inland Steel, became the focus of intense Administration lobbying. Its chairman, Joseph Block, was known to be friendly to the Administration, to believe in 'corporate responsibility' and cooperation with government, and was known to feel, as a Trustee of the CED, that Blough was not the most effective spokesman large capital could have. On 13 April, Inland Steel announced that it was holding its prices and Kaiser and Armco made similar announcements. Bethlehem Steel rescinded its price rises the following day and US Steel immediately followed suit.

No one knows exactly why Block took this stand, or why Bethlehem and US Steel, the two giants in the industry, gave in so quickly. On the one hand, the reasons may have been economic and stemmed either from differences as regards how best to increase investment funds or from fears as to the consequences of a price war in what was becoming a rather fragile industry. On the other hand, they may have been political and have stemmed either from ideological differences amongst corporate leaders or from fears with regard to the possible consequences of prolonged exposure to the negative publicity which they were then experiencing (Rowan, 1972: 104–5). It seems to me that all of these factors were involved. However, in view of the nature of my ongoing argument, the possibility that ideological differences were involved requires a little more discussion.

The nature of the ideological differences involved is clearly indicated by the explanatory statements made by the two corporate antagonists. Here, with Hobart Rowan's helpful comments, is Blough's explanation:

> . . . Roger Blough, as he put it so well himself, is a man who thinks 'in terms of costs'. To such a man, the national interest, as expressed by the President to the United States, was only 'one of the factors' that received consideration. But it was just one factor, weighed along with others – say, the costs of scrap or pig iron. In the world of the Roger Bloughs, costs and prices and profits are the big determinants. Something as fuzzy as a sense of responsibility – the Goldbergian 'national interest' concept – is not very high on the list. After all, how do you show the 'national interest' on a balance sheet? (Rowan, 1972: 107)

Here without any commentary is Block's more modernistic explanation:

> We did not feel that it was in the national interest to raise prices at this time. We felt this very strongly. (Rowan, 1972: 45)

At first glance, the bitterness apparent in the business community's reaction following the crisis suggests that Kennedy's strategy had failed. In April it became known that in the course of the crisis the President had exclaimed in frustration: 'My father always told me that all businessmen were sons of bitches, but I never believed it until now' (quoted in Rowan, 1972: 45). Although the statement was later corrected to read 'steelmen' instead of 'businessmen', the resentment against the President rose to a new intensity. It reached its peak on 28 May, when the Stock Market declined more steeply in one day than it had done since 1929. Because stocks had become overvalued, there were good economic and technical reasons for the crash. Nevertheless, the business community was only too delighted to blame Kennedy personally, as their jokes indicated:

> The Kennedy Cocktail? Stocks on the Rocks.

> Five thousand years ago, Moses said to the children of Israel: 'pick up thy shovels, mount thy asses and camels, and I will lead you to the Promised Land.' Nearly five thousand years later, Roosevelt said: 'Lay down your shovels, sit on your asses, and light up a Camel, this is the Promised Land.' Now Kennedy is stealing your shovels, kicking your asses, raising the price of Camels, and taking over the Promised Land. (quoted in Domhoff, 1970: 144).

However, simultaneous events and some which followed soon after suggest that all this was not to be taken too seriously.

Modernizing the Public Discourse on the Economy

The immediate aim of the Trade Expansion Bill was to reduce US tariffs so as to obtain reciprocal reductions from other countries. Its longer term aim was to reduce the balance of payments deficit, thereby strengthening both the role of the dollar in international finance and the position of growth advocates at home. The close resemblance between the bill and the CED's policy statement 'A New Trade Policy for the United States' makes it clear to whom the Administration intended it to appeal. The point was emphasized by Kennedy's appointment of the CED's chief spokesman on tariffs, Howard Peterson, as his special aide on such matters.

The content of the bill was politically aggressive in that it recommended that tariff policy should be taken out of the hands of Congress and transferred to the executive. The CED had been leading a campaign for the liberalization of tariff policies since the 1950s, but it had been foiled consistently by Congressional opposition on behalf of the smaller companies, which were typically more conservative and parochial. It seems to me, therefore, that the most significant thing about the bill was that modernistic advocates of growth accepted its content and fought for it. In so doing they indicated that they were prepared to take the offensive in the ongoing conflict between the embodiments of competing capitals, spurred on no doubt by a slowly growing fear of the EEC and Japan, as well as by the knowledge that the other side of the Administration's attack on the balance of payments problem was the still pending tax reform package with its tax on the profits of overseas branches and subsidiaries.

They were not to be disappointed as regards the possibility of a quid pro quo on this score, since virtually all of the reform aspects of the tax proposals disappeared and the tax credit remained only in the form of an across-the-board 7 per cent credit for new investment. Even this, it seems, only survived because the Administration also promised to revise the depreciation schedules in the very near future. This, then, helps to explain why the President felt able to lecture the business community as confidently as he did in the course of his Yale Commencement Address of June 1962, despite the recentness of the 'steel crisis'. This speech was later appreciated as a masterly intervention in connection with his greatest, if posthumous, economic policy achievement, the 1964 Tax Cut.

The speech stands out because of its subtlety as well as its boldness. Not only was it Kennedy's frankest espousal of the New Economics, but it achieved its effect coolly and modernistically, that is, by discursively outflanking his opponents rather than attacking them directly. Instead of indulging in a Roosevelt-like denunciation of 'economic royalists', the President spoke to an explicitly managerialist theme. He characterized his opponents as being in the thrall of economic 'myths', to wit: that the federal government was growing too rapidly; that the national debt was also growing too rapidly; that business 'confidence' was the *sine qua non* of economic health; and that federal budgetary deficits necessarily caused inflation. To use his own words:

> . . . the great enemy of the truth is very often not the lie – deliberate, contrived and dishonest – but the myth, persistent, persuasive and unrealistic. Too often we hold fast to the clichés of our forebears. We subject all facts to a prefabricated set of interpretations. We enjoy the comfort of opinion without the discomfort of thought. . .
>
> What is at stake is not some grand warfare of rival ideologies which will sweep the country with passion but the practical management of a modern economy. What we need is not labels and cliches but more basic discussion of the sophisticated and technical issues involved in helping a great economic machinery moving ahead. . .
>
> The debate of the 'thirties had its great significance and produced great results, but it took place in a different world with different needs and different tasks. It is our responsibility today to live in our own world and to identify the needs and discharge the tasks of the 1960s.

If the content of the speech contains clear evidence of Kennedy's commitment to social modernism, its timing clearly demonstrated once again his acute appreciation of the interdependence of the political and economic realms.

In its statement 'Fiscal and Monetary Policy for High Employment', issued in January 1962, the CED had suggested for the first time that under very specific circumstances a conscious increase of the federal budgetary deficit would not only be permissible within the parameters of sound public finance, but it could also be positively beneficial: '(if a depression appears imminent) deliberate enlargement of the federal deficit, over and above the deficit that automatically emerges in recession periods, comprises the chief tool that is available' (quoted in Schriftgeisser, 1967: 103).

In the summer, perhaps emboldened by the Yale speech and certainly galvanized by the deteriorating economic situation, the CED began work on a new statement on taxation policy which was eventually published in December and which recommended a tax cut of $11 billion to be spread over two years. Rather surprisingly, the CED was beaten to the open advocacy of a tax cut by the Chamber of Commerce, which declared its support just two weeks after the Yale Speech. Nevertheless, the President most prized the CED's support, as he showed by asking for a copy of its statement to be sent to every member of Congress.

In December 1962, Kennedy finally reaped the benefits of his reading of Neustadt and his two years of careful and imaginative labour. When he had first floated the idea of a tax cut, he had purposely kept quiet about specifics, hoping to stimulate exactly the sort of debate which had ensued. The possibility of tax cuts excited all sections of the economic community and each group weighed in with its own suggestions and conditions as they sought to influence the Administration. Thus the President gained a great deal of information which would be useful to him when he finally made a formal proposal to the Congress, and diffused responsibility for this radical departure from orthodoxy far beyond its originators in his CEA. The groundswell in favour of a cut became so strong that, when he publicly returned to the topic in December, before the traditionalist Economic Club of New York, he put the straight CEA line and obtained a very favourable hearing. Noting that the economy was now improving again, he nevertheless still argued for a tax reduction on the grounds that:

the accumulated evidence of the last five years [shows] that our present tax system, developed as it was, in good part, during World War II to restrain growth, exerts too heavy a drag on growth in peacetime; that it siphons out of the private economy too large a share of private and business purchasing power; that it reduces financial incentives for personal effort, investment and risk-taking. (Heath, 1969: 117)

By the end of 1962 and just two years after his Inauguration, then, Kennedy had succeeded in gaining general business support for the most radical of the ideas of the New Economics: the diagnosis of 'fiscal drag' as the main barrier to growth, and the suggestion that tax reduction was the cure. Moreover, he had done so in such a way as to gain for himself the political intelligence necessary for the successful administration of the cure in the manner most acceptable to himself and his supporters in the business community.

The CED had wanted a straightforward tax reduction with no strings. They would have been happiest, of course, if the lion's share of the benefits had gone to those in the upper income brackets and to corporate income tax payers. However, responsibly, they accepted the political necessity of doing something for those in the lower income brackets. The conservatives on the other hand wanted any tax reductions to be balanced, to some degree at least, by government expenditure reductions, which the growth advocates thought would be counter-productive. Dillon, the relatively orthodox Treasury Secretary, perhaps unwittingly supplied the means whereby the difficulties created by this difference could be overcome. He suggested another series of loophole-closing reforms which would partially offset the $13 billion reduction in revenues which the Administration eventually proposed. Although many subsequently criticized the decision to tie reduction to reform, on the grounds that it delayed the former, it seems that – ever mindful of such niceties – Kennedy hoped that an insistence on reforms would indicate sufficient awareness of fiscal propriety to undermine the force of the conservative position, satisfy the concern on the part of crucial Congressional figures that the principles of 'good housekeeping' should be respected and, therefore, divide the opposition.

In the course of the subsequent congressional struggle, this hope became a fact. Thanks to the modernistic liberal minority's opposition to expenditure reductions and in the absence of an alternative conservative reform plan, House Ways and Means chair, Wilbur Mills, and other Democratic fiscal conservatives had little choice but to support the President's proposed reforms. This left the Republican fiscal conservatives on their own, wanly complaining that the reforms reduced incentives. In sum, the reform proposals represented a brilliantly conceived 'red herring' which was dragged across the floor of Congress, divided the conservative opposition and facilitated the passage of a tax reduction bill, whose potential stimulative effect was only minimally reduced by a few minor expenditure reductions. In the end, then, The Revenue Act, which President Johnson eventually signed into law in February 1964, was more or less exactly what the New Economists and their more modernistic corporate allies had wanted. The top rate of individual income tax was reduced from 90 per cent to 70 per cent, the rate of corporate taxation was reduced from 52 per cent to 48 per cent, and the additional revenue which was expected to result from the closing of loopholes was a mere $300 million.

By early 1963, then, it seemed that President Kennedy had modernized both the state's mode of economic management and the economic views of both the Congressional majority and large-scale capital. Business was already taking advantage of the tax credit on new investment, it was pleased by the support given by the President to the tax reduction and trade expansion bills and it was reassured by Attorney General Robert Kennedy's preference for cleaning up the unions, especially the

Teamsters, over searching out anti-trust violations (Navasky, 1971). As one financial columnist wrote: 'The Kennedy Administration is cooperating and trusting US business to a degree unprecedented in modern times. . . . To accuse Mr Kennedy of being anti-business is almost akin to accusing Senator Goldwater of being pro-communist' (Heath, 1969: 125). Even chairman Blough of United States Steel published a pamphlet in September urging greater business–government cooperation and entitled 'The Real Revolutionaries'. That the President was largely satisfied by all this is indicated by his calm response to the steel price rises of April and September 1963. He agreed with Walter Heller's analysis: 'Government–business relations are better than in a long time; any condemnation of steel or intimation of possible "future price crackdowns", could impair confidence, with possibly bad economic and political effects' (Heath, 1975: 105–6).

Conclusion: the Crystallization of Social Modernism

In the course of his vigorous courting of capital, the more populist claims that were also part of Kennedy's social modernist rhetoric had begun to wear rather thin. He had failed to do anything much for the poor, the aged sick, the educationally aspirant, the unemployed and, most damagingly of all, the African-Americans of the South, all of whom he had often and specifically promised to help. This none too benign neglect considerably amplified the rumblings of discontent which had been just audible at the time of the 1960 election. The African-American struggle subsequently entered a new phase.

The Student Nonviolent Coordinating Committee (SNCC) was formed and Malcolm X was attracting larger and larger audiences. In May 1963, a peaceful protest led by Martin Luther King turned into an uncontrollable riot in Birmingham, Alabama, and in August 200,000 civil rights protesters marched through Washington.

Similarly, the radicalization of white 'middle class' youth began to accelerate: in May 1960, 8,000 students had picketed the hearings held by the House Unamerican Activities Committee in San Francisco; during the summer of the same year thousands of young people visited Cuba and joined 'Fair Play for Cuba' groups; in April 1961, nationwide demonstrations took place to protest the Bay of Pigs invasion; later that year many students went south to join the civil rights struggle; in June 1962 Students for a Democratic Society (SDS) issued its Port Huron Statement; and, finally, in April 1963, Dr Timothy Leary was dismissed by Harvard University because of his work on hallucinogenic drugs. In sum, by 1963, most of the disaffected social actors who were to turn the late 1960s into a period of unparalleled social disorder had already taken the stage, and they had been encouraged to do so as much by Kennedy's modernistic promises as by his lack of action on the social front.[1]

Worried by a decline in his popularity which had commenced in

January 1963, the President initiated the process which was finally to result in President Johnson's declaration of a 'War on Poverty'. However, it was clear from the beginning that the tax cut and what was hoped would be its 'trickle down effect' would be the centrepiece of the Administration's strategy:

> Our feeling is that the economy, if sufficiently stimulated, . . . could reduce unemployment to the figure of about four per cent. There will be some hard-core structural unemployment in Eastern Kentucky and West Virginia, particularly the coal and steel centers, which will not be substantially aided by the tax bill or even by the general rise in the economy. I do think, however, that if we could reduce unemployment to four per cent, then those programs which are specifically directed towards these centers of chronic unemployment . . . may be able to make a further dent. (quoted in Schlesinger, 1965: 854)

Thus, right to the end of his life, Kennedy was consciously involved in the process of realizing what was actually quite a 'grand design', the modernization of both the means and rationales for capital accumulation in the United States. Given the lack of powerful social pressures for such a change, its achievement must be largely credited to the President, who centralized his way into 'the thick of things', always considered political and economic factors together, always made his own decisions and always kept his goal firmly in mind. If one has to single out one talent that accounted for the President's success, it must be his facility in the realm of ideology, both in terms of his grasp of its specificity in the United States and in terms of his ability and willingness to boldly enunciate a new and modernistic variant of the hegemonic discourse which was to become the standard liberal Democratic variant of corporate liberalism. As I have written elsewhere:

> This was a variant that saw opportunity not as a reward for living one's life according to the rules laid down by the other, more restrictive signs, but rather one which so stressed it that a certain softening of these rules might be justified; i.e. the category of 'the deserving poor' could be broadened, the quid pro quo allowed to organized labour in return for its responsibility could be enlarged and the constraints upon domestic freedom imposed in the name of loyalty could be relaxed, but only if such actions could plausibly be thought to enhance opportunity and thereby strengthen the pertinent subjects' commitment to corporate liberalism. In an attempt to ensure that it did exactly and only this, Kennedy most assiduously repeated the key signs at every opportunity. (Woodiwiss, 1990b: 218). (For Kennedy's almost obsessive repetition of the need for unions to be responsible, see any entry relating to unions in his *Public Papers*.)

In my view, the extraordinary emotion that President Kennedy's assassination released not only in the United States but also throughout the advanced capitalist world, confirmed that he had come to personify the promises of social modernism. As has already been indicated, the apotheosis of social modernism was reached when, assuming the correctness of the claims made by its economic cousin, a newly self-confident sociology began to make similar claims with respect to its capacity to manage society (Patterson, 1981: chs. 5–9; Marris and Rein, 1967; Moynihan, 1969: chs. 2–5). So encouraged, President Johnson declared to a University of Michigan audience in 1964 that his Administration's aim was to create 'The Great Society':

> Your imagination, your initiative, and your indignation will determine whether we build a society where progress is the servant of our needs, or a society where old values and new visions are buried under unbridled growth. For in our time we have the opportunity to move not only toward the rich society and the powerful society, but upward to the Great Society . . . the Great Society is not a safe harbour, a resting place, a final objective, a finished work. It is a challenge constantly renewed, beckoning us toward a destiny where the meaning of our lives matches the marvellous products of our labor . . . I . . . promise this: we are going to assemble the best thought and the broadest knowledge from all over the world to find these answers for America.

Soon afterwards, the political scientist David Apter penned the following words, which may be taken as representative of the social scientific commonsense of the period:

> The work of modernization is the burden of this age. It is our rock. It is an objective that is not confined to a single place or region, to a particular country or class, or to a privileged group of people.
> Modernization is a special kind of hope. Embodied in it are all the past revolutions of history and all the supreme human desires. The modernization revolution is epic in its scale and moral in its significance. Its consequences may be frightening. Any goal that is so desperately desired creates political power, and this force may not always be used wisely or well. Whatever direction it may take, the struggle to modernize is what has given meaning to our generation. It tests our cherished institutions and our beliefs.
> It puts our country in the market place of ideas and ideologies. So compelling a force has it become that we are forced to ask new questions of our own institutions. Each country, whether modernized or modernizing stands in both judgment and fear of the results. Our own society is no exception. (Apter, 1965: 1–2)

As with Bell in the earlier period and thanks indeed to the mediation of Kennedy's texts (Bell, 1988: 419), one has here a very clear instance of an intertextuality whereby ideological art imitates ideological life. As Johnson had made clear a couple of months earlier when he introduced the legislative package that made up his 'war on poverty', the 'Great Society' and therefore *the* modern society was simply corporate liberal society writ large:

> . . . We have never lost sight of our goal: an America in which every citizen shares all the opportunities of his society, in which every man has a chance to advance his welfare to the limit of his capacities. . .
> There are millions of Americans – one fifth of our people – who have not shared in the abundance which has been granted to most of us, and on whom the gates of opportunity have been closed. . .
> The war on poverty is not a struggle simply to support people, to make them dependent on the generosity of others.

It is a struggle to give people a chance.
It is an effort to allow them to develop and use their capacities . . . so that they can share . . . the promise of this nation. . .

Not surprisingly, the Act which was the centrepiece of the Great Society programme was called The Economic Opportunity Act.

Note

1 This paragraph has been adapted from Woodiwiss (1990b: 221).

4
SOCIAL MODERNISM AND CLASS RELATIONS

If the dramatic events of the late 1960s are to be properly understood, the softness of the ground upon which the earlier capital-positive balance of class relations rested must first be appreciated. In the Introduction, the four principal sites of tension and, therefore, sources of motility in the relations between capital and labour were identified as relating to the following:

1 The value of labour power
2 The maintenance of the circuits of capital
3 The balance between the two departments of production
4 The counteracting influences to the tendency of the rate of profit to fall.

As was also spelt out in the Introduction and will be demonstrated below, each of these sites should be understood to be constituted by ideological and political forces, as well as by economic ones, and therefore each site has also to be understood as susceptible to ideological and political developments which are usually thought to be external to class relations. In this chapter I will do two things: first, outline my reading of how the state of the balances between the two classes changed between 1945 and Johnson's election to the Presidency in 1964. And second, outline the rise and significance for these balances of what has become known as 'military Keynesianism'.

The Value of Labour Power

The changes in the balance between labour and capital at this site of tension must be read as having been almost totally positive from capital's point of view. The main reason for this was the unassertive and highly responsible unionism practised by organized labour. Labour accepted and indeed preferred, a quid pro quo whereby the arbitration of grievances was exchanged for a no-strike pledge (Woodiwiss, 1990b: 248ff.), and capital gained immensely from the predictability that this brought to its relations with labour and therefore to any changes in its labour costs. In addition, Congressional actions such as the passage of the Taft-Hartley and Landrum-Griffin Acts, the trends in the free speech and picketing decisions of the Supreme Court (Shapiro, 1964), the Kennedy Administration's introduction of the Wage–Price Guideposts, and the formation of tripartite government, capital and labour Advisory Committees, all had the effect of enforcing and reinforcing this state of affairs. All this said, each of these developments also rendered capital far more dependent upon the continuance of favourable political and ideological conditions than it had been.

The Maintenance of the Circuits of Capital

Here the changes in the state of the balance between labour and capital must be read as having been somewhat less positive from capital's point of view, at least if the possibility of increased future vulnerability is taken into account. The positive balance as regards the productive circuit was reinforced to some degree by the consequences of the actions undertaken in the circulatory sphere that were outlined in Chapter 3. These accelerated the creation of contradictory class positionings or 'opportunities' in such a way as to secure the loyalty of their embodiments to capital, as well as to ensure that the commodity circuit was maintained. Both the production and commodity circuits were additionally stimulated by the expansion of credit facilities. Moreover, these capital-positive effects were reinforced by the state's housing, transportation and education policies, as well as by its celebration of 'the affluent society' with its promise of a tension-free modernity peopled by 'autonomous' individuals. However, all of this was potentially disruptive in that it vastly increased the demands made on capital's revenues and therefore on the money circuit more generally, some of which were subject to political and ideological, as well as purely economic, forces. Henceforth these revenues would have to meet not only investment needs but also advertising expenses, the rapidly increasing loyalty payments and consumption subsidies promised to 'the middle classes', and, finally, the bank interest charges incurred in trying to finance all this through the recurrent business cycles.

The Balance between the two Departments of Production

Here a reading of the changes in the state of the balance between labour and capital is harder to make. However, it seems that it must be partially negative from capital's point of view. The emphasis on the production of consumer goods consequent upon the rapid growth of contradictory positionings appears to have led to a relative neglect of the producer goods sector and especially of the steel industry, whose plant was on average more than fifty years old (Melman, 1985). In the name of 'modernism', the Kennedy Administration attempted to correct this by expending a great deal of political and ideological effort in pursuit of an investment credit and a radical upward revision of depreciation allowances (see above, p. 56). However, the same Administration chose a demand-led expansion policy based upon a tax cut, instead of directed state investment on the then unregarded Japanese, Miti model. This policy appears to have worsened any extant imbalance between the two departments of production; it certainly threw away the chance to correct it that a policy of directed investment in strategic areas of the economy might have provided. The Administration's failure to do anything effective to stop the high level of capital exports that figured so significantly in the balance of payments deficits, or to reduce the level of military spending must also be regarded as further worsening any such imbalance (Perlo 1973: 169ff.). There was pressure from labour and some sections of capital for more attention to the needs of the producer goods department, but the consumer goods market was so buoyant, and so important in securing the loyalty of those who had been given opportunities, that capital was compelled to resist – a response which proved very costly over the longer term in the context of the increasingly competitive world economy.

The Counteracting Influences to the Tendency of the Rate of Profit to Fall

Under this heading, a separate reading of the changes to the state of the balance between labour and capital will be provided for each influence before a judgement is made as to their overall significance.

The Increasing Intensity of Labour at the Point of Production Thanks to the aforementioned quid pro quo (see above, p. 63), 'responsible unionism' meant that there was no significant opposition to production line speed-ups, or to the dissolution of the job property rights otherwise known as 'restrictive practices'. For example, the United Mine Workers (UMW) actively cooperated in the speed-up process, in the reorganization of jobs, in the de-unionization of many thousands of its members and therefore in the loss of 400,000 jobs. Finally, in the unorganized sectors of industry, women began to enter the labour force in increasing numbers and at lower rates of pay than men (Banks, 1981: 210 ff.). The net result of all this was that productivity rose strongly throughout the 1950s, culminating in an annual rate of increase of 5 per cent between 1961 and 1964.

The Depression of Wages below the Value of Labour Power Under certain rather specific and restricted conditions, this very definitely occurred – in such areas of agricultural production as grape picking and lettuce or citrus fruit harvesting, for example, where many of the labourers were illegal immigrants from Mexico. Moreover, if one takes account of Marx's inclusion of the 'traditional standard of life' (that is, the ability to sustain a family and the opportunity to acquire relevant skills) in his definition of subsistence, then the existence of many millions of 'working poor' and/or 'under-employed', who lived at or below the poverty level, would seem to offer evidence of the operation of this counteracting influence on a more general scale. Further, the extreme unevenness of welfare provision, and the general parsimony that followed from the system being premissed upon 'self-reliance', suggest that the state actively facilitated the operation of this influence to capital's advantage (Piven and Cloward, 1971). One measure of this was that welfare provision of even the minimalist corporate liberal kind failed to expand in any significant way. Not only did federal welfare expenditure rise as a proportion of GNP by only 0.4 per cent between 1940 and 1960, but its financing and control became increasingly regressive as they both became matters for the states and localities to decide (Vatter, 1963: 6–7). All this said, the rise of the civil rights movement raised the possibility that this influence too might be neutralized in the future.

The Cheapening of Elements of Constant Capital This occurred to some degree because of technological developments but most importantly because of Kennedy's aforementioned revision of the Internal Revenue Service's depreciation schedules. Even at its end, this period saw only the beginning of the electronic miniaturization that was subsequently to have such an impact. Nevertheless, capital was able to take full advantage of whatever cheapening took place because of the labour acquiescence to any associated changes in the labour process which followed from 'responsible unionism'.

Relative Over-population As the mechanization of agriculture and mining suggests, this influence was also operative during this period. The high unemployment figures and an estimated job-loss because of so-called automation, of between 30,000 and 60,000 per week in the early 1960s confirm this. However, because more than 50 per cent of the research and development finance provided by the state went to capital-intensive, military and 'high tech' spin-off industries, the increasing relative surplus population was not readily absorbed. Marx suggested that such an increase would represent a counteracting influence because he assumed that any new industries would be labour-intensive. This was seldom the case in the 1950s and 1960s, although it was to become so again in the 1970s with the rise of industries such as fast food. In the period under review, however, the most important consequence of the increase in the relative surplus population was that the embodiments of the working class were further fractionalized by the differential availability of job opportunities, and many women and minority groups were permanently excluded from the better paying jobs. Many of the newly redundant workers, most of them male and white, obtained jobs in the new industries because of their skills and work experience, but to the exclusion of those either waiting at home (Banks, 1981; May, 1989) or in the ghettos. Thus, the rise in the relative surplus population in the 1950s contributed to the political embitterment of some sections of the labour force and therefore to the possibility of a challenge to the ideological insistence on 'self-reliance', and its effect on the state of the balance between the two classes must therefore be read as somewhat ambiguous.

Foreign Trade and Investment   There can be no doubt that, because of the favourable terms of trade then obtaining, foreign trade in the form of imports of foodstuffs, metal ores and oil, etc., was a strong counteracting influence. However, investment abroad probably had an even larger and certainly a more easily quantifiable positive effect. Between 1950 and 1964, the proportion of their after-tax profits which corporations owed to their foreign investments rose from 10 per cent to 22 per cent (Barnet, 1972: 146ff). It was not surprising, therefore, that business opposed Kennedy's proposal to tighten up the taxation procedures relating to overseas corporate earnings, or that it welcomed his Trade Expansion Act. To set against all this, there are strong indications that this influence was over-used during this period. The trade deficits eventually created by the accelerating capital exports depleted the gold stocks, undermined the stability of the dollar and eventually threatened the stability of the Bretton Woods system of international financial management. In other words, they tended to undermine the very market growth required for the profitable utilization of the capital exports. Finally, the considerable domestic job-loss which resulted from these exports reinforced the effects of increased mechanization/automation on the size of the relative surplus population and thereby was yet another contributor to the disaffection of the growing number of permanently under-, sub- and unemployed people who felt they had been denied the possibility of 'self-reliance'.

The Increase of Stock Capital   This counteracting tendency is evidenced by the 100 per cent increase in the number of shareholders between 1952 and 1959. This increase provided not only a wealth of relatively cheap capital (dividends are calculated on net or after-tax income) but also a basis for an ideological offensive on capital's behalf around the theme that 'modern' capitalism was a 'People's Capitalism'.

To summarize, in the context of what was happening on the other sites of class tension, and considering these six counterbalancing influences together, capital's continuing vitality must be deemed to have become markedly less assured by the mid-1960s. Only the politically and ideologically dependent cheapening of constant capital after Kennedy's revision of the depreciation schedules and the ideologically potent increase in the quantum of stock capital may be thought of as unambiguously favourable to capital's continuing profitability. The increase in the size of the relative surplus population, the depression of some wage rates below the value of labour power, the increase in foreign trade and investment and even the growth of contradictory positionings in the class

structure must be considered to have had highly ambiguous consequences, especially for the political or control dimension of class
relations inside and outside the workplace. Moreover, the positive consequences for capital of the increasing intensity of labour cannot be
regarded as having become set and irreversible. The 'responsible
unionism' through whose good offices it had largely been accomplished
could only continue to deliver the goods, and thus routinize economic or
possessory class relations, as long as the other counteracting influences
remained effective. Finally, capital's economic environment contained at
least one other politically and ideologically sensitive factor, never
considered by Marx, which ought to be understood as a counter-
counteracting one as regards not simply the rate of profit but also
capital's very title to this profit: corporate taxation. The latter,
notwithstanding the hopes of the New Economists, appeared ever more
likely to increase, as the embodiments of capital gradually became less
able to manage, not only their own internal disciplinary relations, but
also those they had with the embodiments of contradictory, working
class and racialized positionings.

The Rise of Military Keynesianism

All that said, the greatest single threat to capital's continuing vitality was
an aspect of its political and ideological environment which was almost
completely taken for granted, despite President Eisenhower's valedictory
warning about the burgeoning 'military-industrial complex': namely the
growing dependence of the economy on the state's military budget. I will
therefore complete my account of the increasingly uncertain state of class
relations in the period under review by considering some pertinent
accounts of the role of armaments expenditures in the economies of
advanced capitalist societies. However, before I explain why dependence
upon such expenditures should be so fraught with danger, I will first say
something about the history of the state's armaments spending in the
postwar period and its industrial impact.

   Although some of capital's embodiments explicitly recognized the need
for state aid if prosperity was to be maintained after the end of the
Second World War, they do not appear to have been aware that arms
expenditure could be an effective form of such aid. One reason why the
Employment Act of 1946 was always a dead letter as far as policy-making
was concerned (Bailey, 1950) was that, apart from welfare spending and
tax reductions, which were both ideologically anathema, no obvious,
politically acceptable means of administering any fiscal stimulus was
available.

   With few exceptions, the embodiments of large-scale capital supported
the Marshall Plan and the founding of the World Bank on the grounds
of their potential long-term benefits, but they appear to have been
unaware of any specific, counter-cyclical device that they could support.

This changed in 1948, when Truman asked for, and obtained from Congress, a substantial increase in the military budget in order to counter the Russian threat to Berlin. The beneficial effect of this increase on the then weakening economy was striking. As the *US News and World Report* put it:

> Government planners figure they have found the magic formula for almost endless good times. They are now beginning to wonder if there may not be something to perpetual motion after all. . . Cold war is the catalyst. Cold war is an automatic pump-primer. Turn a spigot, and the public clamors for more arms spending. Turn another, the clamor ceases. Truman confidence cockiness is based on this 'Truman formula.' Truman era of good times, President is told, can run much beyond 1952. Cold war demands, if fully exploited, are almost limitless. (Quoted in Perlo, 1973: 157)

The spigot was turned for the Korean War and then again in 1954, 1958 and 1961. The last turn was different from the others, since Kennedy turned the spigot full on and left it running. Whereas Eisenhower was constrained by his concern to balance the budget and so tried occasionally to turn the tap off or at least qualify its effects by postponing or refusing tax reductions, Kennedy's New Economists convinced him that such inhibitions were unnecessary because full employment had not yet been achieved. For all that Congress remained under the thrall of what Kennedy was soon to term the 'myth' of balanced budgets, it accepted this reasoning with barely a murmur of dissent. Indeed, in some influential circles it was thought that such expenditure, then running at a rate of just below 10 per cent of GNP, could reach 15 per cent without damaging the economy as a whole (Barnet, 1972: 165). By 1965, the rate had in fact fallen to 7.3 per cent, only to rise again with the escalation of the war in Vietnam and as a result to stand at 9.2 per cent in 1967.

A few figures should serve to underline the significance and particularity of this expenditure's impact. Excluding its multiplier and accelerator effects, as well as the 3.4 million service men and women, defence work directly accounted for 4.1 million jobs or 5.9 per cent of total civilian employment in 1967. These jobs were distributed as follows: 16 per cent in the aircraft industry; 7.5 per cent in the radio, television and communications equipment industries; 6.2 per cent in the ordinance industry; and most of the the remainder in the service industries. Some industries were more dependent on these jobs than others: 64 per cent of the jobs in the ordinance industry were dependent on defence contracts, as were 59.1 per cent of the jobs in the aircraft industry and 10.5 per cent of all jobs in manufacturing. In 1965, 55 per cent or $7.8 billion of all the industrial research and development funds were provided by the federal government, and of this fully 80 per cent was used for military purposes (J. Phillips, 1969; 173ff.).

Armaments expenditure also had a substantial effect on regional development, as is suggested by Table 4.1. More specifically still, joint research by the National Planning Association and the US Arms Control

Table 4.1 *Percentage of military prime contract awards by region for selected period*

Region	World War II	Korean War	Fiscal 1961
East North Central	32.4	27.4	11.8
Middle Atlantic	23.6	25.1	19.9
West North Central	5.6	6.8	5.8
South Central	8.8	6.4	8.2
New England	8.9	8.1	10.5
South Atlantic	7.2	7.6	10.6
Pacific	12.3	17.9	26.9
Mountain	1.2	0.7	5.7
Alaska and Hawaii	–	–	0.6
Grand Totals	100.0	100.0	100.0

Source: US Department of Defense, cited in Perlo (1973: 109).

and Disarmament Agency showed that, as of 1967, nine specific and very substantial communities had become especially dependent upon defence-related industries: New London, Groton and Norwich (Connecticut); Binghamptom (New York); Baltimore (Maryland); Charleston (South Carolina); Dallas–Fort Worth, (Texas); San Diego, San Jose, San Francisco and Oakland (California); Seattle and Tacoma (Washington) (Klare, 1972: ch.1).

Apart from leaving the defence tap running, Kennedy was also responsible for a change in the United States' global military strategy. Although he had fought the election with the 'missile gap' slogan, the gap that most concerned him was the one he had discovered in the country's conventional capability. Despite the lessons to be learnt from the Korean experience, the state's defence effort during the 1950s had concentrated on building up a capacity for 'massive (nuclear) retaliation'. Once installed in the White House, and partly as a result of an earlier visit to Vietnam, Kennedy became very concerned by the threat posed by what his aides were soon to call 'Khrushchev's wars of national liberation'. He knew that 'massive retaliation' was an impossible response. Consequently, he fought hard to have the need for a counter-insurgency capacity recognized. In this area, as in his economic policy, he showed himself to be in touch with an influential body of business opinion, since the principal pre-existing proponents of a 'flexible response' strategy were such organizations as the Council for Foreign Relations (the CED's twin) and the Rockefeller Brothers Fund, whose expert in such matters was Henry Kissinger. Kennedy invited one of the initial authors of this policy, General Maxwell Taylor, to join his Administration, first as his principal military advisor and later as Chair of the Joint Chiefs of Staff. The most graphic indication of the President's commitment to the new strategy was his award of the coveted 'green beret' to the Army's Special

Services, a practice that had earlier been discontinued because of its elitism (Stevens, 1976: 14ff.).

The economic significance of this change was that, once again, to quote one source, 'traditional industries such as automotive, mechanical, textile, clothing and rubber have become important military suppliers'. Between 1962 and 1967 the military product-mix shifted nearly 20 per cent in favour of conventional as opposed to more sophisticated equipment. For this reason, then, the Kennedy turn of the Cold War spigot encountered even less Congressional opposition than usual.

The Dangers of Military Keynesianism

Many theories have been developed to explain the whys and wherefores of military spending and its effects on the economy. In what follows only those relevant to the present argument will be considered. Thus I will develop my argument via a brief consideration of the works of Paul Samuelson, J. K. Galbraith, Michael Kidron and David Jaffe. As a New Economist, Samuelson (1973) understands the rise in armaments expenditure to have been an accidental and ironically benign consequence of the threat posed by 'Soviet communism'. In his view, tax changes could have served the same purpose, although the resulting dependence upon something as unpredictable as consumer spending choices would have entailed a loss of managerial precision.

The issue of precision is given more weight by more radical Keynesians such as Galbraith (1967: ch. 29). Whilst Galbraith agrees that the role that military spending had come to play was the accidental consequence of the communist threat, he disagrees with the suggestion that tax-induced changes in consumer spending could ever prove to be an equally effective alternative method of managing a growing economy, especially in respect of its research and development needs. He therefore recommends increased expenditure on space research and social programmes against the hoped-for ending of the Cold War.

On the basis of the work of Piero Sraffa as well as that of Marx, the British economist Michael Kidron (1970: ch. 3) has proposed an 'underconsumptionist' approach to the understanding of the economic effects of state armaments expenditure. He argues that, because of the intrinsic mutual contradiction of its two main dynamic tendencies (the increasing productivity of labour and the narrowing ownership of private property), the viability of the capitalist economy is permanently threatened by the possibility that commodities will be over-produced and the commodity circuit therefore fatally 'interrupted'. For this reason, a mechanism has to be found which stimulates growth without running the risk of disrupting the economy in such a way as to disturb the set pattern of property relations. According to Kidron, 'such a mechanism is to be found in a permanent arms budget'. Spending on armaments both stimulates growth and at the same time reduces the tendency towards over-production, because it wastes both Department I and Department II commodities (producer and consumer goods respectively) by keeping them off the open market. The waste of Department I commodities has the additional advantage of slowing the rate at which the organic composition of capital increases: '. . . arms production is (thus) the seemingly permanent offset to "the tendency of the rate of profit to fall"' (Kidron, 1970: 56).

Kidron's claim that the waste represented by armaments expenditure is neutral with respect to capital's continuing viability has been effectively criticized by David Jaffe. For Jaffe, Kidron so over-emphasizes arms expenditure's demand-management function that he neglects entirely its negative consequences at the level of production:

> The point about state expenditures is that they are financed and paid for out of taxes. If the state finances its expenditures through deficit-spending, to this extent 'future' taxes, which presuppose the future profitability of capital, are assumed. In either case, present or 'future' surplus value is appropriated from private capital by the state, in the form of taxes or loans, to pay for these expenditures. This represents a decline in accumulation and a decline in the rate of growth of the productivity of labour. This is so because the state-induced production is 'unproductive' from the point of view of capitalism as a whole. Although state expenditure 'realizes' surplus value, the products bought by the state do not function, in general, as capital, and therefore do not produce additional surplus value. The finished products that the state buys are acquired with already produced surplus value. The individual private capitalist producing for the state quite clearly gets the average rate of profit and 'surplus value' is produced by his exploited workers. But from the stand-point of society, of total social capital, 'unproductive' state expenditure constitutes a 'drain' of capital. So the profit acquired by the individual capitalist producing for the state comes to him only out of a redistribution of the already produced surplus value. (Jaffe, 1973: 218)

For Jaffe, then, whilst in the short run arms expenditure may bring a certain amount of order to the accumulation process, in the longer run it must undermine the same process, since it wastes both labour power and fixed capital and so reduces that available for capital's expanded reproduction through the making of capital-saving inventions and the increased size of the relative surplus population. In other words, it tends to neutralize not the law of the tendency of the rate of profit to fall, but two of its principal offsets, and so the end result of depending on military Keynesianism must be a fatal weakening of capital's recuperative powers.

Conclusion: Guns or Careers

Although I agree with Jaffe's analysis for the most part, I believe his conclusion is mistaken. The options available to those positioned by capital are considerably more open than he, and indeed Kidron, appear to realize. Thus in Part II I will emphasize both the contribution of armaments expenditure to capital's woes and the role of revenue-saving in relation to the numbers and the salaries of the contradictorily positioned in the alleviation of these woes. The increase in the number and proportion of those members of the labour force who are contradictorily positioned was as much part of the solution to capital's earlier accumulatory problems as colonialism and imperialism and the increases in arms spending which they entailed. Its political, ideological and economic significance was also as great as theirs, if not greater.

PART II
FORGETTING SOCIAL
MODERNISM

5

THE RETURN OF THE REFERENTS

As was made clear above and will become still clearer in Chapter 6, the Great Society programme was primarily a response to pressure from below. Its declaration may have led to the intensification of this pressure but it did not create it. In the context of the somewhat disappointing performance of the capitalist economy that was outlined in Chapter 4, a largely culturally generated critique of social modernism appeared in the course of the 1960s which, whilst it definitely came from below – from those to whom the discourse claimed to refer – was nevertheless largely an imminent one. In other words, the criteria it invoked were almost wholly drawn from within rather than from outside the hegemonic discourse. Ineffective as this critique ultimately turned out to be, it nevertheless made it very difficult for those who continued to enunciate social modernism to respond – having been 'called', so to speak; since denial was impossible, all they could do was forget that they had ever made any of the promises that their critics sought to enforce.

As will be explained in more detail in Chapter 7, it was at this point that, for some, the forgetting of social modernism began. Assuming that the Johnson Administration was in a position to choose whether or not it should do something for the poor, the emerging neo-conservatives began to insist that the prime lesson to be learnt from the 1960s was that government should not make promises (the mature form of this 'governmental overload thesis' is most authoritatively expressed in Crozier et al., 1975). The response of some modernist intellectuals, exemplified by Bell's very influential *The Coming of Post-Industrial Society* (1973), was far more agonized and complex. Appropriately, it began with questions far removed from the hurly burly of political life and ended up by rejecting the very conception of society that it had earlier depended upon. Thus Bell specifically rejected all organicist conceptions of society and declared his preference for a disjunctive (Cubist?) conception of society as an ensemble of three mutually irreducible spheres – the economic, the political and the cultural. As will be explained below (see p. 112ff.), this new starting point allows the possibility that the pressures which produced the demand for the Great Society were cultural rather than economic, and thus had nothing to do with capitalism. And, if capitalism cannot be blamed for the initiation of the crisis, equally it cannot be blamed for the failure to overcome it. Thus the straightforward, ideologically prompted rejectionism of the conservatives was eventually reinforced by the obscurely triggered amnesia of the likes of the once modernistic Bell.

In order to justify this judgement and the analyses of the discursive structures of the texts upon which it depends, the later chapters of this Part will be concerned to make one major point. Chapter 6 will establish that the crisis of the 1960s was in fact a crisis of capitalism. More specifically, it will place the 1960s critiques and the actions that accompanied them in the context of Marxist crisis theory and demonstrate that, though they did not achieve their stated aims, they unknowingly played a significant part in making it impossible for even a modernistic capitalism to fulfil many of the promises made in its name. It is, then, in part understandable, even if it is sociologically entirely unforgivable, that those formerly modernistic intellectuals who could not bring themselves to blame capitalism for its own failures should instead visit their scorn on those who tried harder than they did to make capitalism live up to its promises.

For most of the groups from which the dissidents of the 1960s came, and in a material sense at least, life in the late 1950s and early 1960s was either reasonably comfortable or at least better than it had been for their parents. It was, however, not comfortable enough relative to the promises implicit in corporate liberalism and was rapidly becoming ever more explicit in its modernist variant. This, it seems to me, is the key to understanding two things: first, why the dissidents latterly became so extremely angry, when on the face of it many of them had relatively little to be angry about; and second, why they criticized their society for not living up to its own stated values rather than for not being another and better type of society. Student leader, Meldon Levine, later put the point memorably; at the Harvard Commencement of 1969, he said that the country faced a 'conflict of conscience: our practice of your values' (quoted in Huntington, 1981: 2–3).

As the dissidents became angrier, they broadened and/or intensified their assault but they did not change either their target or the criteria upon which they based their critiques. The fragments of the dissident discourses outlined below will confirm that, even at the moment of its greatest vulnerability, social modernism retained its hegemonic hold in the social formation. It was not so much that the dissidents did not want to shift their target – to capitalism or to patriarchy or racism, for example – as that they were unable to do so and still remain in serious ideological contention. This is confirmed by the rapid demise, in some instances physical as well as political, of those organizations which did make such a shift: for example, the Students for a Democratic Society (SDS) after the Progressive Labor Party (PLP) took over; and the African-American left after the emergence of the Black Panther Party for Self-Defense (BPPSD). Neither the gay nor the women's movements, whose criticisms seldom exceeded those possible within the terms of social modernism, suffered the same fate.

In order to support, if not prove (that would take a far more exhaustive report than the one below) this characterization of the discourses of protest, I will now outline what I believe to be a representative fragment of each of the dissident discourses at early points in their development. This outline will be ordered chronologically and according to the increasing anger present in the texts. This should not be taken to suggest that I necessarily think for example, that all African-American texts were, as a rule, angrier than all rank and file trade union texts. (In any case African-American writers figure prominently amongst the authors of rank and file texts.)

The Rank and File Movement: A Challenge to 'Responsible Unionism'?

As it happens, the first of the texts to be discussed was written by just such an African-American rank-and-filer. Published in 1963, James Boggs' *The American Revolution: Pages from a Negro Worker's Notebook* was in some ways a prophetic book and in others, albeit undeservedly, an anachronism. I have chosen to discuss it first because of both of these qualities.

Boggs' text was prophetic in that, like those of later dissidents, it took as its object of criticism an element within corporate liberal ideology – 'responsible unionism' – and voiced this criticism from the position of one to whom this sign supposedly referred. It was, however, also anachronistic in that, unlike the later dissidents, its critique was inspired, not by the failure of the unions to meet what they themselves might agree were their responsibilities, but rather by their betrayal of a deeper interest. This deeper interest Boggs saw, in the Marxist and socialist manner, as that of the working class. Having said this, it is nevertheless also the case that, in the way in which he defined this interest – as freedom from work, Boggs did anticipate one of the more visionary aims of those who succeeded him (cp. Zerzan, 1974):

Anyone listening and talking to workers in the auto plants today can tell that the workers are through with the union. . . Today the problem of control over production and the solution of their specific local grievances will have to be dealt with by larger sections of the population. These are now more than ever before, questions which require the taking on of the union, the city government, the state government, and the national government. . . As the company regained control of production through bargaining with the union and through automation, the workers have been losing control of the union. So that just as the workers today know that they have to challenge more than the plant management for control over production, so they know that merely taking over the union today would gain them very little. Historically, workers move ahead by the new. *That is, they bypass existing organizations and form new ones uncorrupted by past habits and customs.* (Boggs, 1963: 27–32; emphasis in the original)

In sum, then, Boggs' text is of interest for two main reasons. First, it was one of the earliest instances of a dissident discourse which would later reappear in a surprisingly large number of American workplaces and even elicit significant legal countermoves on the part of the Supreme Court (Woodiwiss, 1990b: 253–6). Second, like the others to be discussed below, its publication accompanied the ascension of modernism into the corporate liberal firmament. However, for Boggs, unlike the vast majority of those who succeeded him, there was an 'other' to social modernism, namely socialism. The disappearance of this 'other' from the dissident discourses of the 1960s will now be illustrated, as will (in the same movement) the strengthening hegemony of social modernism even in the texts produced by its staunchest critics.

The Student Movement: A Challenge to 'Opportunity'?

Amongst the dissidents, perhaps those who ostensibly had least to reproach their modernistic society for were the students, particularly those at the so-called elite universities where their revolt began. However, I intend to argue that what most bothered the students initially was a suspicion that the 'opportunity' they had been given might not be all that it was supposed to be, and that later, illusory or not, its loss came to be even more feared. What the student radicals came to fear most – rightly in my judgement – was that they would lose their promised perquisites – their salary differentials, their lifestyle and their 'cultured' status – and be consigned back to the proletariat whence many of their parents had only recently and in part escaped. The second of these occurrences is inherent in the first, as may be illustrated by quoting from Bradford Cleaveland's seminal, 1964 Letter to (Berkeley) Undergraduates, which addressed the problem of what was soon to be called 'the multiversity' or 'the knowledge factory'. In a passage not quoted below, this boisterous and not yet enraged critique defined its own limits in almost the same terms that Levine was to use so many years later (see above, p. 75); that is, it identified the students' as well as the society's problem as the existence of a yawning gap between 'common (and sometimes beautiful) illusions . . . and what actually happens':

It was like this: on the one hand there was substantial agreement that the University stamps out consciousness like a super-madison-avenue-machine; on the other people saying, 'So what?' or 'Bring me a detailed and exhaustive plan.' *But there is no plan for kicking twenty thousand people IN THEIR ASSES!* No plan will stop excessive greed, timidity, and selling out. At best the

University is a pathway to the club of 'tough-minded-liberal-realists' in America, who sit in comfortable armchairs talking radical while clutching hysterically at respectability in a world explosive with revolution. At worst the University destroys your desires to see reality, and to suffer with optimism, at that time when you most need to learn that painful art. In between those two poles is mostly garbage: Bus Ad; Ph.D candidates 'on the make'; departmental enclaves of 'clever and brilliant' students who will become hack critics; and thousands of trainees for high-class trades which will become obsolete in ten years . . . your routine is comprised of a systematic psychological and spiritual brutality inflicted by a faculty of 'well-meaning and nice' men who have decided that your situation is hopeless when it comes to actually participating in serious learning. As an undergraduate you receive a four-year-long series of sharp staccatos: eight semesters, forty courses, one hundred twenty or more units, fifteen hundred to two thousand impersonal lectures, and over three hundred oversized 'discussion' meetings. Approaching what is normally associated with learning: reading, writing, and exams, your situation becomes absurd. Over a period of four years you receive close to fifty bibliographies, ranging in length from one to eight pages, you are examined on more than one hundred occasions, and you are expected to write forty to seventy-five papers. As you well know, reading means 'getting into' hundreds of books, many of which are secondary sources, in a superficial manner. You must cheat to keep up. If you don't cheat you are forced to perform without time to think in depth, and consequently you must hand in papers and exams which are almost as shameful as the ones you've cheated on. (reprinted in Jacobs and Landau, 1967: 219–20)

In its early days SDS, the major national student organization, generated a sense of what it supposed was an 'other' to social modernism and recommended it as a guide to be used in the effort to overcome the gap which the likes of Cleaveland had identified. This guide was the vision of 'a participatory democracy' contained within its founding document, The Port Huron Statement of 1962 – a vision inspired by the work of such early opponents of the world-weary reading of modernism as C.W. Mills and Paul Goodman (Attewell, 1984; Clecak, 1973; J. Miller, 1987; Pells, 1985):

In a participatory democracy, the political life would be based in several root principles:
   that decision-making of basic social consequence be carried on by public groupings;
   that politics be seen positively, as the art of collectively creating an acceptable pattern of social relations;
   that politics has the function of bringing people out of isolation and into community, thus being a necessary, though not sufficient, means of finding meaning in personal life;
   that the political order should serve to clarify problems in a way instrumental to their solution; it should provide outlets for the expression of personal grievance and aspiration; opposing views should be organized so as to illuminate choices and facilitate the attainment of goals; channels should be commonly available to relate men to knowledge and to power so that private problems – from bad recreation facilities to personal alienation – are formulated as general issues.
   The economic sphere would have as its basis the principles:
   that work should involve incentives worthier than money or survival. It

should be educative, not stultifying; creative not mechanical; self-directed, not manipulated, encouraging independence, a respect for others, a sense of dignity and a willingness to accept social responsibility, since it is experience that has crucial influence of habits, perceptions and individual ethics;

   that the economic experience is so personally decisive that the individual must share in its full determination;

   that the economy itself is of such social importance that its major resources and means of production should be open to democratic participation and subject to democratic social regulation. (Jacobs and Landau, 1967: 160-1)

Although one cannot deny that such figures as Mills and Goodman were opposed to the emerging academic and political orthodoxy, if the Port Huron Statement is an at all accurate summation of their views as to the nature of 'the good society' (and I think that it is), then the social vision which they and it projected, so far from being an 'other', or an 'alternative' (to use the language of the time), was in fact the *same* as that projected by social modernism. (Is this, I wonder, why Mills and SDS, for example, are still so often congratulated by sympathetic historians for their 'indigenous American radicalism'?)

To be more specific, there is no indication either in the document itself or in the wider SDS literature as to what the substantive content of a participatory politics and economics might be: would it be 'business as usual' or material equality? Moreover, the modernistic and pluralist school of political science which was emerging by then (see Dahl, 1961, for example) had already claimed that American politics was anyway quite as participatory as that which SDS envisioned. In addition, 'modern', 'progressive' or 'liberal' industrialists had long asserted that work in their plants should be, and anyway often already was, all the things that SDS hoped for. In sum, the alternative so beloved of the SDSers (and their historians) was simply social modernism deferred. Thus it provided the basis for neither a powerful critique of the hegemonic discourse nor an attractive political programme – why support a group of powerless longhairs, if they are only promising you that some time in the future, and after a lot of 'blood, sweat and tears', you can have what the powerful say you can have today or soon, 'no sweat'? In this way, then, social modernism's hegemony resulted in the formation of an 'other' that was a mirror-image of itself, and the discursive world of the United States closed the door on itself and entered that endlessly self-referring condition which was eventually to become known as hyperreality. Thereafter the United States no longer possessed an 'other', on the 'political' left at least, that could serve as a basis for 'making something else' of itself.

However, even this mirage of an 'other' did, for a time, reassure those who feared that they were about to lose what they considered to be their birthright, that someone was on their side. At least it did until the threat of being drafted to Vietnam turned the occasional boisterousness of the confident into the rage of the terrified. I will argue in Chapter 6 that the justifiably frightened young men who sought to 'dodge' the draft, along with the other dissident groups, did in the event, if still unknowingly, create a radical critique of social modernism, if still not a convincing 'other' to it. Here I want simply to point out that, contrary to the received view, the Port Huron Statement was not such a critique.

The Women's Movement: A Challenge to Social Modernism as a Whole?

If even the most ostensibly radical of the dissidents, who sat down deliberately to produce an 'other' to social modernism, failed to do so, it should not be a surprise that no such 'other' may be found in the early writings associated with either the women's or the black liberation movements. These were derived from discursive heritages in which the 'other' represented by socialism had played a relatively small part, and although their critiques of social modernism were from the start far more comprehensive than those generated within the labour movement and amongst the students, there is little or no trace of any 'other' to social modernism within such texts.

Unknowingly, Betty Friedan acknowledged exactly this quality about her text when she entitled the dramatic opening chapter of *The Feminine Mystique* (1963), 'The Problem that Has No Name', and began it by posing her famous question 'Is this all?' The publication of Friedan's book inaugurated the contemporary discourse of feminism, and at the same time indicated that, at its most potent, this discourse operated within the bounds of social modernism and so figured, not as a substitute for it, but rather as a transgression of its internal sub-divisions. In sum, the feminism of the 1960s represented an early instance of the irony that attaches to all effective criticism in a self-referring ideological world – the more successful the critique, the more secure becomes the hegemonic regime which is the supposed object of criticism. And, as with the Port Huron Statement, this result is brought about by the unconscious adoption of social modernism as the source of the criteria that are used to criticize the self-same discourse. The net result, then, of such criticism is that it doubly validates social modernism, first, by re-endorsing its core values and, second, by repeating the discourse that carries these values. This, I will now show, is what happens as Friedan (1963: 44–7) produces the critique of that staple of popular culture in the 1950s, the 'Happy Housewife Heroine', which is the linchpin of her analysis.

Friedan's first 'typical specimen' is a story from the *Ladies' Home Journal* called 'The Sandwich Maker'. In it, a young housewife seeks to gain a measure of financial independence by making sandwiches and selling them to her husband's workmates. For one reason and another it proves impossible for her to sustain her little enterprise and she is forced to recognize that, in her husband's words, 'You're a mother. That's your job. You don't have to earn money, too.'

Her second specimen is a story from *Redbook* magazine called 'A Man Who Acted Like a Husband':

[In this story a] career-woman-devil tempts Junior [the child-bride heroine] with the lure of a job to keep her from breast-feeding her baby. She even restrains the young mother from going to her baby when it cries at 2 a.m. But she gets her comeuppance when George, the husband, discovers the crying baby uncovered, in a freezing wind from an open window, with blood running down its cheek. Kay [the career-woman-devil], reformed and repentant, plays hookey from her job to get her own child and start life anew. And Junior, gloating at the 2 a.m. feeding – 'I'm glad, glad, glad I'm just a housewife' starts to dream about the baby, growing up to be a housewife too. (p. 47)

Friedan's third specimen, a story from the magazine *McCall's* called 'Almost a Love Affair', is only briefly mentioned as one involving a housewife in a choice between her family responsibilities and 'interest in some international cause'. Her fourth and final specimen is another story from *McCall's*, called 'I Didn't Want to Tell You', in which, a competent, independent-minded woman is shown to be at risk of losing her husband until she heeds a friend's advice to show her husband that she needs him to protect her:

[that night] she hears a noise that might be a burglar; even though she knows it's only a mouse, she calls helplessly to her husband, and wins him back. As he comforts her pretended panic, she murmurs that, of course he was right in their argument that morning. 'She lay still in the soft bed, smiling in sweet, secret satisfaction, scarcely touched with guilt.' (p. 47)

Friedan ends her discussion of these stories as follows:

The end of the road, in an almost literal sense, is the disappearance of the heroine altogether, as a separate self and the subject of her own story. The end of the road is togetherness, where the woman has no independent self to hide even in guilt; she exists only for and through her husband and children. (p. 47)

What is of interest here is not so much the fact of women's exclusion from the world outside the home, which is Friedan's entirely reasonable interest, but instead the fact that what the women in these stories are excluded from is *very precisely*, and no more and no less than, the world of social modernism. Thus, Friedan regrets, perhaps unconsciously, the denial to women of 'self-reliance' (the first story), 'opportunity' (the second story) and the chance to demonstrate their 'responsibility' (the third story), whilst at the same time there is an insistence on their 'loyalty' (the fourth story). Ironically, but of course, Friedan ends her discussion with a scathing reference to the then dominant sign in discourses on the family, 'togetherness', which was but a particular variant of the claims to have achieved a conflict-free society which were then being made by social modernism.

The fact that Friedan subsequently goes on to expound simply how women came to be excluded from the world of social modernism explains the limitations of her text as an interpretation of women's oppression, and, in particular, the limitations that follow from its lack of any analysis of economic or class-structural constraints. Many individual women have subsequently proved the value of the admonition with which Friedan closes her book – get a 'life plan'. No matter how many individual women may have escaped, however, the economic and class-cultural constraints remain in place, constituted in part by sexist discourses and practices which have shut out the vast majority of women from even the social modernist world.

The Black Liberation Movement: Another Challenge to Social Modernism as a Whole?

As was made clear in the preceding part, the exclusion of African-Americans from the world of social modernism was even more complete than that of women. They were often denied the chance to be 'self-reliant'; they were very seldom given any 'opportunity'; they were typically denied 'responsibilities', even to the extent of being excluded from unions; their 'loyalty' was highly suspect (to the FBI, for example); and their pigmentation and African ancestry made them supposed incarnations of the opposite to 'modern'. So complete was this exclusion that many, including some African-Americans themselves, considered African-Americans to be social modernism's automatic 'other'.

One such African-American was Eldridge Cleaver, whose *Soul on Ice* (1967) records his struggle against this self-conception. As is clear from Cleaver's book, perhaps the most difficult aspect of any such struggle is acknowledging that such a negative self-conception exists at all. Cleaver eventually recognized that its presence was shown in him by his denial of his desire for white women – a denial whose symptoms were his repeated rapes of 'The Ogre' that white women had become for him. In the course of a sustained interrogation of his prison environment he was galvanized by what he was hearing about what was happening on the outside, especially to the emerging black leadership (the assassination of Malcolm X, for example) and amongst the white youth. And in this context he gradually discovered the idea that would enable him to understand, and come to terms with, his desire for white women in such a way that he would no longer hate them or be unable to desire black women. He discovered, or better, rediscovered, what W.E.B. Dubois had referred to many years earlier as the 'veil' of racism. However, the difficulties that have to be overcome in making this discovery indicate that the gift of 'second sight', which Dubois had suggested is granted to all those who discover the veil, is not something that comes easily.

In Cleaver's case the veil, or 'myth' as he termed it, rested upon the following structure:

> Blacks and whites being conceived as mutually exclusive types, those attributes imputed to the blacks could not also be imputed to the whites – at least not in equal degree – without blurring the line separating the races. These images were based upon the social function of the two races, the work they performed. The ideal white man was one who knew how to use his head, who knew how to manage and control things and get things done. Those whites who were not

in a position to perform these functions nevertheless aspired to them. The ideal black man was one who did exactly what he was told, and did it efficiently and cheerfully. 'Slaves,' said Frederick Douglass, 'are generally expected to sing as well as work.' (Cleaver, 1967: 78)

This, then, is the discursive matrix which produces black men and white women as apparent opposites – 'the super-masculine menial' and 'the ultrafeminine' – and which, therefore, in Cleaver's view makes them irresistible to one another.

However, once the veil so constructed had been pierced and the 'real' equality of the black 'other' with its white counterpart had been asserted, and notwithstanding the omnipresence of Marxist rhetoric, a programme of social transformation which simply demanded that this equality be recognized in practice was commonly thought to be sufficient. This was the case, for example, even with the programme of the Black Panther Party for Self-Defense, for which Cleaver served as Minister of Information:

Full Employment for Our People
    An End to the Robbery by the White Man of Our Black Community; Payment in Currency as Restitution for Slave Labour and Mass Murder of Black People
    Decent Housing, Fit for Shelter of Human Beings
    Education for Our People That Exposes Decadent American Society
    Exemption of Blackmen from Military Service for a Racist Government
    An End to Police Brutality and Murder of Black People by Organizing Armed Self-Defense Groups
    Freedom for All Black Prisoners Because They Haven't Had a Fair Impartial Trial
    Black Defendants Should be Tried by a Jury of Their Peers
    Land, Bread, Housing, Education, Clothing, Justice, and Peace
    A United Nations Plebiscite in the Black Colony to Determine the Will of Black People as to Their National Destiny. (Blair, 1978: 90)

As it turned out, any possibility that this programme might form the basis for the construction of a positive 'other' to social modernism had disappeared with the assassination of Malcolm X and the intensification of the violent repression of those who might have been its architects. The result was that the hegemonic discourse later made a little office-room available for some African-Americans, in the same grudging way that it was to do for some women.

Conclusion

Whilst the dissidents' scepticism was initially aroused by the the gap between ideological promise and lived reality, they were finally enraged and therefore obsessed by the fact that their critiques were met only by ever greater promises – 'The Great Society'. Given the costs that all had to bear in relation to the waging of an undeclared war in Vietnam, this simply made the hypocrisy of the powerful even starker. In short, social modernism was such an easy target that few felt the need to seek another, regardless of how angry they became.

6

THE VIETNAM WAR, PROTEST AND CLASS RELATIONS

This chapter will address the question: 'How did the actions inspired by an alternative discourse which was of a piece with the hegemonic one come to have such socially disruptive consequences?' As will become apparent, the decisions that Kennedy made most easily, perhaps rather thoughtlessly and probably because he had little choice, must be central to any attempt to answer this question. Chief amongst these were the decisions to increase defence expenditure and commit United States military personnel in Vietnam (anti-communism was after all integral to social modernism). Defence and space expenditures rose by some $11 billion between 1961 and 1965 and thereby contributed almost as much to the post-1964 stimulation of the economy as the tax reductions. Kennedy thought he had chosen tax reduction over expenditure increases, Heller and private initiative over Galbraith and state planning. But in fact he had done all of these things simultaneously and, to make matters worse, the expenditure increases he had initiated were not the planned and controllable ones proposed by such as Galbraith, but the unplanned and, as it turned out, uncontrollable ones that follow from undertaking hubristic, foreign military adventures.

A New Type of Capitalist Crisis

The ideological challenge that occurred in the latter half of the 1960s appears to have been too modest to lead to such dramatic consequences. In what follows, the theory of crisis outlined in the Introduction will be used to show that, largely unknowingly, this modest challenge and the actions that either inspired or were inspired by it happened to strike capital at some of its points of greatest vulnerability.

Over the period 1950–64 tensions within the class structure increased, as evidenced by the readings of the states of the pertinent balances in Chapter 4. At the same time American industry was operating some 20 per cent below capacity. Despite spectacular gains in GNP and the living standards of some, the system had in fact been stagnating at its core, the accumulation process. For this reason I cannot agree with the explanations of what happened subsequently that have been provided by such scholars as Robert Stevens, James Tobin and Arthur Okun, each of whom emphasizes the significance of avoidable policy errors. In my view, even if the principles of the New Economics had been followed correctly,

Table 6.1 *Annual rates of return on nonfinancial corporate capital**

Year	Actual		Cyclically adjusted	
	Net 1	Gross 2	Net 3	Gross 4
1948	13.3	11.9	13.64	12.11
1949	11.6	11.0	13.30	12.05
1950	13.9	12.0	13.44	12.21
1951	13.2	12.3	12.18	11.67
1952	11.5	11.2	10.82	10.78
1953	10.9	10.9	10.22	10.48
1954	10.3	10.6	9.28	11.23
1955	12.4	11.9	12.40	11.90
1956	10.6	10.9	10.94	11.11
1957	9.8	10.5	10.48	10.92
1958	8.5	9.7	10.54	10.96
1959	10.7	11.1	11.89	11.84
1960	9.9	10.6	11.60	11.65
1961	9.8	10.6	11.50	11.65
1962	11.2	11.6	12.22	12.23
1963	11.9	12.0	12.92	12.63
1964	12.8	12.6	13.48	13.02
1965	13.7	13.2	13.70	13.20
1966	13.4	13.2	12.72	12.78
1967	11.9	12.2	11.53	11.97
1968	11.7	12.1	11.36	11.89
1969	10.2	11.1	9.86	10.89
1970	8.1	9.7	9.12	10.33
1971	8.4	9.9	9.42	11.53
1972	9.2	10.4	9.54	10.61
1973	8.6	9.9	8.26	9.69
1974	6.4	8.4	8.10	9.45
1975	6.9	8.9	10.30	11.00
1976	7.9	9.7	10.28	11.17

* All rates of return are before tax and are based on interest paid as well as profits. The net rates of return relate capital income net of depreciation to the net capital stock. The gross rates of return relate capital income before depreciation to gross capital stock. All rates of return exclude real capital gains. (Adapted from Feldstein and Summers, 1977: 216.)

the phenomenon of 'stagflation' that has so mystified Keynesian economists would still have occurred and proved resistant to treatment. Something new was happening, the rate of profit had begun to fall. Developments relating to the newly salient political and ideological dimensions of class relations meant that the old equations 'growth equals inflation', 'recession equals deflation' had ceased to hold. This, plus the early and related abortion of the Kennedy revival which resulted from the escalation of the war in Vietnam, may be confirmed by an analysis of Table 6.1.

Column 2, gross rate of return, is the nearest to the Marxist measure of profitability. The difference between Column 2 and Column 1, net rate of return, shows that the effect of depreciation allowances, which was negative in the late 1950s, became positive after the Kennedy revision in 1963 and then negative again after the Vietnam escalation in 1966. The difference between Column 2 and Column 4, the cyclically adjusted gross rate of return, shows the effect of the level of capacity utilization. Again, it was negative in the late 1950s and only became positive because of Kennedy's stimulative measures. It is clear, therefore, that, although of course it did not itself think in such terms, the assertively modernistic Kennedy Administration was measurably on the right track so far as the rate of profit was concerned.

In addition, as was made clear in Chapter 3, it was at least aware of the problems that were developing around the other counteracting influences. In an attempt to guarantee the loyalty of the responsible unionists and hence secure its possessory advantage, it set up incorporative tripartite advisory committees. In an attempt to contain the threat to its disciplinary control which was emerging because of relative over-population, the depression of wages below subsistence and foreign investment, it began to soften the insistence on 'self-reliance' and formulate a 'war on poverty'. For the same reason it also tried to stimulate commodity exports and so reduce the outflow of capital. Finally, the tax cut and the investment tax credit indicate that it was aware of the problems posed by the counter-counteracting influence of corporate taxation as well as by any imbalance between the two departments of production. However, because of Vietnam, the tax cut had a surprisingly small effect on the rate of profit, and corporate taxation has remained a potent counter-counteracting influence and a significant qualification to capital's right of title, as is suggested by Table 6.2.

It is impossible to know, of course, whether or not Johnson, who was committed to the same policies, would have succeeded in maintaining or increasing the rate of profit had it not been for the war. However, although there are those who suggest that the speed-up in the business cycle after 1945 made a major crisis inevitable, I would argue that continued adherence to Kennedy's policies would have at least postponed such a crisis for a while. In any event it seems to me that the degree of political, ideological and economic strain created by the war in Vietnam is more than enough to explain the initiation of the downward trend in profits, provided of course that the nature of this strain is specified and related to the movement in the balance of class forces. It is apparent from Tables 6.1 and 6.2 that the Korean War did not have the same effect. I would suggest that this was because the political and ideological dimensions of class relations were somewhat less pertinent to the rate of profit at that time, and anyway the balances of class forces were all far more favourable to capital than they were later to become.

Table 6.2 *Genuine rates of percentage return on nonfinancial corporate capital and tax rates 1948–73*

Year	Genuine rate of return		Tax rate on corporate income	
	Before tax	After tax	Genuine	Nominal
1948	17.3	9.7	43.9	27.7
1949	14.5	8.8	39.3	34.9
1950	16.7	7.5	55.1	44.1
1951	16.6	6.4	61.2	45.1
1952	13.8	6.0	56.5	47.9
1953	13.3	5.5	58.7	53.8
1954	12.5	6.2	50.4	47.8
1955	15.5	7.9	49.0	42.2
1956	13.4	6.5	51.4	39.0
1957	12.2	6.1	50.0	38.4
1958	10.4	5.4	48.1	41.3
1959	13.0	6.8	47.7	44.6
1960	12.0	6.3	47.5	44.5
1961	11.8	6.3	46.6	45.8
1962	13.5	7.9	41.5	40.3
1963	14.0	8.1	42.1	39.7
1964	15.0	9.1	39.3	37.1
1965	16.3	10.0	38.7	34.8
1966	16.1	9.9	38.5	33.3
1967	14.0	8.8	37.1	31.4
1968	14.0	8.1	42.1	34.9
1969	11.6	6.4	44.8	31.9
1970	9.1	5.3	41.8	26.9
1971	9.6	5.7	40.6	27.5
1972	9.9	5.6	43.4	28.6
1973	10.5	5.4	48.6	33.3

(From Nordhaus, 1974: 180: the difference between the figures in Column 1 in this table and Column 2 in Table 6.1 is accounted for by Feldstein and Summers' use of a more recent data base.)

The Vietnam War and the Failure of Economic Modernism

In September 1964, the National Security Council sent a memorandum to those engaged in planning the intervention in Vietnam: 'The President emphasizes again that no activity of this kind should be delayed in any way by any feeling that our resources for this purpose are restricted. We can find the money. . .' (Barnet, 1972: 108). The majority of the population did not know there was a war on until the spring of 1966. In January 1966, Johnson told Congress that, 'I am unwilling to declare a moratorium on our progress toward the Great Society (in order to finance the war in Vietnam)'. Even as late as January 1967 Secretary McNamara said, 'There are many . . . prices we pay for the war in South Vietnam . . . but in my opinion one of them is not strain on our economy'

(Stevens, 1976: 53). The difference between the 1964 statement and the later ones is the difference between over-confidence and impotence. By 1966/67, both Johnson and McNamara knew perfectly well that they were riding a tiger. The war in Vietnam meant that military expenditures had to be continually increased, whilst the pressure on profit margins and the inflation that the war had unleashed at home made it impossible for the Administration to finance both wars properly: neither capital nor labour was prepared to pay the bills, and the state lacked the power to force the issue.

At the beginning of 1965 there had been general satisfaction with the state of the economy. Full capacity had nearly been reached and the only problems were that unemployment had not fallen quite as much as had been expected and, luxuriously, the growth rate was too high – 5½ per cent instead of the optimum 5 per cent. This mood was destroyed when, in February 1965, the war in Vietnam was escalated, but, instead of being intimidated by the United States' 'surge' capacity, the Vietnamese miraculously succeeded in matching the escalation. The state's national security managers quickly realized that they were in for a long and costly war. However, they did not communicate this diagnosis to the economic managers, who proved to be incapable of divining it on the basis of their own array of economic indicators. Consequently, the economic results of the escalation were making themselves felt long before the economic managers realized it. As CEA member Arthur Okun (1970: 68) subsequently put it, in strikingly modernistic terms: 'Our intelligence system for tracking current movements did not perform well.'

What had happened was this: defence orders had begun to rise very quickly in early 1965 but, since such orders do not show up as expenditures until they are paid for, many of them did not appear on the accounts until the following year or later. They did, however, show up in the private sector as increases in investment and inventories as industry prepared for the expected bonanza. It was the significance of these latter increases which all but a lonely few of the economic managers failed to pick up. These few were in the Federal Reserve, which accordingly raised its discount rate from 4 to 4½ per cent and thereby called down upon itself the wrath of the White House. However, the Fed maintained its position and its diagnosis was soon, if belatedly, accepted as correct.

In sum, the economy had taken off amidst general ignorance and with little planning. Instead of declining, the growth rate soared to 8½ per cent in the nine months following mid-1965. Once the dangers in the situation had been recognized, a policy was formulated to cool things down. It consisted of the monetary restraint imposed by the Fed and a proposed tax increase. The problem was that business, labour and Congress had just begun to enjoy the fruits of the tax cut that, against their better judgement in many cases, they had only recently been convinced was what they needed. To suggest, therefore, that they should give these fruits up for the sake of an undeclared war, which they had anyway been told would be over by 30 June 1967, was a political non-starter.

In the event, the proposed tax increase was never even tabled in either chamber of the Congress. After sounding out the Business Council and the House Ways and Means Committee, the President realized that it did not stand a chance and asked his economic advisors to think again about how to finance the war. All they could suggest was that the Administration should bide its time until the evidence of economic overheating became manifest to everyone and so changed the political climate. Unfortunately for this prescription, the tight monetary policy being pursued by the Federal Reserve caused a credit squeeze in mid-1966, which depressed the construction industry, paralysed the market in city bonds, slowed the rate of investment and curtailed the rise in consumer spending. Thus, when in January 1967 the Administration eventually called for a tax increase, the Congress refused – this time on the ground that it was worried by the possibility of a recession.

The state's failure to perform the economic management role assigned to it by social modernism had disastrous consequences for the overall stability of the economy. By 1968, the deficit on the federal government's full-employment budget was three years old, had reached a figure of $25.3 billion and was increasing at the rate of 100 per cent per year. The rate of inflation had doubled, so that by the same date it stood at 4 per cent. The favourable trade balance, excluding such deficit-increasing items as capital exports and military expenses, was halved. Given these facts and the ever-mounting social unrest associated with the war, the political conditions necessary for taking the measures needed to gain control of the situation had at last appeared, as Okun has so clearly explained:

> The need for economic restraint became clear to the Congress and the public early in 1968 when the horror stories of the economic forecasts began to come true. Prices accelerated to a 4 per cent rate of increase; interest rates rose far above their 1966 peaks; and our world trade surplus again shrank. The economy moved into a feverish boom with a huge advance in GNP of $19 billion in the first quarter of 1968.
>
> Even so, it took major efforts by the American business community and the world financial community to dramatize the urgency of the need for fiscal restraint. With gratifying sophistication and public spirit, our business leaders lined up solidly and vocally behind the tax increase. The advocacy of bankers and homebuilders for higher taxes could be discounted because they were so vulnerable to tight money, but when industrialists traveled to Washington to volunteer – indeed, to demand – to pay higher taxes, our legislators were greatly impressed. The plea was so obviously contrary to the immediate selfish interests of the petitioners that it could be attributed only to a deeply felt sense of the public interest.
>
> The threat of international financial crisis may well have been the single most decisive factor in getting Congress to move on fiscal restraint. The devaluation of sterling in November 1967 was an event extraneous to U.S. economic conditions. But, by generating serious uncertainties in international financial markets, it made the dollar particularly vulnerable to attack. As a

result, internal U.S. conditions were subjected to intensive scrutiny throughout the world. Our legislative stalemate on taxes was read about as a threat of failure of the democratic process in the United States and a clear indication that we lacked the will to keep our economic affairs under control. In the spring of 1968, the United States was not a well-managed bank; and its depositors – foreign central bankers – were understandably nervous.

Few Americans comprehend the nature and economic significance of an international financial crisis. But the specter of 'the downfall of the dollar' makes a much more frightening picture than the threat of an acceleration of one or two percentage points in prices or interest rates. The pleas and threats, the cajolery and rebukes of central bankers around the world had a major impact on our political process. Suddenly, the words of conservative international bankers became music to the ears of liberal American economists. Without the world bankers, I seriously doubt that we would have enacted the fiscal program that was so urgently needed for our own good. (1970: 88–9)

In June 1968, President Johnson signed the Revenue and Expenditure Control Act, which imposed a 10 per cent surcharge on individual and corporate incomes and a $6 billion cutback on all non-Vietnam federal expenditures. However, the effort had proved too much for Johnson, and he announced that he would not stand for re-election. It also proved to be the undoing of the Democrats, since Nixon and not Humphrey took his place.

The process of de-escalating the war, at least in the sense of economic de-mobilization, had begun and the new President commenced his long drawn out and somewhat disingenuous effort to achieve 'peace with honour' by 'Vietnamizing' the war. In addition, Nixon's increasingly 'Friedmanesque' or 'monetarist' economic advisors had what may usefully be referred to as some 'pre-modern' ideas of their own on the topic of how to bring the economy and especially inflation under control (see above, p. 21). On their advice, non-Vietnam federal expenditures were cut and the growth of the money supply was dramatically slowed. In this way they hoped to take the heat out of the economy by creating a 'mild recession'. The result was the most serious recession for twelve years and, contrary to all previous experience, record levels of inflation. In sum, because of their hurry to prove their points against the New Economists, the Friedmanites had failed to properly gauge the consequences of combining a de-escalation of the war and increasing taxes. They had responded to the inflation as if it were still 'demand-pull', when it had in fact become 'cost-push'.

Within a year, they were forced to reverse their policies, and under 'game-plan II', they increased the money supply by more than 30 per cent in an effort to combat unemployment. When this too failed, a strange reversal of economic parts took place. In 1971, Arthur Burns of the Federal Reserve declared that he had lost faith in the efficacy of monetary policy in such a situation and suggested a voluntary prices and incomes policy. The President, however, was still committed to 'game-plan II' and threatened to deprive the Federal Reserve of its independence if such heresy continued to issue from it. This strong affirmation of the existing policy prompted some to dub it 'Nixon's Four-Point Do-Nothing Plan':

1 Not going to institute a wage-price review board.
2 Not going to impose mandatory wage-price controls.
3 Not going to ask for tax relief.
4 Not going to increase federal spending.
(quoted in Stevens, 1976: 181)

No sooner had this plan been reaffirmed than it was replaced by 'game-plan III', which featured what else but a wage–price 'freeze'. This turnaround may be accounted for by reference to developments in the international financial system, which, because of the massive trade deficits consequent on the war and an accelerating flight of capital, was flooded with dollars. Had all these been redeemed for gold, as was technically possible, the United States' gold reserves, which had already been halved, would have suffered still greater depredations, thus endangering the solvency of the entire economy. For this reason, in August 1971, Nixon not only introduced the aforementioned 'freeze' in order to restore world confidence, but also declared that the dollar was no longer convertible against gold. In this way he at least began to get to grips with inflation but at the cost of destroying the trade-encouraging Bretton Woods system of fixed exchange rates (Block, 1977; Wolfe, 1981b: ch. 6).

Stevens has summed up the economic consequences of the war in the following words:

> The results for the nation's economy of the Vietnam war duplicity were the most virulent inflation in American history, the highest interest rates in history, a series of balance of payments crises worse than any that had gone before, an unnecessary recession in 1970–71, two serious declines in stock prices (in 1970 and 1972–73), two major liquidity crises at home (in 1966 and 1969–70), a collapse of the housing industry (1966), financial market distortions that bore extremely heavily on small business and that forced state and local governments to retrench on education and other vital services, and the eventual defeat of the most imaginative experimental approach to the problems of impacted poverty that had ever been tried. (1976: 13)

Stevens also neatly summarizes the size of the war's impact on the economy by pointing out that its cost represents 'a figure so enormous that it defies comparison except with the US GNP itself, which was $900 billion in 1969' (1976: 187).

The one economic cost that Stevens does not refer to is that suggested by the coincidence of the escalation of the war with the decline of the profit rate: namely, the damage done to the very core of the economy, to the accumulation process. In my view the war weakened the economy in fundamental ways and rendered the state impotent in the face of this weakness, as well as intensifying social discontent in just those areas that are most critical to the maintenance of the rate of profit and accumulation more generally. This discontent subsided because of both systematic repression and the intrinsic ideological and political weaknesses of a divided opposition which lacked any strategic leverage in either the economy or society more generally. The rate of profit stabilized once the social crisis had subsided, and capital, if not the state, regained control of the economy.

The Vietnam War and the Balances of Class Forces

In order to support these propositions, I will now outline my readings of the changing state of the balances of forces between the two classes for the period 1965–74.

The Struggle over the Value of Labour Power

The balance that had been so favourable to capital on this site was disturbed by the rapid, war-related increase in investment and production which commenced in 1965 and by the related increases in the wages and prices of non-unionized industries. These developments fuelled demands on the part of rank and file trade unionists for wage increases substantially in excess of those which they had obtained in the early 1960s. Thus, in the latter half of the 1960s, organized labour demanded and won successive increases of 4, 5, 6, 7 and 8 per cent, as compared to an average increase of 3 per cent in the first half of the decade.

In addition and reflecting a more general 'revolt against work' (Zerzan, 1974), the rank and file demanded a shorter working week and numerous improvements in conditions. Worried by the threat to their 'responsible' strategy which the latter set of demands represented, the union leaders went flat out for the wage increases and, because sales and so the demand for labour were both expanding rapidly, they were successful. All the same, the number of strikes, excluding wildcats, rose consistently until 1970, when there were 5,600, involving some 3,300,000 workers, or double the number involved in 1965. Not surprisingly, the Wage–Price Guideposts became inoperative, until Nixon made them mandatory in 1971, and so too did President Johnson's major campaign promise to labour, namely the repeal of section 14b of the Taft-Hartley Act, which allowed the states to prohibit even the post-entry 'closed shop' if they so wished.

Beginning in 1967, and no doubt encouraged by responsible unionism's failure to maintain its side of what William Serrin (1973) has called, somewhat ironically, 'the civilized relationship', capital accelerated the southward relocation of its productive capacity that had begun in the course of World War II. The timing and the rate of this acceleration both strongly suggest that this relocation was part of a strategy by capital's embodiments to regain control over the price of labour power, and indeed to reactivate the counteracting influences to the tendency of the rate of profit to fall. Not only were wage rates some 10–20 per cent lower in the South than in the North-East, but the level of unionization was between 30 and 70 per cent lower than the national rate of 28 per cent. Moreover, the existence of the 'right to work' laws allowed by section 14b of the Taft-Hartley Act, plus the general social conservatism of the region suggested that these advantageous conditions were likely to be sustained into the future. There were other advantages, too: land was cheaper, local taxes were lower, energy supplies were closer, transportation was sometimes cheaper – thanks to the Mississippi – and, perhaps most surprisingly, racial strife could be avoided:

> . . . manufacturing firms are favoring the white South–Northern Mississippi, the white hill country and north-western Arkansas. They are not locating in the black Delta Towns. There are a number of reasons for this new form of racial discrimination. . . Relocating manufacturers find the hill country white workers are free thinkers who reject unions, while black workers seek the protection of unions. With white labor, there is neither a union problem nor a racial problem. (Sternlieb and Hughes, 1976: 157–8)

Thus, as social modernism got tied up in the jungles of Vietnam and responsible unionism failed to control labour – symbolically the United Auto Workers (UAW) left the CIO-AFL in 1968 to form a short-lived Alliance for Labour Action with the Teamsters, which was committed to what it termed 'social unionism' – the embodiments of capital sought their own long term solution to their problems, supported not only by the federal government's disposition of defence contracts but also by the 'boosterism' of state and local governments.

The Maintenance of the Circuits of Capital

In the latter half of the 1960s, the state continued to pursue the transportation, housing and educational policies which had so effectively reinforced the destructuring effects on the embodiments of the working class of the emergence of a large number of contradictory positionings during the 1950s. However, these policies no longer had the unambiguously positive consequences for capital that they had had hitherto. Instead, they highlighted the new and surprising ways in which capital's defensive stratagems could now become socially visible and therefore that much harder to pursue. In this instance a significant minority of the young embodiments of 'the middle class' became the bearers of a radical, if not very thorough-going, critique of their society and even of their own most likely roles within it. For a short time it appeared to many that the society was on the verge of a total transformation. Revulsion against a war which was indefensible, in terms of the idealistic and thoroughly 'modern' values which they had been taught during their schooldays, coincided with the dim but gradually spreading realization that many of the lower level contradictory class positionings no longer represented such great opportunities. Thus many of the young began to reason that, if their loyalty was no longer considered worth paying for, then the society which the corporations dominated was no longer worthy of their loyalty.

This critical stance spread beyond the war as, drawing on the insights of the civil rights movement and the beats, the young 'middle classes' contemplated the still largely abstract possibility of proletarian status. The constrained life of the wage-worker was recognized as the truth behind the American Dream. From a position one generation and half a step away from the proletariat, the constraints, with regard to personal life, education and culture, that are implicit in the wage suddenly became very clear. The nuclear/extended forms of the family were criticized for their repression of sexuality, their manipulation of childhood and their oppression of women. Education was criticized as a mechanism whereby the individual was prepared for society rather than for self-development. Culture – 'consumer culture' – was criticized as fetishist, pacifying, racist and mind-destroying. These, then, were the themes of the amalgam, comprising the anti-war movement, the women's movement, the commune movement, the gay movement, the student movement and the hippie movement, which became known as THE MOVEMENT. The content of these critiques and the histories of the movements which produced them are so well known by now that they will not be discussed further here.

It is perhaps not so well known that there was a more general critique implicit in the otherwise rather specific critiques, namely a rejection of the capital-serving component of the contradictory class positionings. Present in the discourse of the movement as a whole, if not in the minds of many of its individual adherents, was the figure of a social being who should neither serve capital nor submit to the degradations forced upon the proletariat. S/he should be without those supports to the exercise of power provided by sexism, heterosexism, racism, credentialism and sobriety. S/he should be, instead, 'authentic', egalitarian and hedonistic. Although some 'movement people' were revolted by one aspect or another of their present or expected future contradictory positionings, not unreasonably their fear of descent into the proletariat was even more strongly felt. This fear, as I have already suggested, led them to pose an alternative to social modernism that was not its 'other'. What they enunciated was, in Marx's negative sense, a utopianism, since it rested on the belief that significant change was possible by merely accentuating the positive in their condition, namely their individual capacities to reject the supports of power. Not surprisingly, given the one-dimensional ideological universe in which they lived, they failed to recognize or understand that their very possession of such capacities depended upon the prior existence of the contradictory positionings with which these supports were intertwined.

As was indicated in Chapter 5, the incubator of this heady but limited vision was the university, more precisely the elite university. Perhaps because they were the most self-confident and had the most to lose, 'upper middle class' students were the first to perceive the change represented by the coming of what was termed the 'multiversity'. The student movement had begun in the early 1960s by supporting other people: African-Americans, victims of the House Un-American Activities Committee, and Cubans. Under the circumstances obtaining in an 'affluent society', and with a President who constantly emphasized his concern for those who had been left out, the growth potential of a movement which was purely altruistic was not very encouraging. However, once the implications of the 'multiversity' were understood and underlined by the threat of the draft – that is, by a sense of their individual expendibility, the movement grew very rapidly as a vehicle for self-defence, spreading first to the less glamorous universities and then throughout the country with the anti-war protesters, the hippies, the feminists and the gay rights activists.

The proletarianization which lay at the root of the fear which first galvanized and then transformed The Movement had its roots in the early years of the century, with that separation of mental from manual labour in the office which had been made visible by the feminization of the clerical labour force (M. Davies, 1974). It continued during the 1950s, as the skill and income differentials obtaining between some of the lower-level contradictory positionings and the skilled and/or unionized solely working class ones shrank. However, the potentially damaging effects of such shrinkage on the claim that the United States was becoming more and more a 'land of opportunity' were countered by a very rapid growth in the number of, and advantages associated with, such middle and higher level sets of positionings as technicians and professionals. Thus any potentially disruptive consequences proletarianization might have had were inhibited by a lengthening of the aspirational and promotional corporate ladder and a broadening of some of its higher rungs.

However, despite the speed-up in economic growth, the early 1960s saw the arrival of what Bowles and Gintis have called 'The Great American Dream Freeze' (1976), when a rapid increase in the proportion of the 18–21 age group enrolled on degree courses coincided with a radical slowing down of the growth of contradictory positionings, especially at the highest levels of the career ladder. Put numerically, a 6 per cent increase in degree enrolments, from 33.2 per cent of the age group in 1960 to 39.1 per cent in 1965, coincided with a 10 per cent reduction in the rate of increase of contradictory positionings, so that the latter stood at roughly 20 per cent per year. Most dramatically, the rate of increase of the critical professional and technical positionings declined from 60–70 per cent per year in the 1950s to 30 per cent per year in the early 1960s.

Although the Vietnam boom restored the average rate of increase in contradictory positionings to the level of the 1950s, its composition was rather different. Specifically, looking back from 1970, the annual rate of increase in the 1960s for the highest positionings increased again to around 55 per cent, whilst that for the lowest positionings, clerical, rose to over 40 per cent, almost double the rate for the 1950s. Thus, whilst the number of positionings at the top increased somewhat, that in the middle remained more or less constant and that at the bottom radically increased: the dream freeze of the mid-1960s became what the Manpower Administration (1974) called the 'promotion squeeze' of the 1970s. Analysis of the income data for the second part of the 1960s suggests that the profit squeeze as well as technological developments may have contributed to the changing distribution of contradictory positionings, since the same period also witnessed what David Kraus (1976) has called 'a devaluation of the American executive'. The unions were successfully pursuing an aggressive wages policy, and the state was concentrating its resources elsewhere as well as threatening a tax increase. Apart from relocation, one of the few options left to corporations worried by their declining profitability was the retrieval of some part of the revenues which they had hitherto been distributing amongst the embodiments of contradictory positionings in order to secure their loyalty.

Beginning in the mid-1960s, the productivity of white-collar employees, or 'overhead value analysis', became an object of some concern to capital (Burris, 1980; Newman, 1975: 116ff.). Whether as a result of such analysis or for reasons of more immediate necessity, the embodiments of capital not only reduced the rate at which they created contradictory positionings, but also generally reduced the size of the income differential between them and solely working class ones. For example, the salary paid to a middle-level executive rose by an average of 3.1 per cent between 1964 and 1974, whilst that of a factory worker rose by an average of 5.5 per cent, which meant that the gross pay of the former, as a multiple of the latter, fell from 5.7 to 4.6. Consequently, once one takes account of taxation and inflation, the purchasing power of the typical executive fell by 20 per cent, whilst that of the factory worker rose by 5 per cent (D. Kraus, 1976).

The effects of this on the morale of some of those who embodied the contradictory positionings are suggested by the movement of the Survey Research Center's Index of Consumer Sentiment, which measures consumers' optimism concerning their own economic situation and that of the country as a whole. This declined in 1966, recovered a little in 1967 and plunged in 1969 (Katona, 1975). More concretely, house prices soared as the tightening of monetary policy in 1967 made mortgages harder to find and reduced the number of houses available. In this situation many of the lower paid middle classes found themselves unable to leave suburbs which were becoming much more heterogeneous in their social composition: whereas only 1 per cent of the poor lived in suburbia in 1959, 20 per cent of them lived there by 1970. The resulting 'slurbs' or 'sloppy, sleazy, slovenly semi-cities' hardly seemed the stuff of the American Dream (Murphy and Rehfuss, 1976), nor indeed did the processed food, 'canned' entertainment and ever-increasing shopping which passed for leisure and which Tibor Scitovsky has summarized in the depressing statistics of *The Joyless Economy* (1976).

It seems to me that all of this, followed as it was by the de-escalation of the war and so the decline in the draft threat, is very relevant to any

explanation of what happened afterwards to the contradictorily positioned, that is, the decline of student protest and the increase in general
social disengagement. By all accounts, students entering higher education
in the mid-1970s became much more vocationally oriented as the number
of contradictory positionings and therefore career opportunities increased
again, but under conditions of more intensive competition (Wright and
Singelmann, 1982; Wright and Martin, 1987). More noticeably, the
already employed, the future 'yuppies', began to seek meaning in the
diffused and commercialized development of Movement themes: greater
drug use, but for the sake of the 'sharpness' that comes from cocaine
rather than the 'mind expansion' associated with marijuana and LSD;
self-awareness, but through commodified and individualized therapies
rather than 'tribal' rituals; feminism, but through the pursuit of a
pragmatic Equal Rights Amendment rather than a romantic 'liberation';
civic activism, but in the cause of ecology rather than civil rights; in sum,
a 'new age' rather than a 'revolution' was sought.

This said, because of the continuing utopianism of this stance, as well
as because of the increased uncertainty faced by even the relatively
successful, the contradictorily positioned are not now the predictably
modernistic or even corporate liberal political constituency that their
parents were in the 1950s. Their immediate response to capital's reduction in their opportunities and devaluation of their loyalty was to loosen
their commitment to the work ethic, whilst their linked response to the
state's abuse of its power was the tax revolt (Fitzgerald and Meisol, 1978;
Terkel, 1974). Thus, the 'ironic self-detachment' consequent on their
parents' failure to understand the sources of their often new-found
affluence (Vidich and Bensman, 1969: 122) was replaced by an ironic and
arguably proto-postmodernist social detachment resulting from the
failure of capital to maintain and expand this same affluence (cp. Baritz,
1989; Lasch, 1978; Sennett, 1977; Terkel, 1988).

The revolt and disengagement of the 'middle classes' were not the only
important events pertaining to the maintenance of the circuits of capital
in this period. Accompanying and intertwined with these events there was
a developing problem of liquidity in the money circuit, which finally
became explicit in New York City's 'fiscal crisis'. The immediate cause
of the problem was an increase in indebtedness throughout the economy,
which accelerated during the 1960s. *Business Week* summarized what had
happened in the following words:

> . . . what happened during the 1940s and 1950s was only a prelude to what
> happened after 1960. It took 15 years, from 1946 to 1960, for total U.S. debt
> to double, but only 10 years, from 1960 to 1970, for it to double again. The
> key economic indicators – gross national product, personal income, corporate
> profits, and the like – have all grown by 500% or so since World War II. The
> key debt indicators have all grown by three and four times that amount, and
> the sharpest gains have come since 1960.
>
> Corporations have tripled their debt in the past 15 years. Treasury debt,
> which hardly grew at all in the late 1940s and 1950s, has jumped by $180

billion since 1960. Installment debt, mortgage debt, and state and local government debt have all climbed by 200% or more since 1950, and the debts of Federal agencies have climbed by more than 1,000%. New demands for money bred new sources: the commercial paper market, which was a nickel-and-dime affair until the 1960s, and the Euro-currency markets, which were not even born until the 1960s. Leasing became a billion-dollar business during the 1960s. The neighborhood bank became a multinational bank holding company that frequently became as voracious a borrower of funds as the companies to which it lent. . . So now the nation's burden of debt is like a string drawn very taut: $2.5 trillion in debt outstanding and more money needed to keep the economy growing, while the ability of borrowers to repay what they owe and find more and more money is very much in question. (reprinted in Mermelstein, 1975: 181–2)

The underlying cause of this massive increase in indebtedness was the same sharpening of inter-class tensions whose consequences will be further examined in the remaining sections of this chapter. The money capital which could have financed productive investment was siphoned off ever more rapidly as armaments expenditure and capital exports both increased and so made additional demands on capital's revenues. Increasingly, therefore, investment needs had to be met by borrowing from banks, which in turn could only satisfy the demands made on them if they too borrowed. The increasing interest and inflation rates which were a product of this spiralling indebtedness not only further stimulated this process, but also encouraged labour's continuing wage-related aggressiveness and undermined all efforts to constrain the growth of consumer debt. Indebtedness could only be sustained by still more indebtedness, since profit rates were still falling, the stock market was declining and foreign owners of capital lacked confidence in the United States' economy. At the centre of this tightening circle, and holding both ends of the by then very taut string, were the banks. It seems hardly surprising, therefore, that some of them should try to avoid the additional weakening of their positions that might follow from taking a further risk on New York City. Refusing to finance the city's mounting indebtedness had other advantages, too, in that it provided an opportunity for the bankers to exercise political power directly rather than remain dependent on the increasingly unreliable and impotent apparatuses of the local and federal state.

New York City's financial problems represented a classic example of a 'fiscal crisis' in the simple sense of O'Connor's (1973) famous term: tax revenues failed to keep up with the demands made on them in connection with the local management of the conditions necessary to continued accumulation. Since 1961, the city's expenses had been growing at double the rate of its revenues. This gap had been managed by a combination of financial jiggery-pokery – such as over-estimating revenues, underestimating expenses and raiding reserve funds – and issuing bonds, most of which had been bought by banks as tax-efficient investments. Eventually, in 1974, these techniques ceased to be sufficient because the banks

refused to buy any further bonds. A body called the Municipal Assistance Corporation was formed by the city's most powerful creditors, and
in June 1975 it virtually took over the city. Its cure for the city's
problems was to greatly reduce city employment, welfare costs and
educational expenditure, and to increase the interest rate payable on city
bonds (Alcaly and Mermelstein, 1977: pts 1,2). Although many have
criticized this so-called 'good housekeeping' approach as totally inadequate as well as socially oppressive, it nevertheless proved to be fiscally
effective.

The problems that underlay the crisis were indeed far more profound
than the simple fiscal irresponsibility implied by the bankers' actions.
Nevertheless, given the ideological and political conditions then prevailing they were clearly not as intractable as O'Connor and many other
critics appear to have thought. As with the New Economists' full-
employment surplus, there is nothing inevitable about such fiscal crises.
The claims on state revenues do not have to exceed the funds available,
despite the private appropriation of profits. O'Connor's 'structural gap'
does not necessarily exist. In line with what has already been argued in
this chapter, each of the sources of New York's fiscal crisis was related
in one way or another to changes in class relations: for example, the
suburbanization and industrial relocation that undermined the city's tax
base were a consequence of the way in which the state had responded to
the increase in the number of contradictory positionings; and the
increases in wages, welfare rolls and inflation that devoured the city's
revenues were similarly consequences of the Vietnam War and the
associated wider changes in class relations that have already been
outlined. Thus, as the ideological challenges subsided, as new taxpayers
(in the financial services industry, for example) arrived, and as the
national and local balances of class forces came to favour capital once
again, so the fiscal crisis disappeared, for the time being.

In conclusion, the integrity of the circuits of capital was maintained
throughout the crisis period, although it was threatened for a time by an
unexpected but short-lived ideological challenge with its roots in the
onset of a decline in the number and proportion of contradictory class
positionings in the social division of labour, and an associated bank
liquidity problem which was intensified by the slow pace of this decline.

The Balance between the Two Departments of Production

The already well-established tendency towards an asymmetrical development of the two departments of production in favour of Department II
continued until 1971. It was propelled by the diversion of resources to the
war effort, the reduction in the value of depreciation allowances because
of inflation, and the consequent collapse in business fixed investment,
which increased by only 2 per cent in 1969 as opposed to 11 per cent in
1968. In 1971, stimulated by industry's ongoing southward relocation,

investment in fixed capital began to increase again, but not before
bottlenecks in the supply of Department I commodities had become
apparent. The beneficial effect that this should have had for the
producer goods sector was, however, limited by the continuing operation
of all the above-mentioned factors. The only reason that bottlenecks in
the supply of Department I goods did not recur was of the onset of
Nixon's recession (see above, p. 90). Instead, there appeared gluts and
shortages of Department II commodities, because of the absence of
anything approaching perfect competition in certain markets; for example, an over-generous Federal subsidy system led to the massive over-
production of wheat at a time when market conditions would otherwise
have forced a redeployment of resources. In addition, oligopolistic conditions prevented the entry of new companies into markets where there was
strong demand, with the result that there were much publicized 'shortages' of meat, coffee and oil (Mermelstein, 1975).

All in all, it remained as difficult as ever to achieve a balance between
the two departments of production and for a time this stimulated considerable consumer disquiet, as symptomized by product boycotts, talk of anti-
trust suits and oil company divestiture, and renewed Congressional discussion of national planning around the Humphrey-Hawkins Bill (Graham,
1976: chs. 5, 6). The capital-negative effect of all this was, however, in no
way sufficient to counteract the positive effects of the collapse of the
ideological challenges with respect to the first two sites of tension.

The Counteracting Influences to the Tendency of the Rate of Profit to Fall

The Increasing Intensity of Labour at the Point of Production   This may
be gauged by considering the figures relating to the growth of productivity
per person in manufacturing industry (Manpower Report to the President,
1973: 373). Between 1965 and 1970, the average rate of productivity
increase declined to under 2 per cent per year. Since it is known that
investment in constant capital was rising rapidly in the first two of these
years, because of the war, it may safely be assumed that, contrary to
'responsible unionism', labour was successfully resisting the attempts then
being made to increase the intensity of labour. After 1970, as the level of
social unrest inside and outside the plants (Woodiwiss, 1990b: 225–7), as
well as what might be called the excess war investment all declined, the
productivity rate improved substantially to an average rate of more than
6 per cent per year. In other words, capital successfully reimposed
'responsible unionism' and increased the intensity of labour across the
board. The relevance of these changes to the rate of profit is indicated by
comparing their trajectory with that of the gross rates of return given in
Table 6.1. The gross rate of return increased steadily from 1961 to 1965,
held steady in 1966, then declined until 1970. From then until 1973 it
remained stable and even rose fractionally.

The Depression of Wages below the Value of Labour Power   The War on Poverty may not have succeeded in dramatically reducing the number of poor people or in dislodging 'self-reliance' from its dominant position in the discourse pertaining to welfare, but it does seem to have neutralized the operation of this counteracting influence. The proportion of the working population living on wages below either the poverty level or the 'low family-income level' of the Bureau of Labour Statistics appears to have held steady or even to have declined (Ginsburg, 1975: pt. 5). The precise size of this population depends upon which poverty line one chooses: that of the Social Security Administration, which was $4,000 per household in 1970, or that represented by the Bureau of Labour Statistics 'low family-income level', which was $7,183 in the same year. If the former is chosen, the number of people living in poverty was roughly 17 million, whilst if the latter is chosen it was 41 million. In terms of Marx's theory, with its emphasis on 'the traditional standard of life', the second definition is the more appropriate, Helen Ginsburg has said in relation to the first:

> Physical survival is possible on a poverty budget. But it does not represent a minimum level of social adequacy in this country, as perceived by most Americans. According to the Gallup Poll, the public thinks a non-farm family needs much more than the poverty budget to make ends meet. . . In 1971 . . . the public thought it took at least $127 per week ($6,490 annually) just for the basic necessities. (1975: 93; see also Gordon 1972)

Many commentators have rightly criticized the Great Society programme for its failure to break with traditional stereotypes of the poor in either its philosophy or its specific policies. Contrary to the views of today's conservative critics, most of the money expended went into programmes that were premissed upon the assumption that the poor were idle, ignorant and, for these reasons, trapped within an enervating culture of poverty which made them incapable of self-reliance. Thus there were increases in funds for education, manpower development, job-training and medical care (the Medicaid part of the Medicare programme). Even the ostensibly more radical Community Action Program ended up guided by the same assumptions. Pre-packaged programmes such as Headstart were substituted for those that might otherwise have arisen from the anyway very restricted 'maximum feasible participation' recommended by the Economic Opportunity Act, which was later so bizarrely blamed for the failure of the entire programme by those who were at the same moment losing faith in social modernism.

However, until recently (see Murray, 1984, for example) even such critics have shied away from making the point that even these minimalist programmes tended to undermine the accumulatory effectiveness of capital. Those most likely to benefit from them were the under-employed and their families. From the state's point of view, this was rational enough, given that the under-employed accounted for 70 per cent of the non-aged poor, and that, as dramatized by successive riotous summers and the rise of the welfare rights movement, something had to be done to quieten them (Piven and Cloward, 1971). However, it was not so rational from the point of view of capital's embodiments, since improving the standard of living of the under-employed made it hard for capital to depress their wages any further. Indeed in Arthur Okun's view it was precisely in this area of employment that 'the initial burst of price and wage pressures occurred' (Okun, 1970: 68) that set off the inflation of the late 1960s. Moreover, the pressure from the under-employed was not restricted to demands on employers, as was indicated by the popular slogan: 'Decent Wages or Welfare'. Thus the working poor were amongst those who fuelled the welfare rolls explosion of the late 1960s, as they claimed the income supplements which some state and local governments had been forced into offering and which could result in a doubling of the incomes of those on the minimum wage and so bring a family up from the poverty level to the 'low family-income level' (Cloward and Piven, 1975: 141ff.). The welfare rolls explosion as a whole also, of course, indicated an improvement in the situation of the non-working poor and so raised the floor below the low-wage sectors of the economy. Thus the War on Poverty contributed to the neutralization of this counteracting influence. It is therefore somewhat ironic that the War on Poverty was at the time commonly supposed to have finally established the hegemony of social modernism, when in fact it represented very precisely the promise that American capitalism could not keep.

The War on Poverty ceased because, as the 1968 tax increase together with the reduction in non-Vietnam spending shows, it became too expensive (Stevens 1976: ch. 5). Since estimates of the rate of under-employment were not made after 1970, one can only guess that the position of the under-employed deteriorated as a result of the triple assault represented by inflation, recession and Nixon's workfare programmes. One may guess that these three occurrences also contributed to the reimposition of 'self-reliance', the reactivation of this counteracting influence and therefore to the stabilization of the rate of profit.

The Cheapening of the Elements of Constant Capital Kennedy's revision of depreciation schedules lowered the cost of renewing fixed capital until 1969 and so ensured that until then this counteracting influence worked in capital's favour. However, after 1969 these schedules were not further revised, in spite of inflation, and became such a drag on profits that not taking account of this fact would cause one to overstate the revival of profitability by as much as 3 per cent (Nordhaus, 1974: 171–2). Thus the effect of the war, as mediated through the inflation it caused, was first to neutralize, and then to make negative, a counteracting influence which had been operating positively in capital's favour. However, the cheapening of capital that resulted from war-spawned technological advance would seem to have reversed this movement. As the war escalated, resources that could have been used for non-military technological development were siphoned off, but as it de-escalated they once again became available. Although the so-called 'peace dividend' appears to have been an illusion, nevertheless the private retention of patents obtained as a result of state-financed research and development – especially in the area of micro-electronics – promised that the United States might be able to retain its modernistic technological lead into what Bell was already calling the 'post-industrial' era.

Relative Over-population As was argued above, this counteracting influence was already becoming inoperative in the early 1960s. In the late 1960s and into the 1970s, the embitterment which resulted from dependence on this counteracting influence came to have explosive consequences, as the relative surplus population became part of a larger and larger absolute surplus population, concentrated in the minority-dominated ghettos of the inner cities, for whom self-reliance was not an option. Probably the most important single cause of relative over-population was the mechanization of agriculture, which had been the impetus behind the African-American migration to the north (Piven and Cloward, 1971: ch. 7). Initially, the menial jobs available in the cities were tolerated but, as a new generation grew up, the bitterness engendered by racism grew deeper. In the words of Claude Brown: 'The children of these disillusioned colored pioneers inherited the total lot of their parents – the disappointments, the anger. To add to their misery, they had little hope of deliverance. For where does one run to when he's already in the promised land?' (quoted in Gordon, 1972: p. 9).

By 1964, when these words were written, many young African-Americans had clearly discovered a new promised land with the Muslims and the civil rights activists. Despite the fall in unemployment generally, that of young African-Americans increased even while the war escalated and took more and more of them to their deaths in Vietnam. Unsurprisingly, when the de-escalation began, this growth in unemployment accelerated still further (Manpower Report to the President, 1973: 273). The War on Poverty had little effect on this situation because whatever benefits it produced tended to go to the under-employed rather than to the unemployed or to those entering the labour market for the first time. Besides, it simply wasn't conceived on the scale necessary to have any impact on the complex of social and institutional forces which had created the ghettos – forces such as those that produce segregated labour markets, unions, educational facilities, and housing (Forman, 1971). However, although even the gains made by older, employed African-Americans largely disappeared after 1970, so also did much of the politicized bitterness (Blair, 1978). Thus, in this way too, 'self-reliance' was reimposed and the effectivity of this counteracting influence was restored as the ranks of the poor swelled quietly throughout the 1970s.

Foreign Trade and Investment The manner in which this counteracting influence was neutralized by the over-use of the capital export option has already been described (see above, p. 67). However, not only did balance of trade problems cause about-turns in war and domestic policy in 1968 and 1971 respectively, but the United States' worsening trade position also contributed significantly to radical changes in the world financial system, which in turn contributed to the inflation of commodity prices, most spectacularly that of oil (Mermelstein, 1975: sections D, E). The increased costs which then resulted cancelled out any positive effects that the cheapening of labour might otherwise have had on profits in the first half of the 1970s.

The Increase of Stock Capital The two market crashes of 1970 and 1972 seriously hampered the effort to restore profitability by increased use of this relatively cheap form of capital. Insofar as these crashes alienated many small, middle-class savers, who believed that 'modern' capitalism was a 'People's Capitalism', they also undermined the positive ideological effects that this notion had earlier had.

Conclusion

It can be seen that the war contributed significantly to the neutralization of the counteracting influences and intensified the challenges that were anyway being made along the political and ideological dimensions of class relations. The escalation of the war coincided with an increase in the level of labour's resistance to any efforts to intensify labour, with a politically embittering reduction in the wage levels of some of the low-paid and a worsening of the condition of the relative surplus population. Moreover, each of these problems was in turn exacerbated by the escalation: the first because the escalation stimulated investment way beyond the capacity of the extant system of industrial discipline to ensure that it was used profitably and so contributed to the intensification of the challenge then being made to 'responsible unionism'; and the second because the escalation caused such a level of political embitterment that, because of the rioting that ensued, the waging of the War on Poverty also became a much more expensive undertaking than had had been initially envisaged.

In addition, the diversion of capital resources caused by the two wars, plus the inflation that was a product of the way in which they were financed, undermined the effectiveness of the modernist economic strategy that had so recently been adopted: (1) they slowed the cheapening of capital that technological development might otherwise have brought and so undermined the effectiveness of Kennedy's revision of the depreciation schedules; (2) they transformed the effect of the capital exports from a positive to a negative factor; (3) they increased the cost of imported commodities; (4) they made stock capital very hard to obtain; and (5), because they led to an increase in corporate taxation, they reversed what had otherwise been the declining effectiveness of that counter-counteracting influence represented by the taxing of profits.

In sum, then, the war contributed in so many ways to the undermining of capital's political and ideological conditions of existence and to the lessening of its possessory, significatory and, critically (Jones, 1982: 277ff; Woodiwiss, 1990b: 271–2), its control advantages in the workplace, and, therefore, to the neutralization of the counteracting influences, that it moved capital towards an accumulation crisis. However, because of the rather rapid subsidence of the political and ideological challenges that it, alongside capital's attempts at retrenchment vis à vis the 'middle classes', had helped spawn, the move was only a small one. Significant amounts of capital did not become unusable, although some large individual units came close, such as Lockheed and Pan Am. Nevertheless, capital was over-produced and therefore became cheaper (Nordhaus, 1974: 198ff.). The embodiments of the working class may have refused to work any harder or longer than they had been doing, but the historic level of labour intensity was such that even this double refusal was not sufficient to plunge capital into a full-blown accumulation crisis. The counteracting influences were partly neutralized but they were not rendered inoperative. Productivity increased again after 1970, as did the number of people who were paid wages below the value of their labour power. The relative surplus population continued to increase but, like the increasingly detached embodiments of contradictory class positionings, they represented less and less of a political threat.

To conclude, by the mid-1970s the state of the balances between the classes had once again come to favour capital. Nowhere was this clearer than in the ideological realm, where, although the challenges to social modernism had disappeared, the discourse itself lay in verbal ruins, having destroyed its chances of lasting social significance by prompting two wars, neither of which capital could afford. This said, because no other discourse was immediately available and precisely because it lacked all but a vestige of referential adequacy, the shards of social modernism that remained were available to be recombined in new and increasingly distracted ways, as will become apparent in the chapter which follows.

7

THE DISCOURSE OF FORGETFULNESS

As was indicated in Chapter 4, the economic problems which beset capital as a result of the turmoil of the 1960s were intertwined with an ideological inflation every bit as significant as the economic inflation which it accompanied. As it happens, and as was indicated in Chapter 6, the process whereby the ideological bubble was gradually and successfully deflated began some time before its economic equivalent reached its maximum size, specifically when Richard Nixon was re-elected to the presidency. In this chapter I will describe the course of the decline in the ideological inflation through a variety of texts, as a possible forgetfulness became a definite amnesia, thanks to the ever more effective ministrations of the 'new conservatism' in calming the buried anger of the powerful (Coser and Howe, 1974; Clecak, 1977; Crawford, 1980; D. Green, 1987; Hoover and Plant, 1989; King, 1987; Nash, 1979; K. Phillips, 1981; J.K. White, 1988; Wolfe, 1981a, 1983, 1988). In the course of this decline, the claims of social modernism lost whatever substantive content they may once have possessed, but their continued repetition imparted that pronounced unreality to the ideological realm which has been confused with its qualitative transformation. In Chapter 8, I will describe the consequences of these developments for class relations in the period from the mid-1970s to 1990.

Towards a more Amnesiac Presidency

President Nixon's first Inaugural Address contained both a ringing endorsement of the claims made by social modernism and signs that its promises were about to be forgotten. As an endorsement, it spoke approvingly of the discovery of 'new horizons on earth', of wealth that was 'shared more broadly than ever', and even of a society which had 'learned at last to manage a modern economy to assure its continued growth' and had also ensured that freedom's 'promise [had been made] real for black as well as for white'. As a portent of forgetfulness, it also spoke of America's problem as a spiritual rather than a material one; it declared that 'greatness comes in simple trappings' and it judged that: 'In these difficult years, America has suffered from a fever of words; from inflated rhetoric that promises more than it can deliver; from angry rhetoric that fans discontents into hatreds. . .'. Finally, as an alternative to all this 'shouting', it introduced but did not name the entity that was to provide the excuse for forgetfulness, namely the thinly disguised white lower-middle and working classes – the supposed 'great silent majority' of his later speeches: 'For its part, [this] government will listen . . . to the voices of quiet anguish, the voices that speak without words, the voices of the heart – to the injured voices, the anxious voices, the voices that have despaired of being heard.'

Significant as the coexistence of these two discourses within one speech was, the way in which Nixon articulated them with one another turned out to be even more significant, since this provided forgetfulness with its cover and so initiated a new and, as I shall term it, social (post)postmodernist discourse – one that, because it reasserted the primacy of 'self-reliance', proclaimed both the continuing validity of the modernist goals and the state's retreat from their active pursuit:

> The American dream does not come to those who fall asleep.
> But we are approaching the limits of what the government alone can do. . .
> To match the magnitude of our tasks, we need the energies of our people – enlisted not only in grand enterprises, but more importantly in those small, splendid efforts that make headlines in the neighborhood newspaper instead of the national journal. . .
> The essence of freedom is that each of us shares in the shaping of his own destiny.

This, then, was the moment when the United States officially gave up on trying to make its ruling discourse refer to anything in the reality of the daily lives of its poorer citizens. This Nixon confirmed when, in his second State of the Union Message and before he repeated each of the other social modernist signs, he gave priority to the need for welfare reform (that is, to the calling of a halt to the War on Poverty) on the basis of establishing 'an effective work incentive . . . [so as to] provide the means by which more can help themselves'.

Nixon was unsuccessful in his attempt to replace the Great Society's anti-poverty programmes with his preferred alternative of a so-called 'guaranteed income'. Nevertheless, his reassertion of the priority of 'self-reliance' was not subsequently challenged, with a result which was probably even worse for the poor than if he had been successful – the programmes were left to die a death of a thousand cuts over the next twenty years with little debate and less selectivity. In other words, neither Nixon's resignation in disgrace nor the subsequent election of a Democratic president produced any widespread questioning of the correctness of Nixon's opening of the era of social (post)modernism. (As it happens, Watergate appears to have reflected worse on the state as such than on Nixon since; although he appears to have been forgiven, the state continues to be mistrusted.)

President Carter appears to have been every bit as determined as Nixon to insist on the need for renewed primacy to be accorded to 'self-reliance'. Thus, in the first of what with wholly unintended irony, he described in Rooseveltian terms as his 'fireside chats', and despite an opening which featured a touch of Kennedyesque high modernism – '. . . we must . . . allow time for citizens to participate in careful study, in order to develop predictable, long range programs . . . that we know will work' – Carter too insisted on the existence of limits to what even a 'competent and compassionate' state could do. Again like Nixon, he argued that this was no bad thing since 'Our nation was built on the principle of work not welfare.' Drawing on yet another theme of Nixon's, Carter later (in his 1977 'moral equivalent of war' speech on the energy crisis) explained that the reason for the general disregard of this principle (that is, by others as well as by the poor) was the existence of a 'moral and spiritual crisis' brought about by the 'worship [of] self-indulgence and consumption'. Given all this, it should have come as no surprise to anyone that, when Carter finally unveiled his strategy for overcoming the energy crisis, its critical points turned out to have been dictated by a distinctly (post)modernist reading of corporate liberalism:

> . . . beginning this moment, this nation will never use more foreign oil than we did in 1977 ['self-reliance'].
> . . . These efforts will cost a lot of money. . .These funds will go to fight, not to increase, inflation and unemployment ['opportunity'].
> . . . Every act of energy conservation . . . is an act of patriotism ['loyalty']
> . . . We can succeed only if we tap our greatest resources – America's people, America's values, and America's confidence ['(post)modernism'].

The arrival at the White House in 1981 of Ronald Reagan – a veritable incarnation of the by then well-established retro-culture (J.K. White, 1988) – confirmed that the United States remained in love with itself, even though it no longer acted upon its most cherished beliefs. Reagan was both frank about, and extreme in, his social (post)modernism. He said in his first Inaugural Address: 'Government is not the solution to our problem; government is the problem.' He went on to say that, once 'elite' government has given way to 'self-rule', 'this breed called Americans', these 'heroes', will once again dream their 'heroic dreams' and get the country moving again so that it can provide 'equal opportunities for all', as well as 'reach out a hand when they fall, heal them when they are sick, and provide opportunity to make them self-sufficient so they will be equal in fact and not just in theory. . .'. To recreate such a society, he concluded, would both require a loyalty and patriotism akin to that shown by those who had died defending their country in time of war and justify the latters' sacrifices.

As if to reflect an unconscious acknowledgement of the emptiness of the promises he was making, an emptiness which became clearer and clearer with each policy move, Reagan appears later to have sought to give some substance to his increasingly blurred vision of America by developing a sharp contrast between it and that of the 'evil empire' represented by the Soviet Union.

George Bush was more correct than he realized when, as a competitor for the Republican nomination, he referred to Reagan's economic policy proposals as a species of 'voodoo'. For, in the same way that these proposals promised to increase governmental revenues by reducing them and hoping for a miracle, so Reagan's social policy promised, as I have just shown, to restore the capacity for self-reliance to those who lacked it by denying them any chance of regaining it and hoping for another miracle. Nevertheless, despite his insight into the grandiose vacuity of (post)modernist politics, Bush himself soon fell under its spell, first as a two term Vice-President and later as President in his own right. Unfortunately for him, it appears that he allowed his head, which he had dutifully filled with the ideas of the 'new conservatism' (see Gilder, 1981; and Novak, 1983, for example), to rule his heart, with the result that, despite his sustained attempt to simulate a Texan, he proved to be a totally inept practitioner of (post)modernist politics.

An exemplary instance of his shortcomings in this regard is provided by his Inaugural Address. After the customary pleasantries and a not so customary prayer, Bush straight away reaffirmed America's modernity by talking of its 'other': 'The totalitarian era is passing, its old ideas blown away like leaves from an ancient, lifeless tree.' And then, immediately afterwards, he reaffirmed the Nixonian account of the sources of this modernity: '. . . a nation refreshed by freedom . . . [and illuminated by] a thousand points of light . . . the community organizations that are spread like stars throughout the nation, doing good'. In so doing, he placed his repetitions of the most potent incantations of the social (post)modernist spell at the beginning of his speech, instead of saving them for his peroration, as had been his predecessors' practice on such occasions. In other words, he mistook the rhetorical function of these ideas by thinking of them as providing a guide to the solving of problems, when in fact their power lies in their capacity to make them disappear. The difficulties he so created for himself rapidly became apparent as the speech proceeded. Shortly after he identified the ultimate source of America's strength somewhat carelessly in a 'new conservative' manner, as 'free markets', he equally carelessly took a leaf out of Carter's Democratic book and defined the source of America's still continuing spiritual crisis by posing the following rhetorical question: 'Are we [not] enthralled with material things, [and therefore] less appreciative of the nobility of work and sacrifice?' His problem was that, having defined freedom concretely as the buying and selling of goods and services, his discourse became contradictory when he went on to blame the spiritual crisis on the buying and selling of the self-same goods and services.

The consequences of this contradiction were immediate and, in my view, catastrophic for one who, one must imagine, intended to enunciate America's hegemonic ideology – he could not invoke the greatest of all American, let alone social modernism's, talismans, the promise of enhanced opportunities for all. Instead he found himself saying: 'My friends, we are not the sum of our possessions. They are not the measure of our lives. . . What do we want the men and women who work with us to say when we are no longer there? That we were more driven to succeed than anyone around us?' He then compounded his difficulties by making his famous plea for a 'kinder . . . nation' and by thereby admitting the existence of new categories of people in need of such kindness, new categories of people who could not be expected to be self-reliant: 'There are the homeless, lost and roaming – there are children who have nothing, no love and no normalcy – there are those who cannot free themselves of enslavement to whatever addiction: drugs, welfare, the demoralization that rules the slums.' Having thus magnified the social problems the society faced, he had to point out that, given the withdrawal of the state, the result of depending on 'the thousand points of light' is a promise of the opposite to opportunity: 'duty, sacrifice, commitment, and a patriotism that finds its expression in taking part and pitching in'.

This speech represented the sudden, long-delayed and perhaps even unintended irruption of the new conservatism within America's ceremonial discourse. Thanks to the absence of 'opportunity' and given that even 'self-reliance' was hidden by the prominence accorded to the market (invocations of 'responsible unionism' had long since disappeared from the ceremonial if not from the more mundane occasions of social (post)modernist discourse), the only pertinent sign left was 'loyalty'. In other words, in his Inaugural Address Bush actually enunciated classical liberalism tempered by a sense of *noblesse oblige* and certainly not a corporate liberalism of any kind – modernist or (post)modernist. His text presented all the symptoms of a deep amnesia; it contained no trace of the hegemonic discourse of the preceding thirty years, and, even more stunningly, no trace of the discourse of the twenty five years which preceded them – as far as Bush's text is concerned the promises of social modernism were simply never made. The question which necessarily arises, as indeed it did within Bush's text, albeit implicitly, is therefore, 'In what sense, then, may the United States be regarded as *the* modern society?' Not surprisingly, this question caused Bush some difficulty, as is clear in the following very awkward passage, which suggests plain reaction far more clearly than it suggests any recuperative, (post)modernist nostalgia such as Reagan was so adept at evoking: 'The old ideas are new again because they are not old, they're timeless.'

Despite his many famous gaffes, and perhaps because of the very 'pragmatism' which was the despair of some of the more ardent of the 'new conservatives' in his Administrations (see Roberts, 1984; and Stockman, 1986, for example), Reagan never got himself into such a fix, at least not on a ceremonial occasion. He was always careful to follow Nixon's lead and define the ultimate source of the Republic's strength as the self-reliance of its citizenry, and the source of its spiritual malaise as 'big government'. Thus he was able to transform social modernism without contradicting himself, and for this reason was as well served by his 'pragmatism' as Kennedy had been by his (Woodiwiss, 1990b: 217–18).

Similarly, despite his moralistic dislike of the 'worship of consumption', Carter avoided contradiction by talking of it as a threat to 'self-reliance' rather than as a threat to something as profane as the market, and by then arguing that the former could be countered and the latter made to work more efficiently by the actions of a 'competent and compassionate' state. In short and interestingly, the three plebeians proved to be far more competent enunciators of social (post)modernism and its discourse of forgetfulness than the patrician George Bush, who seems indeed to have been one of its principal victims: 'Watch my lips!'

A Floating World

In what follows I wish to suggest that three of the more widely celebrated sociological studies of the 1970s and 1980s were of a piece with social (post)modernism and shared both the forgetfulness and, because of this, the depthlessness apparent in presidential discourse. I do not mean to suggest that they, any more than any other postmodern texts, are without either interest or value, or that the studies I have chosen to examine – Daniel Bell's diptych, *The Coming of Post-Industrial Society* (1973) and *The Cultural Contradictions of Capitalism* (1976), and Robert Bellah et al.'s *Habits of the Heart* (1985) – are alone in possessing this depthless quality. I do suggest, though, that the reasons for their celebrity and influence, both inside and outside academia, are related to the artful ways in which they won their enthusiastic audiences – because of, rather than despite, their depthlessness. And, more important, I suggest that, precisely because they are such popular instances of the discourse they enunciate, a close reading of them promises to disclose much that is of value about the aetiology of the forgetfulness that accounts for their depthlessness.

The depthlessness of which I wish to speak is a product of that same concern with surfaces which Jameson identifies as characteristic of all postmodernist cultural production, and which I have just suggested is *de rigueur* amongst those presidents who would successfully enunciate social (post)modernism – except that, in the case of the academics, it is more likely to be a cause of regret rather than of the celebration apparent in some of the more self-consciously postmodern works (those of Andy Warhol, for example). At first sight, this depthlessness might appear to be simply an artifice of style, but what I want to suggest is that it is also very much a matter of content and of what is absent from this content.

Stylistically, each of the texts of concern here is easy to read on account of that artificially pellucid style so beloved of American academics and their editors – notwithstanding the more recent and remarkable success of Stephen Hawkings' *Short History of Time*, words are still supposed to be equally understandable regardless of the 'difficulty' of the point being made. This said, the collage-type structure, the numerous decorative quotations from otherwise long-forgotten authors, as well as the recurrent, self-glamorizing footnotes describing what might be called 'the natural history' of the text, all give Bell's two books an appearance of difficulty. More than anything else, it seems to me that this appearance reflects the fact that his texts are early and largely unselfconscious examples of full-blown postmodernist writing in the social sciences. Nevertheless, the real difficulty, or the 'horror' as François Roustang (1989: 129) puts it (the irony is intentional), in reading each text comes in trying to understand why they should have been so very well received.

The ultimate reason for their depthlessness, and hence for their peculiar difficulty, is that each of the texts, on my reading at least, lacks any theoretical point. That is, they lack the abstract and theoretical significance which these days is (or should I say 'used to be'?) considered the hallmark of an influential academic text, even in the social sciences (Bell is particularly insistent on this criterion, 1973: ch. 3, *passim*). Thus, since these texts do not satisfactorily explain their own significance, which explanations would anyway and of course be contestable within certain limits, the explanation has to be constructed for them. My point, and therefore my explanation for their popularity, will be that this was, and indeed remains, very easy because these texts were (and are) complicit with the hegemonic discourse and, more particularly, with the forgetting of social modernism which I have suggested is constitutive of the present American conjuncture.

Because Bell's two books were published first, because they have been the more widely influential and because they were written by an avowedly liberal and sometimes even avowedly socialist proponent of social modernism, I will discuss them first. The last of these reasons is the most compelling, since one must assume that the complicity of Bell's texts in the forgetting of social modernism was in no way intended. In sum, Bell's texts may be used to demontrate not simply the discursive fact of the forgetting of social modernism, but also its determinative power even within texts constituted in part by signifying chains which might otherwise have been expected to have provided some resistance to it.

The Coming of Post-Industrial Society

In the course of his uproarious visit to the United Nations in 1960, Nikita Khrushchev banged his shoe on the table and threatened to 'bury' capitalism. In the course of his two books, Bell does a far better job than Khrushchev ever could have done – not because he is anti-capitalist, but on the contrary because, since he could no longer allow himself to criticize capitalism directly, he goes to an immense amount of trouble to hide it from the view of those who would join him in thinking about the past, present and future of the United States. This secreting of capitalism from analytical view accounts, I want to suggest, for the ultimate complicity of

Bell's texts in the forgetting of the very social modernism of which he was once such an articulate and influential enunciator.

To understand how Bell's text hides the fact of capitalism from American view is also to understand why his texts have little, if any, theoretical significance, and certainly not enough to account for their very warm reception within the academic community. Bell's hiding of capitalism begins with his invention of the ideas of 'axial principles' and 'axial structures' in *The Coming of Post-Industrial Society*. The first of these terms refers to the myriad analytical principles which may be used to order social scientific enquiry, such as an emphasis on 'property relations' supposedly recommended by Marx and other theorists of 'capitalism', or the emphasis on 'production and machinery' preferred by Bell and shared with the modernization theorists (cp. Levy, 1966, vol. 1: intro.). According to Bell's formal and thoroughly modernist position, no such principle is inherently more useful than any other, and therefore the choice of one over another is purely a matter of what one is interested in. Thus one can readily imagine that he would dismiss the suggestion that his preference for the axial principle of production and technology, over that of property relations, betrays an unconscious desire to hide capitalism from view. However, any such response on his part would be somewhat disingenuous; as a former Marxist, he must have had reasons for his choice. Indeed, he specifies his reasons in chapter 1, because in the remainder of his text it becomes clear that they have an evaluative component. They comprise a sustained argument to the effect that, as Marx himself is supposed to have realized but latterly felt forced to deny, production and technology long ago came to outweigh property relations as sources of determinant 'pressures' or critical 'questions' in modern societies.

Bell's decision to characterize the axial principle ascribed to Marx as 'property relations' is of course highly controversial, and I for one would not agree. Putting that aside, Bell's next step is his 'analytical' decision to divide society into three parts – 'the social structure, the polity and the culture', each of which is defined descriptively rather than abstractly:

> The social structure comprises the economy, technology, and the occupational system. The polity regulates the distribution of power and adjudicates the conflicting claims and demands of individuals and groups. The culture is the realm of expressive symbolism and meanings. (Bell, 1973: 12)

This step opens his text to the entry of the hegemonic discourse because, in the absence of an abstract definition of what he regards as the axial principles informing these axial structures, he has to define, or better represent (Woodiwiss, 1990a: intro.), these structures using the euphemistic and idealized language of that very discourse:

> In modern Western society the axial principle of the social structure is *economizing* – a way of allocating resources according to principles of least cost, substitutability, optimization, maximization, and the like. The axial

principle of the modern polity is *participation*, sometimes mobilized or controlled, sometimes demanded from below. The axial principle of the culture is the desire for the *fulfillment and enhancement of the self*. (Bell, 1973: 12)

Never mind all the doubts which arise when one considers, for example, the applicability of the third of these principles to Japan; these definitions make clear exactly why 'capitalism' has to disappear from Bell's text. The pressure for it to disappear becomes palpable in the awkward use of the term 'social structure' to refer to 'economy, technology and occupational system', and the homely rendering of the exploitation that for Marxists is the consequence of the operation of 'the principles of resource allocation' in the labour market, as 'economizing'. The source of this pressure, quite simply, is Bell's acceptance of the terms, as well as the self-denying ordinances, of non-Marxist economics – if the question is how the market operates in general rather than why it operates in a particular way, there is no need to enquire further into questions of possession and their consequences.

All of this has at least one ironic consequence. It leaves Bell working within the analytically crippling representationalist terms set by what I have termed elsewhere (Woodiwiss, 1990a: 54) 'the geological metaphor'. According to this metaphor, derived from the base/superstructure model of classical Marxism, societies are understood to comprise three distinct levels of phenomena – the economic, the political and the ideological – each of which is understood to be embodied in particular concrete institutions. The result is that one has to believe, for example, that politics and what Bell calls 'culture' are unknown in factories. This result is doubly ironic since at the very same time that Bell was writing his text, some Marxists were engaged in an equally public endeavour to free themselves from both the metaphor and its disabling consequences. Apparently, Bell preferred to reread the Marxist writers of the 1930s and 1940s, who wished simply to refuse some of the consequences of acting on the metaphor, rather than to refuse it *tout court*.

Be that as it may, the principal and entirely predictable result of Bell's method of proceeding is to make his picture of post-industrial society a ringing endorsement of four in particular of the claims made by social modernism – the claims that the United States is *the* modern society; that it is a society ruled by the principle of equal opportunity; that it is a society in which all 'who are able are expected to' be self-reliant and those who are not are taken care of; and, finally, that it is a society wherein there is every reason to expect that the citizenry will be loyal. (Although a reassertion of the need for and the value of 'responsible unionism' does not have a place in Bell's conclusion, it is clear from his numerous references to unions that he thinks they would, and probably should, have a place, even if a greatly reduced one, in any post-industrial society. See for example section III B of the schema, 1973: 375.)

The endorsement of the first of these claims occurs early on in the book when Bell (1973: 117, Table 1-1, for example) argues that the United States is the first and, as of 1973, the only post-industrial society. The endorsement of the second claim occurs in a rather more leisurely fashion but is prefigured in Bell's initial definition of 'the post-industrial society':

> The concept of the post-industrial society is a large generalization. Its meaning can more easily be understood if one specifies five dimensions, or components, of the term:
> 1 Economic sector: the change from a goods-producing to a service economy;
> 2 Occupational distribution: the pre-eminence of the professional and technical class;
> 3 Axial principle: the centrality of theoretical knowledge as the source of innovation and of policy formulation for the society;
> 4 Future orientation: the control of technology and technological assessment;
> 5 Decision-making: the creation of a new 'intellectual technology'. (1973: 14)

Because of Bell's eschewal of any abstract, let alone critical, principle of analysis other than the pseudo-abstract ones provided by the hegemonic ideology itself, the argument which irresistibly emerges as he sets out his immensely detailed representation of the United States and its likely future under these headings in chapters 2 to 6 is utterly unsurprising. It is the argument that, as the society develops, and in line with a social-structural shift from an 'economizing' to a more humanistic, 'sociologizing' axial principle, the axis of stratification will cease altogether to be 'property' and instead become 'knowledge' (1973: 375). In this way, then, Bell repeats, albeit whilst projecting it into the future, the well-established social modernist promise that, because of the society's commitment to equal opportunity, merit will become the most important principle justifying differential rewards in the United States. Thus he concludes a long discussion and critique of Rawls' theory of 'distributive justice' and its far from unambiguous conception of equality of condition (Woodiwiss, 1990a: 84–5) by restating his (or should I say the official American?) preference for a meritocracy:

> The United States today is not a meritocracy; but this does not discredit the principle. The idea of equality of opportunity is a just one, and the problem is to realize it fairly. (Bell, 1973: 450)

And an important part of the solution to any such fair resolution, he goes on to argue, would be the maintenance and even enhancement of the existing welfare system, so that:

> each person is entitled to a basic set of services and income which provides him with adequate medical care, housing and the like. These are matters of security and dignity which must necessarily be the prior concerns of a civilized society. (1973: 452)

With such a safety net in place, it is Bell's fervently expressed hope that a rigorously maintained meritocratic system would reground both a long overdue renewal of respect for, and deference to, authority (1973: 453) and, implicitly, a renewed emphasis on its obverse, loyalty, albeit a loyalty owed to those of 'superior competence' rather than to those who simply possess greater wealth or power. The need for these renewals arises and will intensify because, thanks to the ever more marked disjunction between society's axial structures, the approach of a meritocracy has had the ironic effect that:

> . . . as disparities have decreased, as democracy has become more tangible, the expectations of equality have increased even faster, and people make more invidious comparisons. . . The revolution of rising expectations is also the revolution in *ressentiment*. (1973: 451)

And what, finally, will make the consequent social quandary inescapable is Bell's conviction that, even more significantly, the approach of the post-industrial society will still further enhance the disjunction between the social spheres:

> The post-industrial society is essentially a game between persons. . . For most of human history, *reality was nature*, and in poetry and imagination men sought to relate the self to the natural world. Then *reality became technics*, tools and things made by men yet given a separate existence outside himself, the reified world. Now *reality is primarily the social world* – neither nature nor things, only men – experienced through the reciprocal consciousness of self and other. Society itself becomes a web of consciousness, a form of imagination to be realized in social construction. . . The constraints of the past vanish with the end of nature and things. (1973: 488)

In this remarkable passage, which links some of Riesman's earlier conclusions in *The Lonely Crowd* with some of Lyotard's later thoughts about 'the postmodern condition', the depthlessness that, I have argued, characterizes Bell's text becomes a literal presence within it as, projectively, the cultural sphere finally floats free of the social structure (economy) and drifts heavenward, borne aloft on a cloud of words, as Lyotard might say, and, as I would say, social modernist promises. In sum, Bell's text was not simply stylistically but was also substantively postmodern *avant* a considerable number of *lettres*.

The Coming of Post-Industrial Society, then, repeats in a new and more sophisticated, because more rarefied, mode the promises made by social modernism, which in an earlier period were summarized by Joe Hill in the phrase 'pie in the sky'. This said, it also provides the means to forget that these promises had already been made, and remained on the table. This is made possible by the notion of the disjunction of spheres, and comprises a variant of the ploy that became known in the more assertively liberal corners of American social science during the 1960s as 'blaming the victim'. In this instance the fault lies in the inability of the needy to suppress their disloyal feelings of *ressentiment* and simply accept what is coming to them.

The Cultural Contradictions of Capitalism

Bell's ideological unconscious had gone to so much trouble to hide capitalism from the view of those who would join him in his effort to think about America's future, that it is at first a little surprising to see the word 'capitalism' figuring so prominently in the title of the second part of his diptych. The sense of surprise quickly evaporates, however, as one reads the text. The titular presence of 'capitalism' does not indicate that Bell has changed his mode of analysis, any more than his misplaced and perhaps somewhat sentimental attachment to such slippery and, I would have thought, discredited terms as 'contradiction' and 'dialectic' indicates that he remains an orthodox Marxist. Indeed, thanks to an audacious discursive somersault, propelled by the exigencies created by the signifying effects unleashed in the earlier text, 'capitalism' becomes the explanation, not for such phenomena as exploitation and inequality, but for the destructive rage associated with what he terms 'the *ressentiment*' of some of those who will not accept the exploitation and inequality visited on either themselves or others – in one sense, then, for Bell the last remnants of the bourgeoisie were the protesters of the 1960s!

Cultural Contradictions begins by discussing the suggestion which Bell finds in Nietzsche and Conrad, that nihilism is what is left of bourgeois culture once rationalism and modernism (in the philosophical/aesthetic sense) have exhausted themselves. As opposed to the postmodernists proper, Bell sides with Conrad rather than Nietzsche in profoundly regretting rather than joyously welcoming this possibility. More important, however, he rejects the apocalyptic tone of the whole debate, finding the tone's source in outmoded conceptions of societies as organic wholes. As an alternative to such conceptions, he repeats his own 'disjunctive' conception of society and concludes with a brief statement of its significance for understanding the present state of industrial societies as they move towards post-industrialism:

> The two realms which had historically been joined to produce a single character structure – that of the puritan and his calling – have now become unjoined. The principles of the economic realm and those of the culture now lead people in contrary directions. (Bell, 1976: 15)

More specifically and unconsciously self-critically (see above, p. 28), Bell suggests that gradually and paradoxically the two personifications of these principles – 'the bourgeois entrepreneur' and 'the independent artist' – have become highly conscious of each other, have come to fear each other and finally have sought to destroy one another:

> Radical in economics, the bourgeoisie became conservative in morals and cultural taste. The bourgeois economic impulse was organized into a highly restrictive character structure whose energies were channeled into the production of goods and into a set of attitudes toward work that feared instinct, spontaneity and vagrant impulse. . . The cultural impulse – I take Baudelaire as its exemplary figure – thus turned into a rage against bourgeois values. (1976: 17)

As a result of a number of 'sociological [should it not be social?] crossovers', the most important of which was the undermining of the protestant ethic by capitalism itself thanks to – a bathetic touch this – 'the invention of the installment plan', artistic modernism became 'exhausted', 'an empty vessel' and consequently 'only the hedonism remained, and the capitalist system lost its transcendent ethic' (1976: 21). Later, Bell argues, this 'unrestrained appetite' crossed over into the political realm, where societies are faced with the contradictory forces represented by 'the revolution of rising entitlements', the recognized 'incompatibility of various wants', damaging 'spillover' effects of economic growth on the environment, a worldwide inflation and the requirement that any attempt at reconciling these forces should take place in the public arena of politics (1976: 23–4). For the problems thus posed to be soluble, Bell argues, 'Western society' must find a new political philosophy which has something of a religious character to it (to ensure a sense of limits), and new institutional means of embedding any such philosophy into the social routine, such as those he envisages when he uses the term 'public household' (to ensure a sense of equity) (1976: 26–30).

These themes are taken up again and elaborated upon in the succeeding chapters. The first, historical, part of the book climaxes in a critique of 'the sensibility of the sixties' which is so negative that it might be better described as a denunciation (see also Bell, 1988). It seems to me that Bell's fury is disproportionate, suggesting that the real object of his rage must be something other than the youthful, 'counter-cultural' revolutionaries of whose activities and motivations he gives such a *ressentiment*-charged and dismissive account. 'Do [their] exhortations add up to anything other than the lost gratifications of an idealized childhood?', he asks (1976: 144). 'But who', I ask, 'gets so angry with children?' Not Professor Bell, I am sure.

It seems to me that what Bell is really angry about is capitalism and its failure once again to deliver on its promises. The emergent forces summarized in the term 'post-industrialism' should have made delivery easier, but capitalist individualism, the elixir which turned into a poison, had one more trick to pull and it found the perfect instrument in the idiot youth of the 1960s. In his own youth Bell vented his anger on capitalism directly, but by the 1970s this was no longer an option: he had 'chosen the West' (Brick, 1986: ch. 4), and had done so in the United States where capitalism is, almost literally, sacrosanct. Instead he too became what he terms, following Irving Kristol and in a doubly ironic allusion to Hegel, part of 'capitalism's unhappy consciousness'.

If Marx's very sociological 'dull compulsions' of everyday capitalist life cannot be admitted as sources of, let alone sufficient for, social order in industrial societies, Bell must and does have resort to what were thought, before sociology, to be the principal supports of the social order, namely religion and the state. His concept of the needed new religion is unacknowledgedly Durkheimian in character, stressing as it does 'some new rite of incorporation' (1976: 170). More significantly, however, in setting it out, Bell makes explicit his desire to see loyalty validated once again, and not just where it concerns those of greater and lesser competence (see above, p. 115):

> . . . a religion of incorporation is a redemptive process whereby individuals seek to discharge their obligations that derive from the moral imperatives of their community: the debts incurred in being nurtured, the debts to the institutions that maintain moral awareness. (1976: 170–1)

In the first political essay of *Cultural Contradictions*, in which significantly, he returns to what he terms the 'turbulence' of the 1960s, Bell may finally and inevitably be found forgetting social modernism. In a move which should become known as a classic of sociological avoidance, the Great Society programmes figure in his analysis not so much as small promises to right great wrongs, but rather as massive sources of finance for revolutionary movements (pp. 178–9). From this multiply dubious fact, Bell draws the following exculpatory conclusion:

> The classic trajectory of expectations . . . tells us that no society that promises justice and, having admitted the legitimacy of the claims, slowly begins to open the way, can then expect to ride out the consequent whirlwind in a comfortable fashion. (1976: 179)

Then, as if even this is to admit too much as regards promises made but not kept, Bell quickly moves off into the more comfortable realm of large sociological generalizations and suggests that the deeper causes of the turbulence of the 1960s were:

> the simultaneous creation of an urban society, a national polity, a communal society, and a post-industrial world . . . [and] three other areas of difficulty . . .: the relation of democracy to empire . . . the participation revolution . . . and a profound change in the culture with the development of a fundamentally anti-rational and anti-intellectual bias in the arts and in modes of experience and sensibility. (1976: 179–80)

Quite how comfortable this realm is becomes apparent as one reads Bell's discussion of these 'causes' and realizes that they lack anything more than a hint or two of the existence of widespread privation and suffering. One is left with the distinct impression that there was little need to have made any promises in the first place:

> Many blacks, for example, claimed that conditions for them had 'worsened'. But what they clearly meant was that they were not where they expected to be. . . The rising new leadership of the blacks was young militant and aggressive. In this there is a curious psychological paradox, in that a second [sic] generation which has not experienced the kind of direct humiliation inflicted on its elders . . . is psychologically more assertive and more outspoken and extreme. (1976: 185)

Bell's last words on the Great Society programmes are as follows:

> In social policy, particularly in the United States, the record of social scientists is . . . dismal. In the areas of education, welfare and social planning, social scientists have reluctantly begun to admit that the problems are more complex than they thought. The failure of liberalism, then, is in part a *failure of knowledge*. (1976: 203, emphasis in the original)

It becomes clear in these words just how unhappy a part of the consciousness of capitalism Bell is. That portion of the blame deserved by capitalism but still remaining after most of it has been laid off onto its victims and critics is here accepted by Bell as a social scientist who has failed to provide knowledge. Finding that peace of mind is not to be gained by blaming the victims alone, Bell tragically resorts to blaming himself, like countless other Americans (Cobb and Sennett, 1973). We can find in this move, it seems to me, the source of both his unflagging intellectual energy and his particular interest in the not entirely respectable pastime of 'social forecasting' – the hope of avoiding future guilt, the hope of redemption that comes from confessing one's sins.

Habits of the Heart

If Bell's two books may be taken as representative of the process – somewhat uncomfortable in his case – whereby liberal American social science forgot social modernism, then that of Bellah and his associates (1985) may be taken as representative of the same social science in the amnesiac mode. Their text exhibits almost all the qualities that Jameson has suggested are characteristic of more self-consciously postmodern cultural products; that is, it is weightless because, like Bell's text, it is depthless despite being highly decorated, and passionless despite being utopian. The one characteristic that it very definitely does not share with the texts of the self-consciously postmodern is the latter's fascination with social and psychological fragmentation. As an instance of the hegemonic ideology, it is written to recommend wholeness of and to the nation, as well as of and to the person. In sum, it comes close to be being a 'New Age' sermon – an effect intensified by a title which intentionally harks back to a time when sermons were significant texts, and to the rhetorical devices upon which they depended, as well as by a writing style which, quite unlike that of the nineteenth-century preachers, surrounds each of the sometimes mildly criticized individuals whose stories it recounts with an indiscriminately loving aura which denies any possibility of anger.

A particular 'horror' one confronts when attempting to grasp the overall meaning of *Habits* (Bellah et al., 1985) is the sense of one's own inner violence which accompanies any attempt to dismantle so modest, so kindhearted and so coherent a text. Be that as it may, this is not an occasion for sentimentality and so I must begin by saying that the reason for the text's depthlessness is not so much its failure to say anything of theoretical significance as its choice of theoretical stance. The nature of this stance is not made explicit, indeed an eclectic clutch of theorists from

Toqueville, through Marx, Weber and Durkheim, to Mead, Riesman, MacIntyre, Habermas, Gadamer and Bell are acknowledged.

Although the authors insist that 'society . . . [is] a reality in itself, not . . . something merely derived from the agreement of individuals' (1985: 303), their choice of methods (participant observation and interviews) tends to deprive this insistence of much force, let alone analytical substance. Economic and political structures are alluded to on occasion and, rather predictably, cultural ones are discussed in some detail. However, because the core of the book is based upon observation of, and interviews with, particular people, and because of the situations Bellah et al. choose to focus on, one does in fact get the distinct impression that society for them is not only rather precisely something 'derived from the agreement of individuals', but is also something that in the American case is currently in some trouble because such agreement is not forthcoming across a wide enough range of concerns. Moreover, by also insisting on the conversational nature of their methods and of their text, as well as upon how much they learnt from the enterprise, Bellah et al. would seem to be sceptical as to whether or not much of actual substantive, as opposed to methodological, value may be provided by theory as opposed to experience anyway – 'Even the social scientist may know more about our society from the common experience of living in it than from any number of monographic studies' (1985: 307).

Thus, although Bellah et al. (1985: 271, for example) on several occasions use the terms 'post-industrial' and 'postmodern' to describe the times in which we live, and although they would agree with Bell that in such times 'reality is primarily other people' (see above p. 116), they arrive at this position in their own rather distinctively American and even transcendentalist, or as they might put it 'biblical republican', way. Although, yet again like Bell, they end by invoking the necessity of religious faith, the route to redemption which they recommend is, unlike Bell's, fraternal and even Franciscan rather than patriarchal and either rabbinical or jesuitical.

Whatever the differences between the theoretical stances of Bellah et al. and Bell, the consequence is the same, namely the openness of their text to the entry of the hegemonic discourse, which again explains its depthlessness as well as its apparent readability. Because, thanks to their methodology, Bellah et al. are frankly representationalist, the fact of the hegemonic discourse's entry is particularly clear (although not to them), as are the lack of analytical depth which results and the somewhat more conscious but equally depthless effort which the authors make to counter it. The existence of such a discourse is also frankly acknowledged – 'everyone in the United States thinks largely in middle-class categories, even when they are inappropriate' (1985: ix). However, because for this reason they choose to 'concentrate . . . their research on white, middle-class Americans' (1985: ix), and because the discourse which interpellates these Americans is much more preconstructed and particular than they imagine, the fact that their text must therefore repeat the same discourse escapes them.

Quite how preconstructed and pervasive the hegemonic discourse is becomes immediately apparent in Bellah et al.'s accounts of their archetypal respondents. At a remarkably small risk of losing anything of significance, each of their stories may be summarized in social modernist terms, several of which are indeed used by the respondents themselves. Brian Palmer, committed to self-reliance, took his opportunities but eventually came to realize that there was more to life than making money, and that these things were not just a matter of shouldering responsibilities but were most importantly a matter of being loyal (he uses the term 'commitment'). Likewise, although Joe Gorman's story revolves rather more narrowly around his sense of his responsibilities to family and community, one is left in little doubt that he also values self-reliance and is grateful for his opportunities. However, his refusal to go along with a campaign against the siting of a low-income housing project in his town suggests that he does not put loyalty to family and community above all other values.

Again, the terms and/or ideas of self-reliance, responsibility and opportunity figure prominently in the discourse of Margaret Oldman as she talks about her life and beliefs. She, too, appears only to question loyalty, in the sense of responsibility to and for others. Finally, even for Wayne Bauer, a Vietnam-era deserter and avowed radical, finds his greatest satisfaction seeing the tenants he organizes gain a sense of what might be termed 'collective self-reliance' and 'collective opportunities', whilst he himself has gained what Bellah et al. (1985: 19) term 'a broadened . . . sense of responsibility'. This is not surprising when one discovers that he is a member of an organization, the Campaign for Economic Democracy, which 'grew', with Tom Hayden, out of SDS and its philosophy of 'participatory democracy' (see above, pp. 78–9).

For Bellah et al., the only problem with the approaches to life of their four archetypes is that each seems to be preoccupied with means rather than ends. But what, they ask, closing the social modernist door behind them, is the meaning of 'success' (defined as taking one's opportunities), 'freedom' (defined as self-reliance) and 'justice' (defined in terms which directly recall the promises of social modernism)? In other words, Bellah et al.'s aim is to transform social modernism (they call it 'individualism') from a simple code of conduct into something worth believing in.

To this end, and in chapter 2 they commence their contribution to the 'conversation' by outlining two strands of American culture – the biblical and the republican, which they suggest coexisted in earlier times with an individualism which, partly because of this, came in an 'expressive' or self-developmental form as well as the more familiar 'utilitarian' or economic one. Gradually, as the utilitarian tradition overwhelmed the others, the 'independent citizen', who so struck De Toqueville, gave way, as people became more and more exhaustive of reality, to 'the entrepreneur', 'the manager' and 'the therapist' in turn, as the 'representative characters' of American society. However, the victory of utilitarian individualism has not been complete. Bellah et al. claim to detect elements of the other traditions surviving in the 'habits of the heart' or mores of their archetypal respondents: elements which they suggest prefigure both the possibility of the final arrival of Riesman's 'autonomous' character-type (the truly modern type, see above, p. 29) and the communal restoration of some sort of 'equilibrium' between the cultural strands (1985: 49–50).

The two parts of the book which follow are devoted to documenting these prefigurations and showing their interconnection in the continuing 'habits of the [American] heart' as the latter show themselves in love and marriage, therapeutic relationships, community involvement, active citizenship and religious communion:

> ... however much Americans extol the autonomy and self-reliance of the individual, they do not imagine that the good life can be lived alone. Those we interviewed all agree that connectedness with others in work, love and community is essential to happiness, self-esteem and moral worth. (1985: 84)

And again:

> ... the realm still survives, even though with difficulty, as an enduring association of the different. In the civic republican tradition, public life is built upon the second languages and practices of commitment that shape character. These languages and practices establish a web of interconnection by creating trust, joining people to families, friends, communities, and churches, and making each individual aware of his [sic] reliance on the larger society. They form those habits of the heart that are the matrix of a moral ecology, the connecting tissue of a body politic. (1985: 251)

More than this, Americans have over the past one hundred years produced at least six visions of how this interconnection might be achieved and so have these resources at their disposal too. Bellah et al. list these visions as: 'The Establishment', 'Populism', 'Welfare Liberalism', 'Neocapitalism', 'The Administered Society' and 'Economic Democracy'. However, the shared problem with all of them is that, like Bellah et al.'s archetypal respondents, they are each far stronger on means than ends.

To my way of thinking and for reasons that have already been explained, the middle two of these visions, the reigning pair, are but the Democratic and Republican variants of social modernism.

Posing 'Welfare Liberalism' against capitalism of any kind, including 'Neocapitalism', obscures the fact that the former was a promise made by the latter, and in this way the forgetting of social modernism that is implicit throughout the text, especially in its insistence on remembering a pre and early capitalist past (1985: 152ff.), is finally made explicit. This judgement as to their forgetfulness is confirmed by the sudden appearance of the term 'modernity' in the conclusion, where it plays the role allotted to 'capitalism' in Bell's discourse. For Bellah et al. (1985: 275), like Bell, modernity is identified with that elixir turned poison called individualism, so deeply buried is the thought that capitalism might be in part responsible for the pathological consequences of America's downing of large quantities of the poison draught.

For Bellah et al., capitalism is simply a problem for the working class, minorities and the poor. It is what makes them hungry and unequal and what denies them both individuality and community. It is not, as it is for me, also the source of individualism, the consequent impossibility of community, and the angst of the embodiments of the so-called middle class, that Bellah et al. document in their soft-focused way. For this reason, then, and contradictorily, capitalism retains a place in the future they hope for. Thus the 1960s figure in their text not as a time of hypocrisy but as the dreamtime (see the comments by Wayne Bauer, Bellah et al., 1985: 17, and by the authors on Martin Luther King, pp. 251–2), during which the seeds of their Franciscan vision first began to germinate. The utopianism that is the inevitable consequence of their sociological depthlessness is made starkly apparent by the similarity of their concluding words to those which President Bush was later to deliver in the course of his Inaugural Address (see above, p. 109):

> We have been called a people of plenty. . . Yet [o]ur material belongings have not brought us happiness. . . We have imagined ourselves a special creation, set apart from other humans. In the late twentieth century we see that our poverty is as absolute as that of the poorest of nations. We have attempted to deny the human condition in our quest for power after power. It would be well for us to rejoin the human race, to accept our essential poverty as a gift, and to share our material wealth with those in need. (Bellah et al., 1985: 295–6)

Finally, their continuing confinement within the mirrored walls of America's hegemonic discourse is confirmed by the tenacity with which, largely silent about capitalism and committed to the continuation of the corporation, they cling to Riesman's ideal of the 'autonomous' character-type, as well as in the enthusiasm with which they repeat the promise of some ill-defined form of 'distributive justice':

> . . . becoming one's own person, whilst always a risky, demanding effort, takes place in a community *loyal* to shared ideals of what makes life worth living. (1985: 252, emphasis added)

Is this not where social modernism came in?

'She wore bluuuue velvet . . .'

Watching David Lynch's *Blue Velvet* in the mid-1980s, it occurred to me that one of the many things that this remarkable and apparently nerveless and affectless depiction of evil is about is the way in which the United States had negated itself, or at least its image of itself, during the preceding twenty-odd years. This thought had been gestating for a long time and, therefore, to have it crystallize in the course of watching a film that made me feel extremely uneasy was both shocking and cathartic, to use an old-fashioned term. In my view, *Blue Velvet* is a film about, to use a rather more modish term, 'the unpresentable', which is a synonym for another old-fashioned, but these days once more current term, namely 'the sublime'. Put another way, as an unsentimental and rigorously self-consciously postmodern text, it is a film about that of which Bellah et al. cannot speak.

If, paraphrasing Lyotard, 'the sublime' signifies that which can be thought but not represented – the holy grail of traditional aesthetics – then *Blue Velvet* is an instance of what used to be called, emphatically, 'a work of art'. Moreover, because of the catharsis it is capable of engendering, it also appears to fulfil the redemptive mission ascribed to such objects by traditionalist modes of criticism and revalidated by the likes of Bell and Bellah et al. I will leave until later the task of pondering and assessing the fact that such a traditionalist critical judgement can result from the deployment of ostensibly avant-garde, postmodern concepts. My more immediate and important concern is with neither aesthetics nor metatheory. Rather it is with what Lynch's film signifies as a sociological allegory and more specifically with what it suggests is, and indeed instances as, unpresentable about what has happened in the United States since the 1960s.

Blue Velvet tells the story of two thoroughly nice 'middle-class kids', Jeffrey, the son of a store owner, and Sandy, the daughter of the police chief, who try to find out how and why someone lost the ear that Jeffrey finds on some waste ground. Their search leads them into a very dangerous world, in which the principal protagonists are Dorothy, a night club singer, and Frank, her greatest fan, who is also the kidnapper of her child and, we are left to assume, the murderer of her husband.

Read as a sociological allegory, *Blue Velvet* is about a social condition which engenders anxiety in those who are positioned in and by it. Besides all the usual cinematographic devices, such as those summarized by the terms montage and *mise en scène*, two far less common devices are used to convey this anxiety. First, there is no certainty as to when the events pictured in the film are supposed to be taking place, thanks to the inconsistent cues given by the soundtrack and set dressings. However, since none of these cues refers us to a period outside that stretching between the late 1950s and the present, it seems reasonable to read the film as being about that whole period. The second source of anxiety for the audience is an additional uncertainty as to the genre to which the film belongs, again because the stylistic cues it offers are inconsistent – sometimes one thinks one is watching a 'teen movie', sometimes a thriller and sometimes a horror film. The net result is that, bereft of historical and stylistic reference points, one has no idea what will happen next and not much confidence as to whether or not one will be able to take it.

What there is to be anxious about is suggested by a remarkable absence from the film's verbal narrative. There is nothing in it that directly and unambiguously validates whatever one might regard as the core American values. Rather, because the nastiness upon which the film focuses occurs almost exclusively at night, one is allowed to think – as naturally as night follows day – that the nastiness is of a piece with the very lightly sketched-in all-American life of daytime Lumberville with its white picket fences, its sentimental songs and its work ethic – 'at the sound of the falling log it will be . . .', incants the radio. This impression is reinforced by the fact that towards the end of the film it is realized that Frank was the person wearing 'the well-dressed man disguise' in the daytime drug deal, and that the other party to the deal was a police officer and friend of Sandy's father.

What justifies this jaundiced view and relates it to the events of the 1960s is suggested by the nature of the nodal points of the narrative and the way in which they are connected with one another. The film opens with a fire engine (a beneficent government) driving down (protecting) an archetypal small town/suburban street ('the good life'). Next, Jeffrey visits his father's sick-bed and later discovers the severed ear, which soon afterwards the camera enters (we pass into the American unconscious – its unpresentable side). The discovery of the ear is juxtaposed with brief scenes in which Jeffrey is seen interacting in a friendly but somewhat paternalistic way with the only two African-Americans in the film, both of whom work in his father's store. In the second interaction, the African-Americans unknowingly equip Jeffrey for what turns out to be his voyage of discovery. Thus the discovery of the ear may be read as a metaphor for the discovery of something else that was unpleasant, namely racism and by extension all the other evils uncovered in the course of the 1960s.

Thereafter, like the young of the 1960s, the film's two young protagonists probe ever more deeply and riskily into their middle-American surroundings, discovering evils – the kidnapping of Dorothy's child – and ambivalences in and about themselves – Jeffrey's only slightly hesitant responsiveness to Dorothy's sado-masochistic desire. The latter both suggests that Jeffrey is, like Dorothy, a product of a culture of narcissism which, as Christopher Lasch has suggested, predisposes all of its subjects to sado-masochism, and is a moment of particularly intense anxiety for the audience, or at least for that part of it that identifies with Jeffrey.

What, however, makes this voyage of discovery really dangerous is the fact that the man (the rogue state) that holds Dorothy's child and therefore controls her too, Frank, is not simply a sado-masochist too ('mummy, mummy', he screams as he catches sight of, and recoils from, Dorothy's vagina [cp. Lasch's 'vagina dentata']), but one with something to hide, namely murder, mayhem and drugs (the war in Vietnam). At one particularly tense point, Sandy tells Jeffrey of a dream she had the night before, which features a host of robins (Christmas-time with its presents and general plenty – the American Dream/the hippy dream).

Just before the film's denouement, Jeffrey echoes the all too familiar words of exhausted and embittered radical disappointment as he refuses to complete the clean-up for the representatives of respectable Lumberville, 'I'm going to let you find (out) on your own.' The twist, however, is that it is made very clear that respectable Lumberville only appears to clean itself up. The film ends with Jeffrey's miraculously recovered father enjoying a family party, to which Dorothy, now an implausibly perfect mother, has been invited, and with a repetition of the opening sequence with its fire engine and white picket fences. To complete this scene of all-American bliss, a robin lands on the kitchen window – clearly a mechanical robin, a simulacrum (Reagan and/or the New Agers).

On my reading, then, *Blue Velvet* is about, and itself instances, a knowing but involuntary retreat from social modernism. In a way which is strongly reminiscent of the 'cool' stance recommended by the beats, Lynch's text thus seems to conclude, not with a socialist-like, 'you have been lied to, get mad', but rather with a zen-like, 'see how ugly the world is and get wisdom'. It is doubtful, however, that a *koan* like *Blue Velvet* will have the same self-contradictorily activistic or 'seductive', even if ultimately short-lived, consequences in relation to the society's amnesiac condition as those which followed from the 'howl' of the beats as they reasserted the prerogatives of the imagination in the 'bromo-seltzer' world of incipient social modernism. In that world, if you believed your eyes, upset stomachs were a major social problem which was manifestly absurd. Today, knowledge of both the nature and extremity of real social problems is widespread. However, so marked has been the retreat into the inner space of which psychology speaks that neither Lynch nor anyone else with the public's ear thinks it worth shouting, let alone asking whether or not capitalism is implicated in the societal self-loathing that is engendered by the existence and apparent intractability of these problems. This stance is especially apparent in Lynch's very private paintings, wherein all manner of fears and unpleasantness are juxtaposed with childlike 'matchstick' people – 'minimal selves' (Lasch, 1984).

Conclusion

To conclude, on the basis of the foregoing, I am prepared to wager that, wherever one may look within the mainstream discourses produced in the United States in the course of the past twenty years, one would discover the same forgetfulness, amnesia and deeply buried, anti-capitalist anger that has been instanced above; that is, the same always nostalgia-tinged oscillation between Bellah-like celebrations of the possibilities of the American surface (see the work of Richard Rorty, for example), and Lynch-like ruminations on the shadows of the same (see the work of Bret Easton Ellis, for example). All that now remains to be done is to relate the ideological deflation of which these developments are symptomatic to the state of class relations over the same period.

8
SOCIAL (POST)MODERNISM AND CLASS RELATIONS

As the ideological challenges and the associated social disruption subsided, the value of labour power was reduced, labour's advances in the circulatory sphere were reversed, and, by the same tokens, the counteracting influences to the tendency of the rate of profit to fall once more came to operate in capital's favour. Nevertheless, it is important to bear in mind, as was emphasized in Chapter 6, that the shift of the balance of forces was small and that the main reason for it was the simple failure of the opposition. As a consequence, for the remainder of the 1970s and into the 1980s, American capital remained weak at the level of its core reproductive processes. It continued to depend, for what might be termed 'life support', on the absence of challenges at the level of its political and ideological conditions of existence. However, while they may have been minimal when compared with those in Western European states, the limits on capital's power represented by the balances intrinsic to even social (post)modernism remained intact and surprisingly restrictive of capital's freedom, especially in relation to social security (state pensions).

The emergence of the social (post)modernism outlined in the preceding chapter may thus be understood as symptomatic of the strain created by these limits in the context of a world economy which had become far more competitive, and which had gradually gained a presence within the United States' economy as foreign-made goods became increasingly dominant in some of the more highly visible domestic markets. All this said, the period between the mid-1970s and the mid-1980s nevertheless saw the commencement of a substantial restructuring of the workplace and of the economy more generally. In 1983 this restructuring finally produced the beginnings of a possibly sustained upward trend in the average rate of corporate profitability (Bosworth, 1982; Bowles et al., 1986; Dumenil et al., 1987; Henley, 1990; Weisskopf, 1988). This chapter, then, aims to outline the emergence and self-destruction of social (post)modernism and assess its significance for the American economy at the four class-structurally determined points of tension that provide the analytical foci of the present study. (For outlines and radically differing assessments of the economic policies pursued since the late 1970s, see Boskin, 1987; B. Friedman, 1989; Hoover and Plant, 1989: ch. 6; Krieger, 1986: ch. 7; Nishkanen, 1988; Rostow, 1983; Tobin, 1988.)

The Value of Labour Power

All the signs are that the effort which the embodiments of capital initiated in the late 1960s to shift the balance of forces between capital and labour to the former's advantage have been successful. Both the disappearance of 'responsible unionism' from the society's ceremonial discourse and capital's continuing southward relocation, which now extends into northern Mexico (Baker et al., 1990; Kurtzman, 1988: ch. 6), have had the entirely predictable effect of rather dramatically weakening organized as well as unorganized labour (Goldfield, 1987; Kochan et al., 1986). Additionally, other developments have occurred which have had and continue to have a similar effect. Examples of such developments are: the especially high unemployment levels associated with the recession of 1981–2; the ever-growing labour force participation of women in a still highly sexist society (Bergman, 1984); the development of new and more sophisticated methods of 'union-busting' (Fantasia, 1988: 66–9); and the widely shared and increasing fear of foreign competition. Finally, the interactive effect of all of these factors has been to intensify the pressures towards a more and more dualistic economy in the pursuit of what has been variously termed 'flexible specialization' or 'post-fordism (Aglietta, 1976; Bluestone and Harrison, 1982; Harrison and Bluestone, 1988; Eitzen and Baca-Zinn, 1989: chs. 16–23; Levitan and Conway, 1988; Piore and Sabel, 1984). As a consequence of this complex of factors, traditional features of secondary labour markets, such as low wages and reduced levels of social protection, have come to characterize the so-called primary labour markets, as firms reduce the size of their relatively privileged core labour force and increase the size of their disprivileged, peripheral or 'contingent' labour force of part-time and temporary employees. The latter are now often white and male, as well as minority and female.

The weakening of labour relative to capital has been particularly marked as regards possessory relations – of course, because this had been the only dimension of production wherein labour had been able to sustain any effective constraints on capital. The level of unionization has continued to fall, until it stood at just 15 per cent in 1989, and these days unions are seldom able to set the 'going rate' even in areas where they have traditionally been strong. The unions' hopes that they could follow capital in its southward move came to nought, when even the minor legislative redressing of the balance that they sought through the Labour Law Reform Bill of 1977 failed to occur on account of a Senate filibuster. So too did their efforts to regain some political clout during the 1970s and 1980s (Woodiwiss, 1990b: 282–6). As a consequence, during the late 1970s and early 1980s, unions often had to 'give back' substantial parts of the private welfare packages that they had obtained in the past. This said, it should also be added that in a small number of cases capital was in even worse shape than labour, so that, especially when the latter was unionized, capital was forced to allow labour to encroach somewhat along the dimensions of title and control (Mroczkowski, 1984; Stone, 1988).

Predictably, labour's loss of power in the labour market has reduced the value of labour power and weakened the toehold that ordinary working people had gained in 'Middle America' during the 1950s and 1960s:

> To live like Americans did in the 1950s and 1960s, when we were the envy of the world, now usually requires two wage earners in each household owing to the fact that American wages, income and buying power have actually fallen since the early 1970s. . . According to the US Congress's Joint Economic Committee (JEC) . . . the earnings of the average thirty-year-old worker – when corrected for inflation and converted into today's dollar terms – have plummeted from a before-taxes high of $25,253 in 1973 to only $18,763 in 1987, a decline of nearly 25 percent. Workers in other age categories have experienced similar drops in earnings while at the same time the prices of such basic necessities as housing, food, day-care services, transportation, and medical care have more than quadrupled since the 1970s. (Kurtzman, 1988: 20–1)

This decline in the value of labour power is even more striking because it has occurred during a period in which, it is possible to argue convincingly, the skill levels associated with many jobs have actually increased (Block, 1990: 85–108).

The Maintenance of the Circuits of Capital

The signs are somewhat more mixed when it comes to judging the consequences of the emergence of social (post)modernism with respect to the maintenance of the circuits of capital, and its consequences for the balance of class forces. As befitted a society which was no longer committed to providing opportunities for all, and repeating what occurred in the mid to late 1960s, the number of most of the higher levels of contradictory positionings has declined (Davis, 1984), as have the pay and perquisites of those who embody the lower level contradictory positionings. Moreover, the chief reasons for this ongoing proletarianization remain the same, namely industry shifts (Plunkert, 1990) and revenue-saving.

As regards the number of such contradictory positionings, the new technology, especially computerization, has transformed the administration of capital even more quickly than it has transformed the manufacturing labour process. Despite generally increasing skill levels (Block, 1990: 85–112), the dual labour market, which from their beginnings distinguished the newer 'high tech' and service industries, has become ever more apparent in the offices and technical sections of the older manufacturing and clerical industries. Hitherto, such offices and technical sections had been regarded as the very stuff of the career ladder for all but the most lowly manual employees and the largely female secretarial labour force (Silvestri and Lukasiewicz, 1989). The point was graphically made by a manager of training for the medical insurance company, Blue Cross Blue Shield in the early 1980s:

> In the past, the lowest six levels of our clerical structure looked like an inverted pyramid. At the very bottom were jobs like filing, sorting, mail delivery, and basic data-entry jobs. You'd almost have to try *not* to get promoted in order to avoid rising through the clerical ranks. Most people did get promoted. With good oral and written communication skills, you could move fairly easily into a supervisory or junior management job. Those senior clerical jobs are disappearing, because the computer is taking over much of the decision-making. We have a lot more routine jobs at the bottom, and a few more complex jobs at the top, where you need someone to analyze hundreds of pages of data. (Kuttner, 1983: 90; see also Harrison and Bluestone, 1988)

Although the available statistics do not allow one to speak with precision about the pay and perquisites that go with the declining number of middle-range, contradictorily-positioned jobs, there is little reason to suppose that they have escaped the decline that has been generally apparent since the late 1960s (Blackburn and Bloom, 1985; Grubb and Wilson, 1989; K. Phillips, 1990; Tilly, 1986).

Whilst these developments imply a recentralization and hence a certain simplification of control relations within enterprises and clearly save revenue, their consequences for the strength of capital relative to labour have not been wholly positive. The 'good feelings' generated by especially Reagan's version of social (post)modernism meant that the ever-widening gap between declining opportunities and increasing expectations has been bridged by ever-increasing indebtedness and an apparently deepening anxiety (Ehrenreich, 1990) among the rank and file of the 'middle classes'; 'yuppiedom' and its 'Gucci' delights have proved as chimerical for most of the 'middle classes' as they have always been for those positioned solely by the working class. By 1986, thanks to the availability of such new forms of indebtedness as 'home equity loans', which deprive those who take them up of much of their future security, average wage-earners paid out more than 33 per cent of their income to service their accumulated and still growing debts – an increase of just under 30 per cent in only three years (Kurtzman, 1988: 84).

The same hubristic combination of increasing indebtedness and anxiety, with all the pressure that it places on the circuit of money capital, has also, of course, been observed amongst corporations, as well as on the part of the government. Indeed, they, alongside the wealthy, have been the heaviest consumers and therefore by far the biggest contributors to the nation's indebtedness (Blecker, 1990). Corporations have borrowed in order to take over other corporations or defend themselves against such takeovers, which has had disastrous consequences for their otherwise reviving profitability (see below, p. 137) as well as for their cash-flow – between 1975 and 1986, the average proportion of cash-flow going to meet interest payments rose from 25 to 40 per cent (Kurtzman, 1988: 77).

Similarly, the federal government also increased its indebtedness massively, for two main reasons. First, Reagan's rhetorical inflation of the threat represented by the Soviet Union required a rapid increase in military expenditure (Melman, 1985). Second, even so persuasive an advocate of self-reliance as Reagan was prevented by political difficulties and costs from reducing the substantial benefits provided for the elderly in the way of pensions and health care by the United States' otherwise minimalist welfare state. The net result of all of this indebtedness was a rise in American debt of all kinds from \$1.6 thousand million in 1970 to \$8.2 thousand million in 1986, which latter figure translated into a debt of \$40,000 for each citizen (Kurtzman, 1988: 73). Not surprisingly, the banking sector, which is where most of these bucks stop and which has also seriously over-committed itself as regards loans to the under-developed world, has been showing signs of strain (namely, the collapse of many savings and loans institutions and some banks, as well as the reduced credit ratings of even some of the most famous banks, see Brumbaugh and Litan, 1990; Mayer, 1991; Rousseaus, 1989).

The Balance between the two Departments of Production

The obverse of increasing indebtedness is, obviously enough, decreasing savings. Decreasing savings means decreasing investment (that is, decreasing purchases of the goods produced in Department I of the economy), and decreasing investment is, or should be, bad news for the balance between the two departments of production, especially when purchases of the consumer goods produced in Department II are increasing. In an economy that is as open to the rest of the world as that of the United States, and as numerous under-developed countries have also discovered, the bad news is that another twist is added to the debt spiral and, equally worryingly, title to capital assets and even the levers of national, macro-economic management, tends to move overseas. The chances that any recovery route adopted might be chosen domestically and democratically become ever more remote.

Because American companies had under-invested as explained earlier (see above pp. 99–100) and though they had been reinvigorated by the Reagan military build-up (Melman, 1985), they could not produce either the number, or especially the quality, of goods demanded by consumers. Overseas companies, especially those of Europe, Japan and the rest of Asia, thus became the main suppliers of many consumer goods.

In other words, as Richard Blecker (1990: 26) has put it, the United States has been '"producing below its needs" rather than "living beyond its means"', and the country's resulting indebtedness has served to stimulate other economies, pay for the further improvement of their production facilities and, therefore, help to maintain the balances between their two departments of production. Moreover, because the resulting negative balance of trade has tended, *ceteris paribus* and over the long run, to reduce the value of the dollar, American capital assets have become relatively cheap for the holders of foreign currencies. And, finally, because of the monetarist choice of interest rates as *the* tool of economic management, interest rates have had to be high in order to restrict the dollar's depreciation, as well as in order to keep America's debt saleable. As a result, an ever-increasing proportion of the country's national income has been expended on interest payments to overseas creditors and so is no longer available for domestic, or at least domestically chosen, use (Kurtzman, 1988: ch. 7). In this way, then, the United States' title as *the* modern society has already in part passed into the hands of its creditors.

The Counteracting Influences to the Tendency of the Rate of Profit to Fall

The Increasing Intensity of Labour at the Point of Production: The weakening of even responsible trade unions, the industry shifts and the workplace/labour market restructurings have been outlined above. The underlying official unemployment rate, already historically high at around 6 per cent, increased to more than 10 per cent at the beginning of 1983 before returning to close on 7 per cent by the beginning of 1985. Against this background it is not at all unreasonable to suppose that workers were made to work harder during the 1980s (Bowles et al., 1986: 156; Weisskopf et al., 1983: 38). This would appear to be confirmed by the work of even mainstream economists, who normally cannot bring themselves to mention such things. For such economists, productivity growth is normally explained by reference to such unexceptionable developments as increases in the quantity and/or quality of fixed and human capital. However, in order to explain the doubling of productivity growth that occurred between 1981 and 1985, former CEA chair, Michael Boskin, drawing on the work of John Kendrick, lists several factors that imply, even if they do not explicitly state, that increased intensity of work was a factor:

> About half the increase can be attributed to a rapid growth in output. The rest must be due to other factors . . . these included the effect of disinflation and declining energy prices; relative increases in research and development and in new plant and equipment; regulatory reforms; changes in the labor-force mix; and joint labor-management efforts to increase productivity to meet increased foreign competition. (1987: 233; see also Baumol et al., 1990)

The Depression of Wages below the Value of Labour Power Contrary to the expectations of such free marketeers as Charles Murray (1984), there has been an increase in poverty-level wages (Gottshalk, 1988). This is explained by the same factors as explain the increasing intensity of work, and by the reimposition of 'self-reliance' and the associated relative decline in welfare provision (Gartner et al., 1982; Schwarz, 1988; Weaver, 1988). More and more people have been forced to take up part-time or temporary 'contingent work' both out of necessity and because it is all that is available, not only for the unskilled and for women and minorities, but now increasingly for the semi-skilled and for white males, too (Eitzen and Baca-Zinn, 1989: chs. 16–23; Pfeffer and Baron, 1988; Levitan and Conway, 1988). The poorest tenth of wage and salary earners has seen its real income decline by fully 10 per cent in the course of the 1980s (Krugman, 1990; Sawhill, 1988).

The Cheapening of Elements of Constant Capital   The accelerated but somewhat less generous revisions of the depreciation schedules used by the Internal Revenue Service which were contained in the legislative centrepiece of the first Reagan Administration, the Economic Recovery and Tax Act of 1981, significantly reduced the cost of new capital equipment for most of the remainder of the decade (Boskin, 1987: ch. 8). This effect would have been even greater had it not been for the passage a year later of the Tax Equity and Fiscal Responsibility Act originated by the Democratically controlled Congress, which cancelled the further acceleration of depreciation allowances which the 1981 Act had proposed should take effect in 1985.

The net effect of these measures was nevertheless amplified considerably by the micro-electronic revolution, which, in the 1980s, finally brought about a substantial cheapening of fixed capital costs in many industries. Block has summarized the process involved as follows:

> The development of the microprocessor was not a single event, and it launched a process of continuous innovation. With each successive microprocessor, engineers managed to put many times the number of logic circuits on a chip of the same size, so that the microprocessors could become progressively more powerful in processing information. Since the costs per chip decline dramatically with mass production, the result has been a tremendous increase in information-processing capacity per dollar invested. This has resulted in continuous capital savings across the full range of capital goods that incorporate electronic controls. (Block, 1990: 135)

Block later exemplifies the range of capital goods involved, referring to the increased use of numerically controlled machines in metalworking, the gradual introduction of flexible manufacturing systems more generally, and the increasing level of automation in the computer industry itself. He also indicates that no attempt has yet been made to measure the extent of the capital saving represented by such developments and explains the immense difficulties faced by those who would try to do so. Nevertheless, he gives some indication of the scale of these savings when he reports that, according to one estimate, simply taking account of the reduced costs of computing power, which is something official statistics did not do until 1985, increases the estimated size of the GNP for 1984 by $100 million and the annual growth rate of producers' durable equipment from

5.6 per cent to 12.6 per cent between 1972 and 1982 (Block, 1990: 136–7).

In short, it would appear that the effectivity of this counteracting influence has moved steadily and massively in capital's favour since the 1970s. Provided the immense political and economic difficulties involved in undertaking another 'reconversion' process are overcome, this movement may be expected to strengthen still more with the ending of the Cold War. However, it is very important, as Block also insists, to bear in mind always that capital improvements, no matter how cheaply bought, do not necessarily result in productivity, let alone profitability, gains. In other words, they may simply result in waste if the appropriate software is unavailable or if, to use the chilling Japanese corporate-speak, the 'humanware' is inefficiently utilized.

Relative Over-population   It has already been mentioned that one result of the accelerating economic restructuring of the 1970s and 1980s was the stabilization of the official unemployment rate at the historically high level of between 6 and 7 per cent. Given the interlinked reimposition of 'self-reliance' and the failure of welfare benefits to grow with the increased need bespoken by this figure, what Michael Kalecki once referred to as 'the threat of the sack' regained much of the effectiveness that it had lost in the 1960s as regards labour discipline and the intensification of labour, and there were plenty of takers for the many new low paid and/or 'contingent' jobs created by the restructuring. Rapidly increasing proportions of women and minorities were entering the labour force, both for demographic reasons, including greatly increased immigration (illegal as well as legal), and because the expectations of women, if not their status, were slowly changing (Eitzen and Baca-Zinn, 1989: chs. 16–23). In sum, thanks to the silence that descended once the contradictorily positioned stopped listening to the 'shouting' of the poor that Nixon had so castigated, the increased size of the relative surplus population appears to have become an effective counteracting influence once again.

Foreign Trade and Investment   Until the early 1970s, this counteracting influence had worked in capital's favour by reducing the costs of raw materials and providing more profitable outlets for the investment of money capital. Since then, however, the costs of some of the raw materials upon which the United States has grown most dependent, especially oil, have increased dramatically. Also, the weight of manufactured goods in the country's basket of imports has increased greatly. Thus foreign trade and especially the burgeoning trade and current account deficits which reappeared in 1983 have become a symbol as well as a cause of American capital's current weakness (Boskin, 1987: 104; Kurtzman, 1988: *passim*).

This said, overseas investment by American companies continues to contribute handsomely to their own, if not to their country's, overall profitability; for example 68.1 per cent of Exxon's and 43 per cent of IBM's revenues were earned abroad in 1985 (Eitzen and Baca-Zinn, 1989: intro.). Moreover, by contributing to the acceleration of the United States' deindustrialization (Bluestone and Harrison, 1982; Harrison and Bluestone, 1988), this export of capital has made its own, possibly unintended, contribution to the restoration of 'the threat of the sack', which, in turn, facilitates the ongoing restructuring of the economy and its accompanying intensification of labour. Thus it may be anticipated that, once the restructuring is complete (if one can ever talk of such a thing) and especially once, with the equally unintended help of the likes of Toyota and Honda (Dohse et al., 1985), a new regime of labour discipline has been firmly established, American multinational money capital might once again be invested in the United States in quantities sufficient to help to reduce the trade-related deficits.

The Increase of Stock Capital   Between 1949 and 1964 the proportion of the external funds required by corporations which was raised by means of stock issues rose from 23 to 41 per cent. However, access to this relatively cheap form of money capital decreased considerably and consistently in the years following 1964, with the result that it stood at 24 per cent in 1979 (Stearns, 1990: 186). Stock capital had once represented a cheap form of capital that allowed a corporation to retain the maximum degree of autonomy from financial institutions, but the 1980s saw it become a source of financial and even organizational vulnerability in the deregulated and highly speculative financial markets created by the concentration of wealth in the hands of wealthy individuals and financial institutions that accompanied the restructuring of the economy. As Linda Brewster Stearns puts it:

> The movement of capital out of the stock market meant, however, that corporations could no longer depend on the demand for their stock to increase their stock prices. Instead to keep stockholders from selling their stock (and hence lowering prices), dividends had to be competitive with the high interest rates obtainable in the capital market. This situation simultaneously decreased the internal funds of corporations while increasing their dependence on financial institutions for external capital resources. (1990: 187)

This said, this set of reverses has also – not entirely unintentionally – contributed to the ongoing restructuring of the economy and the accompanying intensification of labour, because it has had consequences at the level of what Stearns refers to as 'the social relations of production'. As she continues:

> Using restrictive loan covenants, financial institutions can prevent corporations from risk-taking ventures as a means of increasing profits. As a result, corporations may be forced independently, or through direct lender pressures, to maximize profits by lowering labour costs. A case in point is International Harvester Company. . . *Business Week* reported [in 1982 that] in spite of [all its other cost cutting efforts], 'If Harvester does request revision of the loan

terms, bankers will attempt to tighten the screws on its operations further by pushing for speeded-up cost cutting efforts. At the top of the list will be intensified demands that Harvester wring concessions out of the United Auto Workers. (1990: 196; see also Mintz and Schwartz, 1990: 206ff.; and for the continuation of the same pressures through much of the remainder of the 1980s, Kurtzman, 1988: 191–3)

Latterly, of course, the invention of the 'junk bond', the accompanying merger mania satirized (?) in Oliver Stone's film, *Wall Street*, and the stock market crash of 19 October 1987, have together caused a further decline in the utility of stock issues as sources of cheap capital. They have also further enhanced the industrial and wider economic leverage of the financial institutions. The latter, however, now deploy their power with more than a hint of desperation as their own asset bases have been eroded by the collapses in stock and real estate values, let alone in what has become known as 'the real economy', which appear to be the end result of their period of economic hegemony.

Conclusion

Although labour has ceased to represent much of a threat to profitability along any of the dimensions of class relations, investment in manufacturing has continued to lag because of the financial sector's preference for short term, high-gain speculative ventures and the state's continuing bias in favour of spending on the development and procurement of new weapons systems. In the context of the new and increasingly open global economy (Chase-Dunn, 1990; Gill and Law, 1989), this failure to invest has meant that, since around 1975, the domestic operations of American corporations have become particularly susceptible to declines in profitability caused by sales difficulties (Henley, 1990; Michl, 1988). More positively, thanks largely to the continuing after-image of social modernism the American market is still the largest, the easiest and the least risky in the world, and its buoyancy as well as therefore the maintenance of American incomes, should increasingly become a key concern of overseas-based multinationals in this global economy. However, although the prognosis for capital in the United States must be positive, multinational capital, wherever its headquarters may be, is increasingly free of the controls exercisable by national governments, so that questions as to the level of this income and its distribution also become the concern of the multinationals. Capital's problem is that it does not want to be burdened with these concerns and cannot and will not deal with them in any effective way (B. Friedman, 1989: intro.). Labour's problem is that it will not be able to take advantage of this weakness, in the way that, for example, it was sometimes able to when the same refusal became apparent in the world of nation states, until it too becomes globally organized – a very distant prospect.

In sum, then, social (post)modernism both saw and contributed to the completion of the process whereby the capitalist class structure finally became a manifestly global structure. However, in the same movement, it also saw and contributed to the completion of the demolition of its own as well as its modernist predecessor's conditions of existence. This, because of the twin deficits which resulted, was the net effect of cutting taxes and believing the state's tax revenues would increase – of, in other words, 'voodoo economics'. The reason the spell had the power it did has been very well put by Benjamin Friedman, an unapologetic social modernist of the old school. Friedman understands very clearly how, in a way which is highly reminiscent of what happened in relation to the economic impact of the Vietnam War, social modernism came to be the negation of itself in Reagan's mesmerizing discourse:

> Taxes . . . really do affect incentives. And when taxes are large in relation to incomes and profits as in postwar America, it is always possible that some effects of taxes on incentives may be very large as well. Reagan's central economic assumption was that these incentive effects were very large indeed. That assumption provided the link that made lower taxes consistent with the basic morality that had traditionally guided America's public choices. With lower taxes, people would work harder and save more, business would invest more, and individual Americans would start more new businesses. Lower taxes, in other words, supported one basic American value after another – in addition to being in themselves most agreeable. And, of course, the emphasis on incentive effects solved the problem of how to pay the cost of all that government does. (Friedman, 1989: 235; for how the coincidence of the 'Reagan Recovery' which began in 1983 and the growth of the deficits obscured the dangers of the latter, see ibid.: ch. 6.)

The end result of the successful administration of this spell has been, not simply a dramatic widening of the gulf between rich and poor (K. Phillips, 1990) and therefore a sharp drop in the percentage of the population who are able to enjoy Riesman's 'possibilities', but also that the American state is rapidly losing the ability to guarantee the delivery of even that minimal financial security promised by the 1935 Social Security Act (Ross and Trachte, 1990). And, as the credibility of this first promise has faded, so too has the interpellative effectivity of each of the social modernist signs: 'self-reliance' has become a necessity instead of a boast; 'responsible unionism' has lost its *raison d'être* since there is so little to be gained from it, and it has been replaced by a much more diffuse insistence on popular 'responsibility'; 'opportunity' has become something for the few rather than the many, since not only has the proportion of contradictory positionings in the occupational structure shrunk, but so too has the proportion of well-paid, solely working-class positionings; 'loyalty' has become something that is demanded rather than earned; and, finally, 'modernism' has become simply yesterday's extremely expensive art.

All this said, although social modernism may have lost much of its overall coherence because of the decline in the referential plausibility of its component signs, no changes have occurred at the level of the discursive formation which would justify any talk of the imminent emergence of any 'new paradigm', whether it be Bushian reaction or something more progressive. (Clearly, President Clinton's proposed synthesis of the Republican and Democratic variants of social modernism by giving equal weight to 'self-reliance' and 'opportunity' in his 'new covenant' is not an instance of the latter, although it equally clearly betokens a renewed faith in Kennedyesque economic modernization.) Because the United States remains a capitalist society, and especially because American capital can no longer afford to bankroll an unusually large middle class, the problems it now faces bear some resemblance to those that it faced in the 1930s, namely a generalized, if depoliticized, threat to social order consequent upon poverty and growing inequalities. Because the United States remains a democratic society, these problems have still to be addressed in a way which takes some account at least of those needs of the poor that are supported by the existing welfare institutions, pressure groups or what remains of the trade union movement. And finally, because notwithstanding President Bush's conservative improvisations, and as is confirmed by President Clinton's choice of words, the predominant concepts, themes and reasoning strategies available to the federal government remain those which were first crystallized in Truman's 'Fair Deal' speech.

In sum no fresh start is possible. And given that the Evil Empire no longer exists and that the so-called issues of 'trust' and 'character' are no substitute for it as contrapuntal images in the hyperreal discourse of American politics, it is only by engaging in an archaelogical investigation of this desert of shattered signs that the people of the United States may finally discover that they have no special claim to deliverance. In addition, it is only in this desert that these same people may finally find the resources necessary to turn this knowledge into a source of sustenance for the society's 'huddled masses'. Moreover, it is only in this desert that the question can be posed as to what kind of social arrangements would at last allow *all*, rather than just the majority of, citizens to be self-reliant, to be responsible, to take advantage of their opportunities, and to want to be loyal.

And finally, the only thing that is certain in this desert, even supposing the absence of the deficits, is that no such outcome is possible so long as the society premisses itself upon capitalist principles of social organization and therefore *must* preserve the inequalities which they presuppose.

CONCLUSION

In this Conclusion, I wish to return to some of the specifically sociological issues mentioned in the Preface and Introduction. In particular, I wish to explain two things: first, the contribution made by the foregoing to my incredulity as regards my former comrades' blanket declaration that we are now living in a qualitatively different and postmodern world; and second, the contribution that I nevertheless firmly believe postmodernism has made to the possibility of a sociology which is capable of understanding what remains in fact a very diverse world. Since in providing these explanations I will also be defining my stance vis-à-vis postmodernism, it seems appropriate that I should frame what follows by briefly and critically outlining Baudrillard's position.

Originally a Marxist, Baudrillard is currently regarded as perhaps the leading postmodernist thinker. Predictably, and like the others so labelled, he rejects this attempt to pigeonhole him. This said, and as one would expect given that he is the only sociologist amongst those who share this allergy, his work nevertheless represents the single most worked-out effort to specify the nature of postmodernity as a social condition.

The occasion of both his break from Marxism and the beginning of his attempt to specify this condition was his prolonged reflection on the nature and significance of what is commonly known as the consumer society. In the three books he published between 1968 and 1972, he tried to elaborate a Marxist account of this new social form and, inspired by Saussure, he conceptualized the array of commodities available in such societies as a systematic structure or code that possessed a meaning of its own – a meaning that is imposed, willy nilly, upon those who possess or even just encounter any of the individual commodities. That is, once the code exists, it is no longer possible to say that a car, for example, is a car is a car. Rather it is inescapable that a Rolls Royce, for example, is a Rolls Royce and is *therefore* superior to a Ford.

In *For a Critique of the Political Economy of the Sign*, the last of his initial trio of texts, Baudrillard developed a Marxist critique of Saussurian linguistics which took the latter to task for its ahistoricity. This was not a wise move, for two reasons. First, it sociologistically refused to recognize that criticisms that apply in one discipline do not necessarily apply in another. (This is an especially pertinent point in this case since, as it happens, Saussure made his breakthrough precisely because he refused the hitherto prevailing historical approach.) Second, once in possession of the history of what he was later to call 'the successive phases of the image' that his move made possible, Baudrillard used it to historicize and so dismiss the very Marxism that had made the same history possible. Thereafter he lost sight of the analytical power and particularity of Marxism and simply regarded it as part of the same narrowly productivist discourse as capitalism. More specifically, he came to regard Marxism as the mirror image of capitalism and as symptomatic therefore of the arrival of what Mark Poster (1989) has termed 'the era of the sign'. As defined in *Simulacra and Simulations*, the 'successive phases of the image' are the following (see Poster, 1989: 170):

1 It is the reflection of a basic reality.
2 It masks and perverts a basic reality.
3 It masks the absence of a basic reality.
4 It bears no relation to any reality whatever:
    it is its own pure simulacrum.

According to Baudrillard, then, the era of the sign, which Saussure (correctly in my view) assumed had been eternal, in fact opened with the commencement of the second phase of the image, which phase was inaugurated by the generalization of capitalist commodity production and the associated first appearance of the mass media. It reached its apogee with the full development of the media and the consequent disappearance of any unmediated experience of reality. The arrival of the last phase, in which reality is unapproachable and truth is therefore unknowable does not, however, end the human craving for a sense of the real. On the contrary, it intensifies this craving with the result that the media have to become more and more multi-dimensional, more and more simulatory – in a word 'hyperreal'. The latter condition may be exemplified by Disneyland and developments in the area of 'virtual reality'. As Baudrillard says of Disneyland:

> [It] is there to conceal the fact that it is the 'real' country. . . Disneyland is presented as imaginary in order to make us believe that the rest is real, when in fact all of Los Angeles and the America surrounding it are no longer real, but of the order of the hyperreal and of simulation. (Poster, 1989: 172)

With the passage of time, Baudrillard's response to hyperreality has grown steadily more pessimistic. Initially, he thought that a return to the era when controllable symbols occupied the position of the uncontrollable signs might still be possible. Later he thought that the power of the sign system could only be countered by turning its oblique and instantaneous power of 'seduction' against itself. Most recently he appears to have decided that only the adoption of a fatal strategy, or the taking up of the stance of the object (such as the silent majority) offers any chance of relief:

> . . . the only difference between a banal theory and a fatal theory is that in the former the subject always believes itself to be more clever than the object, while in the latter the object is always taken to be more clever, more cynical, more ingenious than the subject, which it awaits at every turn. (Poster, 1989: 198)

The Postmodern Condition: Only in America?

There are three main reasons for my sceptical stance vis-à-vis Baudrillard's contentions. First, I do not think it necessary to historicize the coming of the sign in order to be able to conceive of the possibility of hyperreality. All that is required is the refusal of the geological metaphor according to which the ideological, the political and the economic are conceptualized as so many levels of sociality (Woodiwiss, 1990a: 54–5). In the absence of this metaphor, the ideological may be understood to have been always imbricated with the other dimensions of sociality, which other dimensions could therefore be apprehended only through discourse of some kind or another. Thus the implosion of the ideological within the other levels may no longer be taken as definitive of hyperreality. Therefore, instead of being conceptualized as a single condition wherein the ideological realm has become pre-eminent, hyperreality may be understood as a multiply determined and multidimensional condition. In sum, it may be understood as a condition which has always been possible whenever and wherever socially hegemonic discourses are enunciated without concern for their veracity.

Secondly, beguiling though Baudrillard's alternative epistemological/political strategies may be, I am not convinced that only some variant of irrealism is compatible with postmodernism's anti-representationalism and non-humanism. On the contrary I am convinced that not only is realism compatible with anti-representationalism and non-humanism but also that it provides a more fruitful basis upon which to turn them to some good sociological account (Woodiwiss, 1990a: intro. and ch. 1). Thirdly and finally, I doubt the generality of postmodernity/hyperreality amongst even the advanced capitalist nations of the world.

I have written at length elsewhere on the first of the reasons for my scepticism. I will now elaborate on the third before ending with a coda which takes the form of an extended reflection on the positive aspects of the second. My scepticism on the third count is rooted in a prior doubt which has been immensely strengthened in the course of writing the present text. This doubt concerns the always implied, but seldom justified, claim that, before the onset of postmodernity, something called 'modernity' obtained throughout the advanced capitalist world. Startlingly, despite the omnipresence of the term 'discourse' in the debates over postmodernism, none of the participants in these debates has inquired into modernism's genealogy. Rather, sometimes self-contradictorily, they have been content to define modernism in the traditionally denotative and therefore anachronistically representationalist manner of the dictionary entry. That is, they have defined it, depending on the context, by identifying it with Cartesian epistemology, a self-reflexive individualism, and the first and/or second industrial revolutions.

It is commonly agreed that the discourse of modernism emerged as an aspect of a broad and therefore very loosely defined movement within the arts which was indeed informed and affected by all of these developments. In the course of this emergence, the initially negative connotations of the word 'modern' were gradually reversed as the movement slowly gestated during the nineteenth century, became widely visible around the turn of the century, and, in the English-speaking world, belatedly became conscious of itself as 'modernism' in the 1930s (Bradbury and McFarlane, 1991: intro.).

It appears to be far less commonly recognized that, to summarize one of the principal results of the archaeological work reported above, the expansion of the meaning of modernism to include a social condition called modernity was primarily an American enterprise. The United States became the centre of modernist experimentation in the arts in the course of the 1940s. At the same time a stoical, world-weary reading of the social diagnosis implicit in aesthetic modernism took hold of certain sections of that society's cultural intelligentsia, as best exemplified in the works of Bell and Riesman. This was a reading to the effect that knowing self-reflexiveness, competitiveness and changefulness (qualified only by the existence of a welfare state, the representations of responsible trade unions and a societal commitment to equality of opportunity) are *all* that one can or ought to expect in or of the modern world. The result was that aestheticization of the ideology which was first publicly crystallized in President Truman's Fair Deal speech (see above, p. 27), and which in the end became the social modernism of Presidents Kennedy and Johnson.

The academic results of this interchange between aesthetic and sociological discourses were also striking: ideological pluralism disappeared from what became the modernizationist mainstream of American development studies; the entire history of the world over the past four or five hundred years was reconceptualized within that mainstream in Americentric terms as an unequal conflict between tradition and modernity; and, finally, all previous social thinkers came to be thought of, not as the authors of alternative conceptualizations of this transition, but as more or less percipient proto-modernizationists. Because of the United States' intellectual pre-eminence in the postwar period, this modernizationist discourse gradually inscribed itself within the academic discourses of the advanced capitalist societies. However, with the exception of a few areas such as development and Japanese studies, it lay largely dormant within them – until 1979, that is. In that year, focusing on the United States and borrowing a term from what was specifically American literary criticism, Lyotard declared that, epistemologically at least, our condition had become postmodern. The result of this declaration has been that, thanks especially to the reinforcement of its rhetorical effects by the collapse of the Soviet Union, the vocabulary of modernization has, for the time being (?), displaced all the alternative conceptualizations of the history of the past four or five hundred years.

Lyotard's declaration has often been read as meaning, amongst other things, that the United States' cultural imperium has finally come to an end. In the light of the genealogy that I have just outlined, this seems to have been a misreading as far as the social sciences are concerned. Subsequently even many members of the Western European, Marxisant, social-scientific left that had for so long resisted the modernizationist vocabulary have taken it up all of a sudden and apparently without much thought, as they too have become obsessed with the question of whether we are now living in a modern or a postmodern world. Despite the fact that (mistakenly in my view) they continue to depend upon modes of theorizing that are largely unaffected by postmodernism's metatheoretical insights, the likes of Bauman (1992), Berman (1982), Jameson (1991), Harvey (1989), Lash (1990) and Featherstone (1991) have not investigated, let alone challenged, the sociological, as opposed to the aesthetic, validity of the concept of 'modernity' as an analytical term. Indeed, in a state of what would appear to be blissful unawareness of, or in Berman's (1982: 26–7) case carelessness as to, its provenance, they have embedded it in the heart of even what remain in some cases avowedly Marxist discussions of the nature of the present conjuncture.

Now, none of this would matter much except that, once the *jouissance* of no longer having to use the term 'capitalism' wears off, the new protagonists of modernism will find themselves stuck with an analytical vocabulary that will either disappoint or appal them. When it is used carefully in the manner of a Lyotard or a committed modernizationist such as Marion Levy (1966: 35), they will find that it ties them either to an idealism that presents the world as the product of changing epistemes, or to a technological determinism which makes that of even the most vulgar Marxist seem the epitome of sophistication. When, as is most often the case today, it is used more loosely as a way of categorizing whole societies on the basis of a misapplied aesthetic/ philosophical category, they will make three other discomfiting discoveries in addition to the implicit idealism of this move. First, they still face the same problems of relating the different structural orders to one another that they struggled with as Marxists. Secondly, they have unwittingly embraced a whiggish metanarrative that pictures the last four or five hundred years of world history as culminating in a condition that some American sociologists once imagined obtained in the United States during the 1950s and 1960s. And finally, and on the basis of no very clear sociological criteria, they have condemned themselves to producing misleading analyses of the very varied social conditions at present obtaining in the advanced capitalist societies, since the sociological use of the concept 'modernity' in the looser sense homogenizes the circumstances to which it is applied.

Alternatives to Social Modernism

Although social modernism was hegemonic within the United States for much of the postwar period, it cannot be said that it held such a position in other, similarly developed societies over the same period. In Western Europe some form or other of social democracy held sway, somewhat modified by Conservative or Christian-Democratic reservations, of course (Stephens, 1979). In Japan, by contrast, a direct attempt was made to embed a qualified version of the individualistic values of American social modernism in the so-called 'New Constitution' under the tutelage of the Occupation. As in the American case, the Japanese Constitution commits the state to ensuring certain minimum welfare standards, gives support to a responsible trade union movement and proclaims the society's commitment to equal opportunities for all its citizens. The major difference is that it assumes the loyalty of the citizenry rather than provides a basis upon which it might be sought (Woodiwiss, 1992: 70–5).

However, by the mid-1960s, largely because of the economic success which was then becoming apparent, Japan's traditional ideology had been 'reinvented' – reinvented in the form of a largely secular and strikingly sociologized ideological formation which I have termed *Kigyoshugi* (enterprisism) (Woodiwiss, 1992: 87). In this formation the company is seen as the most significant contemporary instance of the patriarchal household, the traditional and supposedly unique form of social organization, and belief in the intrinsic virtue of the company replaced the prewar belief in the intrinsic virtue of the *tenno* (the standard Japanese term for the emperor which appropriately preserves a sense of the continuing religious significance of the office). This gave a particular cast to the values enshrined in the Constitution, and clearly differentiated them from those of American social modernism. As I have argued at length elsewhere (Woodiwiss, 1992: ch. 5), the meaning of these values changes substantially and to the citizens' disadvantage, when, the Constitution is read as assuming, not only the citizenry's loyalty to the state, but also the employees' loyalty to the enterprise.

Now, it seems to me that the United States is literally a postmodern society in that it is a society in which there is an incredulity towards the modernist metanarrative that for the past thirty or so years has explained and legitimated what occurs within it. It also seems to me that it is a society which for this reason has gone hyperreal. And it finally seems to me, to repeat the central thesis of the present study, that these attributes are more the product of an involuntary forgetting of social modernism (that is, of a specifically discursive development), than they are the product of such extra-discursive developments as the arrival of the consumerism, new media and post-industrialism rather bathetically stressed by the postmodernists themselves, or indeed than they are the result of the similarly extra-discursive developments within late capitalism stressed by Jameson, Harvey, Lash and Featherstone.

There undoubtedly exists a globalized, postmodern aesthetic, *Zeitgeist* or 'state of mind' (Bauman, 1992: vii), whose inspiration is largely American for reasons that I hope may now be understood. Nevertheless once the particularity of the American ideological condition is acknowledged it should be clear that, if the societies of Western Europe and Japan, for example, are post-anything, they are not post-modern. In fact, it seems to me that they are neither post-anything nor instances of the arrival of hyper-reality. In Western Europe, despite the rigours of Thatcherism in Britain and the general move in the direction of social modernism amongst the social democratic parties, not only does an ideological pluralism still persist, but also a form of social democracy still holds sway, and it is sometimes acted upon. In Japan, too, an ideological pluralism persists, although perhaps only just, and ever improving, if not converging, living standards indicate that the promises made in the name of *Kigyoshugi* continue to be honoured. Taken together, then, these societies are perhaps on the edge of hyperreality but not yet in it. The postmodernist epigoni commonly suppose that the enhanced salience of difference is a sign of the impossibility of truth; on the contrary, the persistence of a pluralism at the level of countervailing social imaginaries can be seen as a condition of the continuing possibility of the pursuit of truth.[1]

All that said, it is only necessary to say in conclusion that, whilst the United States may be the only literally postmodern society, it is not the only one to have exhibited the more generic condition of hyperreality. For example, many 'communist' societies, in Asia as well as Europe, experienced this condition once they gave up acting upon their never-theless continuously repeated ideologies. I make this point because it suggests both that hyperreality is both full of opportunities, since the desire for truth may become irresistible, and that it is fraught with danger, in that it is very hard to accept the proposition that all one can ever know with certainty is that one can never know the truth – fantasies of blood and soil may seem far more realistic.

CODA

Towards a Non-Representationalist Sociology

As exemplified by Baudrillard's aversion to Marxism, the one-dimensional nature of his travelogue *America*, (1988), and the latter's great appeal in the United States, postmodernism is both implicated in, and a symptom of, the forgetting of social modernism that I have outlined. Nevertheless, I remain convinced that much has been learnt as a consequence of postmodernism's obsession with the autonomous powers of discourse, and that therefore the use of some of its concepts and strategies to rethink more traditional Marxist ones is essential to understanding why and how this forgetting occurred. For this reason, I will now outline in more detail what is at issue between Marxism and postmodernism, before saying a little more about what and how the former may learn from the latter and so create the possibility of producing more satisfying accounts of hyperreality and such local variants as postmodernity.

Depending on the commentator's point of view, postmodernism is either a *very* good or a *very* bad thing. Even in academia, to use Luc Ferry and Alain Renaut's (1990) unconsciously self-critical term, similarly 'hyperbolic' responses abound. This is less because of ignorance than because of a rather surprising fixation, in the theoretical circumstances, with postmodernism's origins and a less surprising one with its ethico-political significance (on the latter, see Norris, 1992). Unfortunately, these fixations have inhibited the investigation of the social correlate of the term (the recent writings of Featherstone, 1991, and Lash, 1990 are an exception to this rule). This, it seems to me, is a product both of the sociological weakness of postmodernist thought and of the concern on the part of its critics, largely Marxists and Critical Theorists, to protect their radical patrimony, whether by denunciation (Callinicos, 1989; Dews, 1987; Eagleton, 1990; Habermas, 1990, for example), or by distraint (Harvey, 1989; Jameson, 1984, 1991, for example) rather than to improve upon postmodernist analyses.

Even when the debate about postmodernism, which interestingly has been joined most fiercely by the Marxists and Critical Theorists, does rise above the level of a blood feud, it has tended to revolve around rather abstract questions, such as whether or not postmodernism has any significance outside the minds of its progenitors, or whether or not there is anything intrinsically bad about the supposedly central Marxist concept of totality. As regards the first question, the Marxists have sought to deny postmodernism any wider significance, whilst, ironically but of course, the postmodernists have sought to affirm the extra-discursive existence of the condition from whence they derive their name. On the second question, the postmodernists have taken the offensive, and they have argued that the concept of totality bespeaks an unconscious, but nonetheless dangerous, 'will to power' on the part of those who deploy it. The Marxists have responded by admitting their sins, whilst at the same time insisting that the advocates of 'detotalization' risk throwing out the conceptual baby of capitalism with the bathwater of economic determinism.

Within this context, the Marxists and Critical Theorists have sought to confine the pertinence of postmodernist ideas to the aesthetic/philo-sophical and, sometimes, the social psychological realms (Harvey, 1989; Jameson, 1991), and/or to denounce it as a pernicious new form of conservatism (Eagleton, 1990; Habermas, 1990), and/or to deny the existence of any such thing (Callinicos, 1989). For their part, the postmodernists have tended either to ignore these criticisms ('Marxism is dead') or, in the case of the epigoni, simply to repeat criticisms of

Marxism which they could not have produced for themselves and which as a consequence appear wan and formulaic. Not the least of the reasons for this weedy response is the fact that, genealogically (that is, when one considers the pertinent readings of, for example, the works of Nietzsche, Freud, Husserl, Heidegger and Merleau-Ponty), postmodernism as a discourse in process of formation was always hostile to sociology, especially in its Marxist, Durkheimian and functionalist variants. All of these thinkers sensed in sociology another form of that idolatry of 'totality', in this instance 'society', which they had come to fear (for a recent example of this hostility, see Laclau and Mouffe, 1985: ch. 4). In its latter genealogical stages (that is, during the 1960s and 1970s), this hostility towards any 'totalizing' conception of the social, to use the appropriately Sartrean term, was profoundly reinforced by a wholly correct loathing of Stalinism in both its Russian and French forms. It is not surprising, therefore, that the proto-postmodernist texts of those decades should show so few signs of any engagement with the new and, in the present author's view, potentially very productive conception of the social associated with the names of Louis Althusser and Nicos Poulantzas, even though the latter conception was made possible by sources of inspiration, and above all by an anti-humanism, shared with the postmodernists.

In the event, of course, the advent of postmodernism and its competitor for peer group leadership, neo-liberalism, regrettably meant that there was little interest in the academic-industrial complex in developing, applying and publishing either the Althusserian or any other supposedly totalizing conception of the social during most of the 1980s. This in itself is a minor corroborative instance of the amnesia with which this text has been concerned. Thus, although what postmodernism might refer to as a body of theory is pretty settled (that is, a selection of texts by such writers as Lyotard and Baudrillard, augmented by a particular reading of a further selection of texts by such as Lacan, Barthes, Foucault and Derrida), it has hitherto been very unclear what postmodernity refers to by way of a social condition.

On my reading, postmodernism's prime achievement has been to rediscover and extend, albeit in a way that is fatally flawed, the possibilities inherent in the Saussurian theory of language as a significatory rather than representational phenomenon. These possibilities were obscured for a long time by the scientistic readings of this theory which dominated linguistics and such other usages as those associated with the likes of Althusser, Poulantzas and Claude Lévi-Strauss. More specifically, its achievement has been to rediscover the possibilities implicit in Saussure's insistence that language is a self-subsisting if not a self-sufficient, social entity: an entity wherein the two aspects of all signs (their signifiers – material images – and their signifieds – mental images) are brought into alignment with one another but not with any referent they may have in the extra-linguistic world. Putting the point another way, the postmodernists have been excited by the analytical possibilities created by the realization that words and signs more generally may mean something without referring to anything in the extra-linguistic world and, therefore, that all language and language-borne phenomena (philosophies, ideologies and even sciences, for example) might be far more autonomous in relation to other social phenomena than had been suspected hitherto.

The scientistic appropriations of Saussure's theory obscured the theory's more radical implications for a long time because, as a minimal, self-imposed but contradictory condition of their own existence, their authors made the precise claim that *their* words, if no others, were verifiably accurate depictions of what they referred to, whether the latter objects were aspects of language, literature, kinship systems or modes of production. However, with the exception of the pioneering Lacan, those thinkers who are now thought of as the precursors of postmodernism (that is, primarily Foucault and Derrida) did not return to Saussure directly and try to rethink what had become known as 'the structuralist tradition' on a non-scientistic basis. Instead, they sought to counter scientism by resorting to bodies of thought located outside the struc-turalist tradition – Nietzsche in Foucault's case and Heidegger in Derrida's. Whichever strategy was adopted, the conclusion was arrived at that there was both more and less to words than met the eye: more in that even individual words always carry traces of other words and texts (Derrida), provide evidence of and for the unconscious (Lacan) and, as elements in discourse, project power (Foucault); less in that, for Lacan and Derrida, if not for Foucault (Woodiwiss, 1990a: 63–4), words were no longer understood to carry aspects of the extralinguistic world into thought.

Marxism after Postmodernism

Now that the intellectual monism that for too long characterized Marx-ism's theoretical and explanatory endeavours may be rejected, thanks largely to the labours of the postmodernists and their precursors, Marxism turns out to provide the essential complement to postmodernism. Unlike any other extant body of social theory, Marxism may, given one proviso, be made to share postmodernism's anti-representationalism and ontological non-humanism. It is thus, ironically, the body of social theory best suited to facilitate the transformation of postmodernism's metatheoretical innovations into a viable social scientific stance – better by far, for example, than a continued dependence on any variety of Nietz-schean thought which, even in the work of such avowed anti-humanists as Deleuze and Guattari (1983), often reads in a way that, like a mirror-image, is highly reminiscent of the assertively humanist writings of such rational choice theorists as Elster and Roemer.

The proviso mentioned above is that postmodernism's distinctive insistence upon giving a new significance to the linguistic and language-borne dimension of social life should be registered metatheoretically at the epistemological rather than, as is most often the case, at the ontological level. Put briefly, if language is ontologically privileged in any way, the difference between the world and what is thought about it becomes very hard to maintain. And this, in turn, creates problems, not simply because it violates the key and, to my mind, still critical realist postulate that the world exists whether or not human beings think about it, but also because in so doing it removes the possibility of error. Where the world and thought about it are not considered to be identical, the possibility of error is ever present, as is, by the same token, that possibility of truth which saves realism from the theoretical paralysis that otherwise appears to follow from the verificational scepticism that it shares with postmodernism. In sum, the critical lesson to be learnt from the postmodernists concerns the non-representational nature of knowledge rather than the mentalistic nature of the world. I will now try to provide an outline justification for this judgement.

The principal reason classical Marxism did not anticipate many of the more striking ideas of postmodernism, I think, is that the intellectual move that, crystallizing many others, made postmodernism possible was a literally post-Marxist one, namely Saussure's aforementioned replacement of a representational account of language by a significatory one. To my mind, Marx's earlier resort to the brilliant metaphor of the fetish in order to understand the relationship between the ideological realm and the economic indicated that he appreciated not only the non-representational character of the ideological realm, but also – by the very force of the denial that it represented – the autonomy of the ideological. If the otherwise apparent freedom of the ideological realm in relation to the economic was not a problem, why go to the very considerable intellectual trouble represented by the figure of fetishism? All this said, a metaphor is an inherently representational construct, which may point us in the direction of an explanation but cannot itself provide such an explanation, because it involves the simple redescription of the relationship to which it refers and lacks the acknowledgement of ontological depth that Bhaskar (1989) has, to my mind convincingly, argued is an essential attribute of scientific explanation. However, it seems to me that the presence of this metaphor in Marx's texts was overdetermined by his wholly understandable, and as far as I am concerned entirely justified, hostility to the idealism which seemed in his time to characterize any attempt to grant any degree of autonomy to the ideological realm.

With the appearance of a realist/materialist theory of language which was not reductionist, because it was not representationalist, this overdetermining force disappeared and so, after a long, long delay, it was possible to formulate concepts such as discourse and discursive formation. It seems to me that such concepts may be substituted for the figure of fetishism, allowing empirical investigations and explanations of the ideological realm and its relations with the economic and political which were not possible before. In the more structurally-inclined texts, this change has been registered to a degree within Marxist discourse as some of its practitioners have taken up anti-humanist stances, moved towards a non-representationalist conception of theory, and engaged in analyses of substantive discourses.

Unfortunately, this is as far as the process of rethinking Marxism has gone. In particular it has stopped short of fully acknowledging that, like the rest of classical social theory with the partial exception of Durkheim, Marxist theory as a whole was constructed on the basis of a now long surpassed, representationalist conception of language. That is, the significance of the Saussurian tradition for contemporary social science cannot stop with the 'discovery' of discourse, since the intellectual revolution that allowed this discovery transforms our approach to all language-borne phenomena including theory itself. The specific point I wish to make here is that it transforms our conception of how one should go about the business of theoretical abstraction. That is, if words in general cannot be understood to *re-present* things in the world, then, first, why should Marxists think that their words are any different? And, second, why should they be excused the challenges and anxieties that accompany the opportunities which arise when one attempts to base theorizing on a more defensible account of how words gain meaning and of how, as a separate question, they come to refer to things beyond themselves?

In other words, why should Marxists or indeed any other school of social theorists, think that modes of abstraction that produce picto-graphic hieroglyphs provide an adequate basis for sociological communication, when they use a proper language in their everyday lives? Why should we restrict ourselves to the equivalent of ancient Egyptian, when we already have a more adequate and demanding linguistic model at our disposal? This model suggests the necessity of two things: first, if we want our sociological signifiers to have specifically sociological signifieds that may be consciously manipulated, then they must be part of a consciously elaborated discourse that imposes its own specific syntagmatic and paradigmatic contraints on their use; and, second, if we wish the signs so formed to refer to anything beyond themselves, then we must be prepared both to identify and to manipulate (that is, by engaging in research as well as by theorizing) the discursive formation that allows any such reference. In sum, as the realist tradition has long maintained against the invariably representationalist empiricist and inter-pretative traditions, even if not for the reasons just given, theory and research ought not to be confused with one another, since they are distinct, if necessarily conjoint, enterprises.

As such post-structuralist precursors of postmodernism as Barthes, Derrida and Lacan have made abundantly clear, it is impossible to free spoken or written language from the meaning-subversive effects of the ever-present possibility of figurative play. Nevertheless, I take the view that the chances of producing a discourse that warrants consideration as the basis of a serious discipline are vastly increased, to the degree that the possibility of connotative play is reduced. And the main way in which this may be done is by excluding, as far as possible, representational and/or figural terms or notions from the discourse's core vocabulary. For example, the central role allowed to the term 'struggle' in Marxist discourse, because of its figural appeal, has for too long obscured the need for a fuller theorization of the concept of class. Also, because of the contingent nature of the figure's appeal, changes in political and other circumstances have come to have as much, if not more, of an effect upon the concept's social scientific acceptability than assessments of its research utility.

There has been a regressive movement amongst those for whom Marxism still possesses some appeal (see Eagleton's recent *Ideology: An Introduction* (1991)). It is caused mainly, it seems to me, by the extreme discomfort of suddenly realizing that postmodernism too was an outcome of taking Saussure seriously. This realization is accompanied by the particularly unsettling fear that to go any further down the road opened by Saussure would lead to the acceptance of a whole array of positions which are assumed, although seldom argued, to be life-threatening to Marxism. Such positions include: (1) not simply an acceptance of the fallibility of knowledge claims, but also an acceptance of the impossibility of such claims, in the sense that they are ultimately unverifiable; (2) not simply an acceptance of the non-representational nature of language, but also an acceptance of the possibility that individual human beings are not what social scientists should be trying to understand; (3) not simply an acceptance of the fragmentation of human knowledges, but also an acceptance of their incommensurability; (4) not simply an acceptance of the fragmented nature of the social world, but also an acceptance of its ultimate incoherence. In short, what appears to many to be at stake is not just Marxism's position as a claimant to metanarrative status, but also the very existence of any such status – the very possibility of so-called 'grand theory'.

As I indicated in the Introduction, it would seem to me that instead of a recoiling in horror and a heading back to whence one came, a more interesting response to all this would be to hang on to one's ontological realism, refuse the panic that such thoughts may otherwise most certainly engender, and pose a series of 'so what' questions:

So what if knowledges are ultimately unverifiable, does it mean that they should not be pursued?

So what if society is composed of non-representable, non-human entities, does this mean that we cannot gain evidence for their existence?

So what if human knowledges are fragmented and incommensurable, does this mean that they are utterly resistant to combination?

So what if human societies are fragmented and ultimately incoherent, does this mean that they cannot be understood?

So what if Marxism has no supportable claims to metanarrative status, does this mean that it has no scientific status?

So what if 'grand theory' is impossible, does it mean that theorizing as such is impossible?

Marx himself anticipated the first two positions to a degree, and it seems to me perfectly possible for a Marxist, such as myself, to accept even the most unsettling of the postmodernists' metatheoretical claims and engage in what I suspect most people would regard as a thoroughly worthwhile activity: the rigorous pursuit of knowledges – fragmented and unassimilable, but nevertheless combinable – about the diverse and apparently disconnected entities that arguably make up the social world.

That said, I do not want to be thought of as saying simply that postmodernism is a paper tiger. More positively, I would like to suggest that the form of social theory and indeed of social science that I have just outlined has much to be said for it – for example, modesty, practicality, cooperativeness and creativity would appear to me to be the principal virtues of a Marxism that took such a form.

I say 'modesty' because, in the absence of a commitment to the realization of visions of social science and society as totalities, such a Marxism would make smaller claims. In my view, the main claim that Marxism could still make would be that, given certain modifications, its particular concept of class explains better than any other much that is central to modern social life. I say 'practicality' because, freed from the crushing demands of being a super-synthetic knowledge of everything, Marxism would be better able to attend to the task of explaining the nature of the class structure and class relations in particular societies. I say 'cooperativeness' because it would become a regional sociology, and its practitioners would have to learn how to use and work alongside the knowledges produced on the basis of other metatheoretically compatible bodies of theory. And finally, I say 'creativity' because, freed from the pictographic shackles of representationalism, it should be capable of inspiring new conceptions of, and therefore new explanations of, the social world.

When the Marxist canon is reread in the light of these ideas, not just its more substantive concepts but also its conceptions of theory, reference, and therefore its very object of study, are found to be in need of a radical rethinking so that they no longer partake of what may now be seen as a disabling representationalism and humanism. On this basis social theory itself may be reconceptualized as a rigorously abstract body of concepts which has to be made to refer to the extra-theoretical world in certain specific ways and under certain specific conditions, so that it may illuminate the operation of certain *sui generis* social forces. Foremost amongst the more substantive theoretical consequences of such meta-theoretical reconceptualization are the rejection of such hitherto hallowed notions as 'economic determination in the last instance' and the socially exhaustive nature of the class structure.

To develop the metatheoretical point somewhat, in Derridean terms Marxism, like all sociologies, positively asserts a conception of the social which depends for its meaning upon its opposition to a *'supplément'* – the individual. However, thanks to its presence in critical metaphors, the latter continues to play a far greater role in the reasoning made possible by its opposite than even many so-called 'structuralist Marxists' have typically been prepared to acknowledge. However, *contra* some Derrideans if not Derrida himself, there is a limit beyond which such a critical rereading need not be taken. Specifically, because of both my rereading of the relationship between law and the emergence of capitalism (Woodiwiss, 1990a: ch. 6), and the persistence of differences between philosophy/literature on the one hand and the social sciences on the other even after the supposed collapse of 'the great narratives' (Woodiwiss, 1990a: 30–5), it seems to me that such criticism reaches, but does not invalidate, the concepts which are Marxism's *sine qua non*, namely 'surplus value', 'class' and 'ideology' – indeed, each of these concepts retains a presence in the discourse of Lyotard and other postmodernists. This should not be taken to mean, however, either that such concepts are not in need of radical rethinking, or that this rethinking has been provided by such as Lyotard. Rather, it suggests very strongly that priority should now be given to ensuring that these concepts should no longer partake of the representationalism which, through the metaphor of 'class struggle', naturalizes and so obscures the presence of that sociologically 'dangerous' (that is, subversive), humanist *'supplément'*, the individual. This metaphor has so often placed the very concept of the social under *'érasure'* (that is, under threat of losing its meaning) even within the Marxist tradition (*vide* some variants of Critical Theory).

When these new methods and rethought concepts are applied in the theoretically critical realm of the ideological (Woodiwiss, 1990a: pt. 2), analysis ceases to be a matter of stripping authors of the disguises with which, consciously or unconsciously, they cloak their economic interests and which may have resulted in these interests shaping texts from which they are supposed to have been excluded. Instead, as I have demonstrated in Chapter 7, it becomes a matter of discovering the structure and dynamics of, as well as the relations between, whatever extra-individual discourses are present in the texts under investigation and then of relating these to their own distinctively social, rather than their authors' more strictly biographical, economic and political conditions of existence.

To develop the point a little, when, as is the case in the present study, the texts and discourses of interest relate to state policy, and regardless of whether they enunciate, criticize or discuss it, they may be understood to be sited in a field of discourse conditioned by the state's structural location and therefore governed by an overwhelming preoccupation with promises made in the name of the state and with judgements as to the credibility, if any, that should be afforded them. Lacan suggests that the unconscious is structured *like* a language. In the case of the discourses concerned with state policy, it seems to me that one may usefully reverse Lacan's analogy and say that the language of these discourses is structured *like* the unconscious. What allows one to speak of such a likeness is the similarity of the role played by promises in state policy discourse to that played by desire in the unconscious. In Lacanian terms, both may be said to arise because of 'lacks' of one kind or another. In both cases, some or even all of these 'lacks' may or, given certain structural conditions, must remain unfulfilled or unfulfillable. The anger provoked by such failures, especially if it is denied or avoided in some way, may then set off a complex series of transformations and displacements within the pertinent 'network of signifiers', with the result that authors' texts are likely to be structured by discursive and other forces and therefore in ways which they are unlikely to be aware of. Again, I exemplified some of these effects in Chapter 7 – specifically, those which occur in texts produced by those who support the assumptions upon which state policies are based and who therefore *cannot* admit their anger at the complicity of these same assumptions in the failure of the policies involved.

Rethinking Surplus Value

Finally, in order to explain how the analysis presented in the substantive part of this text was possible, I now wish to specify the difference made to what is signified by 'surplus value' and, by extension, 'class' and 'capitalist crisis' by adopting a referential rather than a representational conception of theory and by acknowledging the relatively autonomous nature of the ideological (significatory) and political (disciplinary) dimensions of sociality. First, to acknowledge that there are discursive and political dimensions to production, as well as discursive and political conditions of its existence, is to radically diminish and transform the explanatory pertinence of the labour theory of value. The only claim that its supporters need now make for the latter is the following: it *explains* the possibility of capital's appropriation of surplus labour as a function of the 'peculiar property' of labour power as a commodity; that is, of labour power's 'use value . . . being a source of value, whose actual consumption . . . is itself an embodiment of labour, and consequently, a creation of value' (Marx, 1965: 167).

Thus surplus value should no longer be understood in a representationalist and, therefore, humanist manner as referring to a quantifiable substance whose presence or absence accounts for any difference between necessary and surplus labour time and may therefore serve as a measure of exploitation. Rather, it should be thought of simply as a nodal point in the discourse which Marx initiated when he repeated the claim, already made by the classical political economists, that labour is the source of all value – a claim whose significance he greatly enhanced by his further and more novel claim that what those positioned as labourers sell under capitalism is not their labour but their labour power. Understood non-representationally and non-humanistically, surplus value is a critical component in an abstractly specified causal mechanism (Sayer, 1984: 95 ff.), and should be judged, not according to how accurately it in itself represents the conditions to which it is applied, but rather according to how coherently and convincingly the aforementioned causal mechanism may be made to refer to and hence explain such conditions. Thus, whilst the concept of surplus value may be understood to play a necessary role in the explanation of capital's appropriation of surplus labour, it does not in itself comprise a sufficient explanation of such appropriation.

The explanation of capital's appropriation of surplus labour, then, needs to be referentially adequate and to present an empirical justification for the substantive but not substantial claim that there is a difference between necessary and surplus labour and that the size of this difference may vary. (It does not need to overcome 'the transformation problem' and relate phenomena at one representational level – production – to those at another – the market.) It must therefore be made to do two things: first, to make room for, and second to allow the effectivity within production of, the relatively autonomous phenomena referred to by the concepts of what I have called 'the discourses of production' (Woodiwiss, 1990a: ch. 3) and Burawoy (1979, 1985) 'the politics of production'.

For example, to repeat what I have written elsewhere (Woodiwiss, 1990a: 149) the specific contribution made by the concept of the 'discourses of production' is the provision of a means of explaining not just the legal and wider significatory grounds upon which a wage may be demanded and/or paid, but also why particular wages may be demanded or paid, since the latter particularities are constructed in the discourses, including the gendering and racializing ones, which define skills, apportion responsibilities, justify hierarchies and so on. Together with political and other economic determinations, these discourses explain the existence and the structure of internal labour markets and, by extension, contribute to the understanding of external labour markets too. The point is, then, that, taken together, these determinations provide a means of explaining the prices paid for labour power, which preserves the idea that under capitalism a varying proportion of it is not paid for. However, it does not depend upon establishing any quantitative and substantial relationship between value and price, or upon making any assumptions about the illusory or epiphenomenal nature of price as compared to value. Exchange relations and their social dimensions may thus be granted their due reality, their due degree of autonomy and their due determinative power.

Rethinking Class and Capitalist Crisis

In order to bring out the significance of these moves as regards the labour
theory of value, I will now spell out some of the consequences they have
for the position I take vis-à-vis the current debates about the significance
of the class structure and, by extension, capitalist crises in advanced
capitalist societies.

Britons in general and British sociologists in particular are sometimes
thought, by Americans especially, to be obsessed with class. I share this
obsession and I hope I have demonstrated good sociological as well as
social reasons for it. This said, stimulated by the phenomenon we have
come to know as Thatcherism, a debate, which in part has been trans-
atlantic, has raged this past decade about whether or not the salience of
class is decreasing in contemporary British society. In order that the
particularity of the analysis contained in the main body of this text may
be appreciated, I will now briefly summarize this debate and define my
position in relation to it.

The challenges to traditional class analysis, whether in its Marxist or
Weberian forms, have revolved around two major points: first, that the
class structure is changing shape, essentially from a pyramidal to a
diamond form, at an accelerating pace (Bell, 1973, for example); and
second, that the class structure as a largely economic construct has been
displaced from its position of structural primacy by political and
ideological/cultural constructs that have gained a social salience that is
more and more autonomous of any connections that such constructs may
or may not once have had with economic or class constructs (for example:
Laclau and Mouffe, 1985; S. Hall, 1988). For reasons that have been
outlined elsewhere (Woodiwiss, 1991) and do not require repeating here,
both the Marxist and the Weberian defenders of traditional class theory
have argued forcibly that the events of the recent past have confirmed
rather than undermined the utility of their approaches (for example:
Callinicos, 1989; G. Marshall et al., 1989).

In the light of the synthesis of Marxism and postmodernism which I
advocate, I think that this debate represents a missed opportunity.
Regardless of what one thinks the answers should be, the questions posed
by the events of the Thatcher and Reagan years, and which, it must be
said, for so long perplexed sociologists of all schools, should have
prompted a far more radical rethinking of class theory than is apparent
in the texts I have mentioned. The critics of the orthodoxies of class
analysis have not provided alternative conceptualizations that are at all
developed, whilst the defenders of the orthodoxies have responded exactly
as Thomas Kuhn predicts people in such a position always will act,
namely by making *ad hoc* alterations to less central parts of their theories
(in this instance their class 'maps') in order to protect the more central
parts.

To develop the point, it seems to me that the dispute between the critics and the guardians of the orthodoxies has been fundamentally about the degree to which individual beliefs and behaviours are constrained by the class structure. For all the participants in the debate, including the postmodernists, it is individuals, or groups of them, who take up positions in what the Marxists term 'the social relations of production' or in what the neo-Weberians term 'the occupational structure'. The same individuals then supposedly translate (with varying degrees of predictability) the effects of said positions and occupations into political and ideological/cultural class effects. The critics argue that such constraints and translation effects are lessening and they sometimes also doubt that they were ever very great. Meanwhile, the guardians of the orthodoxies respond that such constraints and translation effects remain as powerful as they ever were, even if they were not properly understood before.

After examining the arguments and evidence provided by both sides, my conclusion is not that one side is right and the other wrong, but rather that there is more agreement between them than either side imagines, and that this agreement cannot be acknowledged because both sides make the same basic mistake. They agree that the beliefs and behaviour of individuals are far less predictable than macro-sociologists have generally assumed – the critics give reasons for this that have already been outlined, whilst the defenders of the orthodoxies unconsciously acknowledge it by refining and elaborating their class 'maps' and so increasing the chance that any particular combination of economic, ideological/cultural and political positions that an individual might take up may allow their assignation to a particular class or stratum. Not so long ago, sociologists worked with two, three or four classes and/or strata. Now, in a manner that to me should have evoked fears of Occam's Razor, they sometimes work with six (early Wright), eleven (Goldthorpe) or twelve (present Wright) such categories.

Meanwhile it remains very difficult to assign some individuals and/or occupations unambiguously to classes and/or strata; and it has been admitted that conclusions cannot be drawn about individual beliefs on the basis of data concerning the distribution and structuring of beliefs within groups (G. Marshall et al., 1989: 190–1). These factors and the orthodox defence of refining class maps all seem to confirm that it is, and perhaps always has been, very difficult both to distinguish one person's class position from that of another, and to know anything about the relations between individual economic locations and individual beliefs. Thus the problems encountered as a result of trying to ground a theory of class on the classification of individuals or families continue to defeat even the best efforts of the methodologically ingenious, and on their own terms too.

Should one, though, regard the purpose of class analysis as the representationalist one of classifying individuals and producing class 'maps'? I think not. It seems to me that individual people are always too unpredictable to be ever usefully categorized in this way and therefore to provide any sort of firm basis for sociological reasoning. This unpredict-ability may only be elucidated by recourse to psychology (Woodiwiss, 1990a: 25–7). The shared mistake, therefore, of all the participants in the debate I have outlined is to think that either the individual or a collection of individuals should be the unit of class analysis, is indeed to think that there is any 'unit of class analysis'.

My response to this realization, and to the role of post-structuralist and postmodernist ideas in making it possible, has been to attempt the deconstruction and reconstruction of the pertinent parts of Marxist theory (the theories of production and law as well as that of class) on a rigorously non-representationalist and non-humanist basis. I have tried to do so in such a way that the political and ideological dimensions of sociality are given their proper place and weight without placing the very concept of class under threat of erasure, as always appears to happen when individual subjects are thought of as the only conduits of ideo-logical and political forces. Somewhat more specifically, I have used a variant of Derrida's deconstructive method to criticize and continue the work commenced, but for one reason or another later abandoned, by Althusser, Poulantzas, and Hindess and Hirst. The result is a theory of class which seeks to accommodate the complexity of real class relations whilst retaining the explanatory power and simplicity of Marx's original two-class model.

Shorn of all supportive argumentation, the conception of class upon which I have depended in the foregoing may be summarized in six core propositions: first, that in the absence of another mode of production, there are only two classes in capitalist societies; second, that these classes are not collectivities of individuals, but rather synthetic ensembles draw-ing on but not exhausting economic, political and ideological structures; third, that, as things in their own right, classes are sets of positions, in the sense of imagined structural constants, defined by particular relations of economic possession, particular disciplinary or political relations of control, and particular significatory or ideological relations of title, the results of whose mutual determination is capital's appropriation of surplus labour; fourth, that individuals are not only, or *the* only, class subjects (individuals may also be 'racialized' (Miles, 1989), gendered and idiosyncratic subjects, whilst corporate bodies such as companies and trade unions may also be class subjects); fifth, that if and when individuals and corporate bodies do serve as, and therefore sometimes act as, class subjects, it is as often because of *some* of the things they say and do as it is because of *everything* they say and do (thus, for example, at some times in her day's work and by some of her actions an individual may embody the working class, whilst at other times and in some other of her actions the same individual may embody capital); and sixth, that embodying such contradictory class positionings does not make one a member of a middle class but simply aids the reproduction of the two classes. In sum, for me, people do not have class positions and so are not members of classes, but classes sometimes have people or parts of them and so, because some of their positionings are shared, create the possibility of solidarities between them. And, whilst for this reason (and many others) people and corporate bodies may often be engaged in struggles with one another, classes themselves never engage in struggle but exist instead in a condition of permanent and unavoidable tension with one another.

To conclude this section, I would simply like to comment very briefly on the consequences of this conception of the class structure for the theory of capitalist crisis. Most significant are those consequences which follow from the displacement of the original, quantitative and representationalist understanding of surplus value as something that can be counted and visualized, by a non-representationalist understanding of it as a purely conceptual entity, performing an explanatory rather than a measuring role within Marxist theory. Given this displacement, the plausibility of the so-called 'law of the tendency of the rate of profit to fall' and 'its counteracting influences' no longer depends upon the ability of its proponents to link supposedly quantifiable increases in the organic composition of capital (that is, in the proportionalities of fixed capital to labour power after the effects of the 'counteracting influences' have been taken account of), to the rate of the appropriation of surplus labour, to changes in prices and, therefore, to profits. In terms of the position being enunciated here, prices are viewed, not as transformed quantities of value, but rather as the aggregated consequences of the relatively autonomous discourses and politics of production on exchange relations in the context of capitalist relations of possession and separation.

Conclusion

To sum up, then, I have attempted to save Marxism from the disabling consequences of its economic essentialism by rethinking and elaborating on some of its critical structural concepts, rather than by pursuing the well-established strategy of simply adding in an element of indeterminacy by invoking some variation on the concept of agency. For me, understanding what animates social structures is primarily a matter of understanding inter-structural and intra-structural forces that are often embodied by subjects of one kind or another, but are not reducible to them.

The principal advantages which I would claim for the present approach are the following. First, compared to that of the orthodox Marxists, it neither privileges economic relations nor exaggerates the social import of the class structure. Second, the present approach preserves the critical insight of the Weberians as regards the autonomy of the ideological and political dimensions of class. It does not, however, adopt the humanist ontology that typically underpins concepts of agency and so lands them in the extremely uncomfortable position of continuing to insist that classes are ultimately collectivities of human subjects, even though they cannot meet their own criterion of 'adequacy at the level of meaning', since they are unable to say anything about what actually happens in the minds of such subjects. And third, it depends upon a non-humanist mode of understanding the ideological realm and thanks to the differences just specified, renders moot all the points made by the orthodoxies' critics.

Harking back to what the appearance of social theory after post-modernism, would look like, I hope that the reconceptualization of class that I have proposed clarifies my suggestion that a non-representationalist and non-humanist approach enables one both to simplify things and at the same time to combine otherwise unassimilable knowledges and on this basis, to understand very complex social formations that lack any overall coherence.

My contention here is that the concept I offer suggests a way in which several different knowledges may be synthesized, and specifies several points at which class relations are articulated with, and affected by, such other sets of relations as those that gender, racialize and individualize subjects. This said, it is equally important to stress that it involves no claims either to have displaced the knowledges upon which it draws, or to the effect that non-class relations are subsumable by, or in any sense subordinate to, class relations.

Finally, to my mind, it is able to do all these fine things because it rests upon a refusal of that temptation to omniscience that all too often arises when it is thought that social scientists are about providing accurate representations of human beings as they interact with one another; that is, and to put the point positively, it rests upon the assumption that the sociologist is interested in what human behaviour can tell us about other more specifically social entities, rather than what it can tell us about why particular people and groups do the things they do — just because human beings are only representable as unitary entities, this does not mean that knowledge, whether of them or of what they participate in, need also be unitary. In short, then, all of the foregoing was premissed upon the conviction that Marxism and postmodernism need each other if there is to be any future for radical, *sui generis* sociological analysis, now that the seldom acknowledged and often unwanted guarantee of Marxism's plausibility represented by the existence of the Soviet Union has disappeared.

Note

1. Of course, none of what has just been said should be taken as suggesting that I think that one can no longer aspire to know the truth about America, nor indeed that I think that millions of Americans do not make the effort every day. All it means is that the ruling discourse in whatever sphere, whether it be in the polity, economy, industrial relations, or even philosophy, no longer allows the pertinence of questioning the truthfulness or otherwise of its imagined America. And this, as I argue in the main body of the text, is because this discourse is haunted by a profound but deeply buried uncertainty as to its own veracity.

BIBLIOGRAPHY

AFL–CIO (1985) *The Changing Situation of Workers and Their Unions*. AFL–CIO, Washington.

Aglietta, M. (1976) *A Theory of Capitalist Regulation*. New Left Books, London.

Alcaly, R. and Mermelstein, D. (eds) (1977) *The Fiscal Crisis of American Cities*. Vintage, New York.

Allswang, J.M. (1978) *The New Deal and American Politics*. Wiley, New York.

Altmeyer, A. (1966) *The Formative Years of Social Security*. University of Wisconsin Press, Madison.

Amenta, E. and Carruthers, B. (1988) 'The Formative Years of U.S. Social Spending Policies: Theories of the Welfare State and the American States During the Great Depression', *American Sociological Review*, 53 (5): 661.

Anderson, K. (1980) *The Creation of a Democratic Majority 1928–1936*. University of Chicago Press, Chicago.

Apter, D. (1965) *The Politics of Modernization*. University of Chicago Press, Chicago.

Aronowitz, S. (1973) *False Promises*. McGraw-Hill, New York.

Attewell, P. (1984) *Radical Political Economy since the Sixties: a Sociology of Knowledge Analysis*. Rutgers University Press, Princeton.

Auerbach, J. (1976) *Unequal Justice*. Oxford University Press, New York.

Aya, R. and Miller, N. (eds) (1971) *The New American Revolution*. Free Press, New York.

Bailey, S. (1950) *Congress Makes a Law*. Columbia University Press, New York.

Baker, S., Weiner, E. and Borrus, A. (1990) 'Mexico: A New Economic Era', *International Business Week*, 12 Nov.: 46.

Banks, O. (1981) *Faces of Feminism: A Study of Feminism as a Social Movement*. Basil Blackwell, Oxford.

Baran, P. and Sweezy, P. (1968) *Monopoly Capital*. Penguin, Harmondsworth.

Baritz, L. (1960) *Servants of Power*. Wesleyan University Press, Middletown, Conn.

Baritz, L. (1989) *The Good Life: The Meaning of Success for the American Middle Class*. Knopf, New York.

Barnet, R.J. (1972) *The Roots of War*. Atheneum, New York.

Baron, H. and Hymer, B. (1968) 'The Negro Worker in the Chicago Labor Market', in Jacobson (1968).

Baudrillard, J. (1968) *Le Système des Objets*. Gallimard, Paris.

Baudrillard, J. (1970) *La Société de Consommatian*. Gallimard, Paris.

Baudrillard, J. (1972) *For a Critique of the Political Economy of the Sign*. Telos Press, St Louis.

Baudrillard, J. (1975) *The Mirror of Production*. Telos Press, St Louis.

Baudrillard, J. (1988) *America*. Verso, London.

Bauman, Z. (1989) *Modernity and the Holocaust*. Cornell University Press, Ithaca.

Bauman, Z. (1992) *Intimations of Postmodernity*. Routledge, London.

Baumol, W., Blackman, S.B. and Wolff, E. (1990) *Productivity and American Leadership: the Long View*. MIT Press, Cambridge, Mass.

Becker, J. (1973) 'Class Structure and Conflict in the Managerial Phase', *Science and Society*, 37 (3): 259.

Bell D. (ed.) (1955) *The Radical Right*. Doubleday, New York.

Bell, D. (1960) *The End of Ideology*. Harvard University Press, Cambridge, Mass.

Bell, D. (1967) *Marxian Socialism in the United States*. Princeton University Press, Princeton.

Bell, D. (1973) *The Coming of Post-Industrial Society*. Basic Books, New York.

Bell, D. (1976) *The Cultural Contradictions of Capitalism*. Basic Books, New York.

Bell, D. (1988) 'New Afterword', in Bell (1960).

Bellah, R., Madsen, R., Sullivan, W., Swidler, A. and Tipton, S. (1985) *Habits of the Heart: Individualism and Commitment in American Life*. University of California Press, Berkeley.

Bendix, R. (1956) *Work and Authority in Industry*. Harper Row, New York.

Berger, P. (1974) *The Homeless Mind*. Penguin, Harmondsworth.

Bergman, B. (1984) *The Economic Emergence of Women*. Basic Books, New York.

Berman, M. (1982) *All that is Sold Melts into Air*. Verso, London.

Berman, R. (1968) *America in the Sixties*. Free Press, Glencoe.

Bernstein, B. (1968) 'The New Deal: the Conservative Achievements of Liberal Reform', in B. Bernstein (ed.) (1968), *Towards a New Past*. Random House, New York.

Bernstein, I. (1950) *New Deal Collective Bargaining Policy*. University of California Press, Berkeley.

Bernstein, I. (1960) *The Lean Years 1920–1933*. Houghton Mifflin, Boston.

Bernstein, M. (1989) 'Why the Great Depression was Great: Toward a New Understanding of the Interwar Economic Crisis in the United States', in Fraser and Gerstle (1989).

Bernstein, N. (1972) 'The Presidency and Management Improvement', in Thomas and Baade (1972).

Bhaskar, R. (1989) *Reclaiming Reality*. Verso, London.

Biskind, P. (1983) *Seeing is Believing: How Hollywood Taught us to Stop Worrying and Love the 1950s*. Pantheon, New York.

Blackburn, M. and Bloom, D. (1985) 'What is Happening to the Middle Class?' in Eitzen and Baca-Zinn (1989).

Blair, T. (1978) *Retreat to the Ghetto*. Hill and Wang, New York.

Blecker, R. (1990) 'The Consumption Binge is a Myth', *Challenge*, May/June: 22.

Block, F. (1977) *The Origins of International Economic Disorder*. University of California Press, Berkeley.

Block, F. (1990) *Postindustrial Possibilities: A Critique of Economic Discourse*. University of California Press, Berkeley.

Bluestone, B. and Harrison, B. (1982) *The Deindustrialization of America*. Basic Books, New York.

Boggs, J. (1963) *The American Revolution: Pages from a Negro Worker's Notebook*. Monthly Review Press, New York.

Bok, D.C. and Dunlop, J.T. (1970) *Labor and the American Community*. Simon and Schuster, New York.

Boskin, M.J. (1987) *Reagan and the Economy*. Institute for Contemporary Studies, San Francisco.

Bosworth, B. (1982) 'Capital Formation and Economic Policy', *Brookings Papers on Economic Activity*, 2: 273.

Bouchier, D. (1978) *Idealism and Revolution*. Edward Arnold, London.

Bowen, H. and Mangum, G. (eds) (1966) *Automation and Economic Progress*. Prentice-Hall, Englewood Cliffs.

Bowles, S. and Gintis, M. (1976) *Schooling in Capitalist America*. Routledge, London.

Bowles, S., Gordon, D. and Weisskopf, T. (1983) *Beyond the Wasteland*. Anchor, New York.

Bowles, S., Gordon, D. and Weisskopf, T. (1986) 'Power and Profits: The Social Structure of Accumulation and the Profitability of the Postwar United States Economy', *Review of Radical Political Economy*, 18 (1/2): 132.

Boyer, P. (1978) *Urban Masses and Social Order in America 1820–1920*. Harvard University Press, Cambridge, Mass.

Bradbury, M. and McFarlane, J. (1991) *Modernism: A Guide to European Literature 1890–1930*. Penguin, London.

Braverman, H. (1974) *Labor and Monopoly Capital*. Monthly Review Press, New York.

Brecher, J. (1972) *Strike*. Straight Arrow Books, San Francisco.

Brick, H. (1986) *Daniel Bell and the Decline of Intellectual Radicalism: Social Theory and Political Reconciliation in the 1940s*. University of Wisconsin Press, Madison.

Brinkley, A. (1989) 'The New Deal and the Idea of the State', in Fraser and Gerstle (1989).

Bronner, S. (1990) *Socialism Unbound*. Routledge, London.

Brumbaugh, R., Jnr. and Litan, R. (1990) 'The Banks are Worse Off than you Think', *Challenge*, January/February: 4.

Brundage, P. (1970) *The Bureau of the Budget*. Praeger, New York.

Buckley, W. (1965) *Up From Liberalism*. Honor Books, New York.

Burawoy, M. (1979) *Manufacturing Consent: Changes in the Labor Process and Monopoly Capitalism*. University of Chicago Press, Chicago.

Burawoy, M. (1985) *The Politics of Production*. Verso, London.

Burnham, W.D. (1970) *Critical Elections and the Mainsprings of American Politics*. Norton, New York.

Burris, V. (1980) 'Capital Accumulation and the Rise of the New Middle Class', *Review of Radical Political Economy*, 12 (1): 17.

Callinicos, A. (1989) *Against Postmodernism: A Marxist Critique*. Polity, Cambridge.

Callinicos, A. and Harman, C. (1987) *The Changing Working Class*. Bookmark, London.

Cantor, M. (ed.) (1979) *American Working Class Culture*. Greenwood Press, Westport, Conn.

Caplowitz, D. (1963) *The Poor Pay More*. Free Press, Glencoe.

Carnoy, M. (ed.) (1975) *Schooling in a Corporate Society*. McKay, New York.

Carroll, P. (1990) *It Seemed like Nothing Happened: America in the 1970s*. Rutgers University Press, Princeton.

Carter, P. (1983) *Another Part of the Fifties*. Columbia University Press, New York.

Castells, M. (1980) *The Economic Crisis and American Society*. Princeton University Press, Princeton.

Castrell, R.M. (1981) 'Overhead Labour and the Cyclical Behaviour of Productivity and Real Wages', *Journal of Post-Keynesian Economics*, 3: 277.

Cater, D. (1972) 'The Do it Yourself Nature of Presidential Power', in Latham (1972).

Chambers, W. and Burnham, W.D. (eds) (1967) *The American Party System*. Oxford University Press, New York.

Chandler, A.D., Jnr. (1962) *Strategy and Structure*. MIT Press, Cambridge, Mass.

Chandler, A.D. Jnr. (1977) *The Visible Hand*. Belknap, Cambridge, Mass.

Chapin, F. (1935) *Contemporary American Institutions*. Harper, New York.

Chase-Dunn, C. (1990) *Global Formation: Structures of the World Economy*. Blackwell, Oxford.

Clawson, D. (1980) *Bureaucracy and the Labor Process*. Monthly Review Press, New York.

Cleaver, E. (1967) *Soul on Ice*. McGraw-Hill, New York.

Clecak, P. (1973) *Radical Paradoxes: Dilemmas of the American Left 1945–1970*. Harper & Row, New York.

Clecak, P. (1977) *Crooked Paths: Reflections on Socialism, Conservatism, and the Welfare State*. Harper & Row, New York.

Cloward, R. and Piven, F. (1975) *The Politics of Turmoil: Poverty, Race and the Urban Crisis*. Vintage, New York.

Cobb, J. and Sennett, R. (1973) *The Hidden Injuries of Class*. Random House, New York.

Collier, P. and Horowitz, D. (eds) (1989) *Second Thoughts: Former Radicals Look Back at the Sixties*. Madison Books, Lanham.

Cornard, J. (1966) *The Behavior of Interest Rates*. National Bureau of Economic Research, New York.

Coser, L. and Howe, I. (1974) *The New Conservatives: A Critique from the Left*. Quadrangle, New York.

Crawford, A. (1980) *Thunder on the Right: The 'New Rights' and the Politics of Resentment*. Pantheon, New York.

Crewe, I. (1986) 'On the Death and Resurrection of Class Voting', *Political Studies*, xxxiv, 4.

Cronin, T. (1972) 'Everybody Believes in Democracy until he Gets to the White House', in Thomas and Baade (1972).

Crozier, M., Huntington, S. and Watanuki, J. (1975) *The Crisis of Democracy: Report on the Governability of Democracies*. Trilateral Commission, New York.

Dahl, R. (1961) *Who Governs?* Yale University Press, New Haven, Conn.

Davies, M. (1974) 'Women's Place is at the Typewriter: The Feminisation of the Clerical Labour Force', *Radical America*, 8 (4).

Davies, R. (1966) *Housing Reform During the Truman Administration*. University of Missouri Press, Columbia.

Davis, M. (1980a) 'Why the U.S. Working Class is Different', *New Left Review*, 123.

Davis, M. (1980b) 'The Barren Marriage of American Labour and the Democratic Party', *New Left Review*, 124.

Davis, M. (1981) 'The Rise of the New Right', *New Left Review*, 128.

Davis, M. (1982) 'The AFL–CIO's Second Century', *New Left Review*, 136.

Davis, M. (1984) 'The Political Economy of Late Imperial America', *New Left Review*, 143.

Davis, M. (1986) *Prisoners of the American Dream*. Verso, London.

Deleuze, G. and Guattari, F. (1983) *Anti-Oedipus*. University of Minnesota Press, Minneapolis.

Derber, M. (1970) *The American Idea of Industrial Democracy*. University of Illinois Press, Urbana.

Dews, P. (1987) *Logics of Disintegration*. Verso, London.

Dickstein, M. (1977) *Gates of Eden*. Basic Books, New York.

Divine, R. (ed.) (1987) *The Johnson Years*, 2 vols. University of Kansas Press, Lawrence.

Dohse, K., Jurgens, U. and Malsch, T. (1985) 'From Fordism to Toyotaism', *Politics and Society*, 14 (2).

Domhoff, W. (1970) *The Higher Circles*. Vintage, New York.

Domhoff, W. (1972) *Fat Cats and Democrats*. Prentice-Hall, Englewood Cliffs.

Douglas, P. (1936) *Social Security in the United States*. McGraw-Hill, New York.

Dower, J. (ed.) (1975) *The Origins of the Modern Japanese State: Selected Writings of E.H. Norman*. Pantheon, New York.

Duboff, R. and Herman, E. (1975) 'The New Economics: Handmaiden of Inspired Truth', in S. Rosen (1975).

Dumenil, G., Glick, M. and Rangel, J. (1987) 'The Rate of Profit in the U.S.', *Cambridge Journal of Economics*, 11: 331.

Eagleton, T. (1990) *The Ideology of the Aesthetic*. Blackwell, Oxford.

Eagleton, T. (1991) *Ideology: An Introduction*. Verso, London.

Eakins, D. (1969) 'Business Planners and America's Postwar Expansion', in Horowitz (1969).

Eakins, D. (1972) 'Policy – Planning for the Establishment' in Radosh and Rothbard (1972).

Edsall, T. (1989) 'The Changing Shape of Power: A Realignment in Public Policy', in Fraser and Gerstle (1989).

Edwards, P.K. (1981) *Strikes in the U.S. 1881–1974*. Basil Blackwell, Oxford.

Edwards, R. (1979) *Contested Terrain*. Heinemann, London.

Edwards, R., Reich, M. and Weisskopf, T. (eds) (1972) *The Capitalist System*. Prentice-Hall, Englewood Cliffs.

Ehrenreich, B. (1990) *Fear of Falling: The Inner Life of the Middle Class*. Pantheon, New York.

Eitzen, S. and Baca-Zinn, M. (1989) *The Reshaping of America*. Prentice-Hall, New York.

Ekirch, A. (1969) *Ideologies and Utopias: the Impact of the New Deal on American Thought*. Quadrangle, Chicago.

Enthoven, A. and Smith, K. (1971) *How Much is Enough?* Harper & Row, New York.

Evans, P.B., Rueschemeyer, D. and Skocpol, T. (eds) (1985) *Bringing the State Back In*. Cambridge University Press, New York.

Fantasia, R. (1988) *Cultures of Solidarity*. University of California Press, Berkeley.

Farley, R. (1977) 'Trends in Racial Inequalities: Have the Gains of the 1960s Disappeared in the 1970s?', *American Sociological Review*, 42 (2): 189–207.

Feagin, J. (1975) *Subordinating the Poor*. Spectrum Books, Englewood Cliffs, NJ.

Featherstone, M. (1991) *Consumer Culture and Postmodernism*. Sage, London.

Feldstein, M. and Summers, L. (1977) 'Is the Rate of Profit Falling?', *Brookings Papers*, I, Washington.

Fellman, G. and Brandt, B. (1973) *The Deceived Majority*. Transaction Books, New Jersey.

Ferguson, T. (1989) 'Industrial Conflict and the Coming of the New Deal: The Triumph of Multinational Liberalism in America', in Fraser and Gerstle (1989).

Ferry, L. and Renaut, A. (1990) *French Philosophy of the Sixties: An Essay on Antihumanism*. Massachusetts University Press, Amhurst.

Fine, S. (1956) *Laissez-Faire and the General Welfare State*. University of Michigan Press, Ann Arbor.

Fisher, L. (1975) *Presidential Spending Power*. Princeton University Press, Princeton.

Fitzgerald, P. and Meisol, P. (1978) 'The "Tax Payers Revolt" Takes to the States', *National Journal*, 6 March.

Flacks, R. (1971) 'Revolt of the Young Intelligentsia' in Aya and Miller (1971).

Flash, E. (1965) *Economic Advice and Presidential Leadership*. Columbia University Press, New York.

Forman, R. (1971) *Black Ghettos, White Ghettos and Slums*. Prentice-Hall, Englewood Cliffs.

Franklin, R. and Resnick, S. (1973) *The Political Economy of Racism*. Holt, Rinehart and Winston, New York.

Fraser, S. (1989) 'The "Labor Question"', in Fraser and Gerstle (1989).

Fraser, S. and Gerstle, G. (eds) (1989) *The Rise and Fall of the New Deal Order 1930–1980*. Princeton University Press, Princeton.

Friedan, B. (1963) *The Feminine Mystique*. Dell, New York.

Friedman, B. (1989) *Day of Reckoning: The Consequences of American Economic Policy*. Vintage, New York.

Friedman, M., Jacobson, A. and Schwartz, A. (1963) *A Monetary History of the United States 1867–1960*. Princeton University Press, Princeton.

Fusfeld, D. (1956) *The Economic Thought of Franklin D. Roosevelt and the Origins of the New Deal*. Columbia University Press, New York.

Fusfeld, D. (1972) *The Age of the Economist*. Scott, Foresman and Co., Glenville.

Galbraith, J.K. (1958) *The Affluent Society*. Penguin, Harmondsworth.

Galbraith, J.K. (1967) *The New Industrial State*. Penguin, Harmondsworth.

Galbraith, J.K. (1969) *How to Control the Military*. Doubleday, New York.

Gane, M. (1988) *On Durkheim's Rules of Sociological Method*. Routledge, London.

Garrett, C. (1961) *The LaGuardia Years: Machine and Reform Politics in New York City*. Rutgers University Press, New Brunswick.

Gartner, Greer, C. and Reissman, F. (eds) (1982) *What Reagan is Doing to Us*. Harper & Row, New York.

Gelfand, M. (1975) *A Nation of Cities: The Federal Government and Urban America 1933–1965*. Oxford University Press, New York.

Georgakas, D. and Surkin, M. (1975) *Detroit: I Do Mind Dying*. St Martin's Press, New York.

Gersuny, C. (1981) *Work Hazards and Industrial Conflict*. University Press of New England, Hanover, NH.

Gettleman, M. and Mermelstein, D. (eds) (1967) *The Great Society Reader*. Vintage Books, New York.

Gettleman, M. and Mermelstein, D. (eds) (1971) *The Failure of American Liberalism after the Great Society*. Vintage, New York.

Gilbert, J. (1972) *Designing the Industrial State: The Intellectual Pursuit of Collectivism in America 1880–1940*. Quadrangle, Chicago.

Gilder, G. (1981) *Wealth and Poverty*. Buchan and Enright, London.

Gill, S. and Law, D. (1989) *The Global Political Economy*. Columbia University Press, New York.

Ginsburg, H. (1975) 'Unemployment, Subemployment and Public Policy', mimeo, New York University School of Social Work.

Gitlin, T. (1987) *The Sixties: Years of Hope Days of Rage*. Bantam Books, New York.

Goffman, E. (1959) *The Presentation of Self in Everyday Life*. Doubleday, New York.

Goldfield, M. (1987) *The Decline of Organized Labour in the United States*. University of Chicago Press, Chicago.

Goldthorpe, J. (1980) *Social Mobility and Class Structure in Modern Britain*. Oxford University Press, Oxford.

Gordon, D. (ed.) (1972) *Theories of Poverty and Underdevelopment*. Lexington Books, Lexington.

Gordon, D., Edwards, R. and Reich, M. (1982) *Segmented Work, Divided Workers*. Cambridge University Press, Cambridge.

Gordon, M. (1958) *Social Class in American Sociology*. Duke University Press, Durham.

Gottshalk, P. (1988) 'Retrenchment in Antipoverty Programs in the United States: Lessons for the Future', in Kymlicka and Matthews (1988).

Graham, O. (1976) *Toward a Planned Society*. Oxford University Press, New York.

Green, D. (1987) *The New Conservatism*. St Martin's Press, New York.

Green, J. (1980) *The World of the Worker*. Hill and Wang, New York.

Greenstone, D. (1977) *Labor in American Politics*. University of Chicago Press, Chicago.

Gross, B. (ed.) (1966) *A Great Society?* Basic Books, New York.

Grubb, W.N. and Wilson, R.H. (1989) 'Sources of Increasing Inequality in Wages and Salaries', *Monthly Labor Review*, 112 (4): 3.

Guttman, A. and Ziegler, B. (eds) (1964) *Communism, the Courts and the Constitution*. D.C. Heath, Lexington.

Habermas, J. (1990) *The New Conservatism*. MIT Press, Cambridge, Mass.

Hall, B. (ed.) (1972) *Autocracy and Insurgency in Organized Labor*. Transaction Books, New Brunswick.

Hall, S. (1988) *The Hard Road to Renewal: Thatcherism and the Crisis of the Left*. Verso, London.

Hall, S. and Jacques, M. (eds) (1985) *The Politics of Thatcherism*. Lawrence and Wishart, London.

Hall, S. and Jacques, M. (eds) (1989) *New Times: The Changing Face of Politics in the 1990s*. Lawrence and Wishart, London.

Hamby, A. (1973) *Beyond the New Deal*. Columbia University Press, New York.

Harrington, M. (1963) *The Other America*. Penguin, Harmondsworth.

Harrington, M. (1986) *The Dream of Deliverance in American Politics*. Knopf, New York.

Harris, H.J. (1982) *The Right to Manage*. University of Wisconsin Press, Madison.

Harris, S. (1964) *The Economics of the Kennedy Years*. Harper & Row, New York.

Harrison, B. and Bluestone, B. (1988) *The Great U-Turn: Corporate Restructuring and the Polarizing of America*. Basic Books, New York.

Harrison, D. (1988) *The Sociology of Modernization and Development*. Unwin Hyman, London.

Harvey, D. (1989) *The Condition of Postmodernity*. Blackwell, Oxford.

Hayden, T. (1980) *The American Future*. South End Press, Boston.

Hayes, E.C. (1977) *Power Structure and Urban Policy: Who Rules in Oakland?* McGraw-Hill, New York.

Heath, J. (1969) *John F. Kennedy and the Business Community*. University of Chicago Press, Chicago.

Heath, J. (1975) *Decade of Disillusionment*. Indiana University Press, Bloomington.

Heller, W. (1966) *New Dimensions of Political Economy*. Harvard University Press, Cambridge, Mass.

Henley, A. (1990) *Wages and Profits in a Capitalist Economy*. Edward Elgar, Aldershot.

Herding, R. (1972) *Job Control and Union Structure*. Rotterdam University Press, Rotterdam, Netherlands.

Hoffer, E. (1989) *The True Believer*. Harper & Row, New York.

Hoover, K. and Plant, R. (1989) *Conservative Capitalism in Britain and the United States*. Routledge, London.

Horowitz, D. (ed.) (1969) *Corporations and the Cold War*. Monthly Review Press, New York.

Hoselitz, B. (ed.) (1952) *The Progress of Underdeveloped Areas*. University of Chicago Press, Chicago.

Huber, J. and Form, W. (1973) *Income and Ideology*. Free Press, Glencoe.

Huberman, L. (1938) *The Labour Spy Racket*. Left Book Club, London.

Hunnius, G. (ed.) (1973) *Workers' Control*. Vintage, New York.

Hunt, A. (1977) *The Sociological Movement in Law*. Macmillan, London.

Huntington, S. (1981) *American Politics: The Promise of Disharmony*. Harvard University Press, Cambridge, Mass.

Hutchinson, J. (1970) *The Imperfect Union: a History of Corruption in American Unions*. E.P. Dutton, New York.

Isserman, M. and Kazin, M. (1989) 'The Failure and Success of the New Radicalism', in Fraser and Gerstle (1989).

Jacobs, P. and Landau, S. (eds) (1967) *The New Radicals*. Penguin, Harmondsworth.

Jacobson, J. (ed.) (1968) *The Negro and the American Labor Movement*. Doubleday, New York.

Jacobson, P. and Jacobson, J. (eds) (1983) *Socialist Perspectives*. Karz-Cohl, New York.

Jacoby, R. (1977) *Social Amnesia*. The Harvester Press, Hassocks.

Jaffe, D. (1973) 'The Marxian Theory of Crisis, Capital and the State', *Economy and Society*, 2 (2): 186.

Jameson, F. (1984) 'Post-Modernism, or the Cultural Logic of Late Capitalism', *New Left Review*, 146.

Jameson, F. (1991) *Postmodernism, or the Cultural Logic of Late Capitalism*. Duke University Press, Durham, N.C.

Jones, K. (1982) *Law and Economy*. Academic Press, London.

Kariel, H.S. (1967) *The Decline of American Pluralism*. Stanford University Press, Stanford.

Karl, B. (1963) *Executive Reorganization and Reform in the New Deal*. Harvard University Press, Cambridge, Mass.

Katona, G. (1975) *Psychological Economics*. Elsevier, New York.

Katz, M. (1971) *Class, Bureaucracy and Schools*. Praeger, New York.

Katznelson, I. (1989) 'Was the Great Society a Lost Opportunity?', in Fraser and Gerstle (1989).

Kavanagh, T. (ed.) (1989) *The Limits of Theory*. Stanford University Press, Stanford.

Kaysen, K. (1957) 'The Social Significance of the Modern Corporation', *American Economic Review, Papers and Proceedings*, 47: 311.

Kennedy, J. (1936) *I'm For Roosevelt*. Reynal and Hitchcock, New York.

Kennedy, P. (1987) *The Rise and Fall of the Great Powers*. Random House, New York.

Kerr, G. (1977) *Labour Markets and Wage Determination*. University of California Press, Berkeley.

Kidron, M. (1970) *Western Capitalism since the War*. Penguin, Harmondsworth.

Kimmel, L. (1959) *The Federal Budget and Fiscal Policy 1789–1958*. Brookings Institution, Washington.

King, D. (1987) *The New Right: Politics, Markets and Citizenship*. Dorsey Press, Chicago.

Klare, M.T. (1972) *War Without End*. Vintage, New York.

Kochan, T. (ed.) (1985) *Challenges and Choices facing American Labor*. MIT Press, Cambridge, Mass.

Kochan, T., Katz, H. and McKersie, R. (1986) *The Transformation of American Industrial Relations*. Basic Books, New York.

Koenig, L. (1972) 'Kennedy's Personal Management' in Latham (1972).

Kolko, G. (1962) *Wealth and Power in America*. Praeger, New York.

Kolko, G. (1967) *The Triumph of Conservatism*. Quadrangle, Chicago.

Kolko, J. and Kolko, G. (1972) *The Limits of Power: The World and United States Foreign Policy*. Harper & Row, New York.

Kraus, D. (1976) 'The Devaluation of the American Executive', *Harvard Business Review*, May/June: 84–94.

Kraus, S. (ed.) (1962) *The Great Debates: Kennedy vs. Nixon 1960*. Indiana University Press, Bloomington.

Kraus, S. (ed.) (1979) *The Great Debates: Carter vs. Ford 1976*. Indiana University Press, Bloomington.

Krieger, J. (1986) *Reagan, Thatcher and the Politics of Decline*. Polity Press, Cambridge.

Krugman, P. (1990) 'The Income Distribution Disparity', *Challenge*, July/August: 4.

Kuczynski, J. (1973) *A Short History of Labour Conditions and Industrial Capitalism*, vol. 2. Muller, London.

Kurtzman, J. (1988) *The Decline and Crash of the American Economy*. Norton, New York.

Kuttner, R. (1983) 'The Changing Occupational Structure' in Eitzen and Baca-Zinn (1989).

Kymlicka, B.B. and Matthews, J. (eds) (1988) *The Reagan Revolution?* The Dorsey Press, Chicago.

Laclau, E. and Mouffe, C. (1985) *Hegemony and Socialist Strategy*. Verso, London.

Larrowe, C. (1972) *Harry Bridges: the Rise and Fall of Radical Labor in the United States*. Lawrence Hill and Co., New York.

Lasch, C. (1978) *The Culture of Narcissism*. Norton, New York.

Lasch, C. (1984) *The Minimal Self: Psychic Survival in Troubled Times*. Norton, New York.

Lash, S. (1990) *Sociology of Postmodernism*. Routledge, London.

Latham, E. (ed.) (1972) *J.F. Kennedy and Presidential Power*. D.C. Heath, Lexington.

Lekachman, R. (1969) *The Age of Keynes*. Penguin, Harmondsworth.

Lester, R.A. (1958) *As Unions Mature*. Princeton University Press, Princeton.

Leuchtenburg, W. (1963) *Franklin D. Roosevelt and the New Deal,*.Harper & Row, New York.

Levitan, S.A. and Conway, E. (1988) 'Part-timers: Living on Half Rations', *Challenge*, May/June: 9.

Levy, M.J. (1966) *Modernization and the Structure of Societies*. Princeton University Press, Princeton.

Lichtenstein, N. (1975) 'Defending the No-Strike Pledge: CIO Politics during WWII', *Radical America*, 9 (4) and 9 (5).

Lichtenstein, N. (1983) *Labour's War at Home: the CIO in World War II*. Cambridge University Press, Cambridge.

Lichtenstein, N. (1989) 'From Corporatism to Collective Bargaining: Organized Labor and the Eclipse of Social Democracy in the Postwar Era' in Fraser and Gerstle (1989).

Liebfried, S. (1973) 'US Central Government Reform of the Administrative Structure during the Ash Period (1968–1971)', *Kapitalistate*, 1.

Liebman, R.C. and Wuthnow, R. (eds) (1983) *The New Christian Right*. Aldine, New York.

Lipietz, A. (1985) *The Enchanted World*. Verso, London.

Lo, C. (1975) 'The Conflicting Functions of U.S. Military Spending after World War II', *Kapitalistate*, 3.

Lockwood, D. (1958) *The Blackcoated Worker*. Allen and Unwin, London.

Lowi, T. (1969) *The End of Liberalism*. Norton, New York.

Lowi, T. and Stone, A. (eds) (1978) *Nationalising Government*. Sage, Beverley Hills.

Lubove, R. (1968) *The Struggle for Social Security 1900–1935*. Harvard University Press, Cambridge, Mass.

Lynch, D. (1991) *Paintings and Drawings*. Tokyo Museum of Contemporary Art, Tokyo.

Lynd, H. and Lynd, R. (1956) *Middletown*. Harvest Books, New York.

Lynd, R. (1933) 'The People as Consumers', in *The Report of the President's Research Committee on Social Trends*, US Government, Washington.

Lynd, S. (ed.) (1973) *American Labor Radicalism*. Wiley, New York.

Lyotard, J.F. (1984) *The Postmodern Condition*. University of Minnesota Press, Minneapolis.

McAdams, A.K. (1964) *Power and Politics in Labor Legislation*. Columbia University Press, New York.

McClure, A. (1956) *The Truman Administration and the Problems of Postwar Labor 1945–1948*. Fairleigh Dickinson University Press, Rutherford.

McConnell, G. (1962) *Steel and the Presidency*. Norton, New York.

McConnell, G. (1967) *Private Power and American Democracy*. McGraw-Hill, New York.

Machlup, F. (1962) *The Production and Distribution of Knowledge in the US*. Princeton University Press, Princeton.

McKinley, C. and Frase, R. (1970) *Launching Social Security 1935–1937*. University of Wisconsin Press, Madison.

Magdorf, H. and Sweezy, P. (1975) 'Banks: Skating on Thin Ice', in Mermelstein (1975).

Manpower Report to the President (1973), 178, 183.

Mansfield, H. (1972) 'Reorganizing the Federal Executive Branch: the Limits of Institutionalization', in Thomas and Baade (1972).

Marable, M. (1980) *Race, Reform and Rebellion: The Second Reconstruction in Black America*. University Press of Mississippi, Jackson.

Marris, P. and Rein, M. (1967) *Dilemmas of Social Reform*. Atherton, New York.

Marshall, G., Rose, D., Newby, H. and Vogler, C. (1989) *Social Class in Modern Britain*. Unwin Hyman, London.

Marshall, R. (1986) *Unheard Voices: Labor and Economic Policy in a Competitive World*. Basic Books, New York.

Marx, K. (1965) *Capital*, vol. 1. Lawrence and Wishart, London.

Mattick, P. (1971) *Marx and Keynes*. Merlin, London.

Matusow, A. (1984) *The Unraveling of America: A History of Liberalism in the 1960s*. Harper & Row, New York.

May, E.T. (1989) 'Cold War – Warm Hearth: Politics and the Family in Postwar America', in Fraser and Gerstle (1989).

Mayer, M. (1991) *The Greatest-Ever Bank Robbery: The Collapse of the Savings and Loan Industry*. Charles Scribner's Sons, New York.

Melman, S. (1985) *The Permanent War Economy* 2nd edn. Simon and Schuster, New York.

Mermelstein, D. (ed.) (1975) *The Economic Crisis Reader*. Vintage, New York.

Michl, T. R. (1988) 'The Two Stage Decline in U.S. Non-financial Corporate Profitability', *Review of Radical Political Economy*, 20 (4): 1.

Miles, R. (1989) *Racism*. Routledge, London.

Miller, A.S. (1968) *The Supreme Court and American Capitalism*. Free Press, New York.

Miller, H. (1966) *Income Distribution in the United States*. Bureau of the Census, Washington.

Miller, J. (1987) *Democracy is in the Streets: From Port Huron to the Siege of Chicago*. Simon and Schuster, New York.

Miller, W.E. and Levitan, T.E. (1976) *Leadership and Change: The New Politics and the American Electorate*. Winthrop, Cambridge, Mass.

Mills, C.W. (1951) *White Collar: The American Middle Classes*. Oxford University Press, New York.

Mills, C.W. (1956) *The Power Elite*. Oxford University Press, New York.

Milton, D. (1982) *The Politics of US Labor: From the Depression to the New Deal*. Monthly Review Press, New York.

Mintz, B. and Schwartz, M. (1990) 'Capital Flows and the Process of Financial Hegemony', in Zukin and DiMaggio (1990).

Miroff, B. (1976) *Pragmatic Illusion*. McKay, New York.

Mkrtchian, A. (1973) *US Labor Unions Today*. Progress Publishers, Moscow.

Moynihan, D.P. (1969) *Maximum Feasible Misunderstanding: Community Action in the War on Poverty*. The Free Press, Glencoe.

Moynihan, D. P. (1973) *The Politics of a Guaranteed Income*. Random House, New York.

Mroczkowski, T. (1984) 'Is the American Labour–Management Relation Changing?', *British Journal of Industrial Relations*, 22 (1): 47.

Murphy, T. and Rehfuss, J. (1976) *Urban Politics in the Suburban Era*. The Dorsey Press, Homewood.

Murray, C. (1984) *Losing Ground: American Social Policy, 1950–1980*. Basic Books, New York.

Naples, M. (1981) 'Industrial Conflict and its Implications for Productivity Growth', *American Economics Association Papers and Proceedings*, 71: 36–41.

Naples, M. (1986) 'The Unravelling of the Union–Capital Truce and the U.S. Productivity Crisis', *Review of Radical Political Economy*, 18 (1/2): 110.

Nash, G. (1979) *The Conservative Intellectual Movement in America since 1945*. Basic Books, New York.

Navasky, V. (1971) *Kennedy Justice*. Atheneum, New York.

Neustadt, R. (1960) *Presidential Power: The Politics of Leadership*. Wiley, New York.

Newman, J. (1975) 'Make Overhead Cuts the Last', *Harvard Business Review*, May/June.

Nishkanen, W. (1988) 'Reflections on Reaganomics', in Kymlicka and Matthews (1988).

Nordhaus, W. (1974) 'The Falling Share of Profits', *Brookings Papers*, 1, Washington.

Norris, C. (1992) *Uncritical Theory: Postmodernism, Intellectuals and the Gulf War*. Lawrence and Wishart, London.

Novak, M. (1983) *The Spirit of Democratic Capitalism*. Simon and Schuster, New York.

Novick, D. (ed.) (1965) *Program Budgeting: Program Analysis and the Federal Budget*. Harvard University Press, Cambridge, Mass.

Nye, J. (1990) *Bound to Lead: The Changing Nature of American Power*. Basic Books, New York.

O'Conner, L. et al. (1973) *The Office Workers Manifesto*. Freeway Press, New York.

O'Connor, J. (1973) *The Fiscal Crisis of the State*. St Martins, New York.

O'Connor, J. (1984) *Accumulation Crisis*. Basil Blackwell, Oxford.

Offe, C. (1976) *Income and Inequality*. Arnold, London.

Oglesby, (1977) *The Yankee Cowboy War*. Medallion, Berkeley.

Okun, A. (1970) *The Political Economy of Prosperity*. The Brookings Institution, Washington.

O'Neill, W.O. (1989) *American High: The Years of Confidence 1945–60*. Free Press, New York.

Parker, R. (1973) *The Myth of the Middle Class*. Harper Colophon, New York.

Parsons, T. (1964) *Essays in Sociological Theory*. Free Press, Glencoe.

Patterson, J.T. (1981) *America's Struggle Against Poverty 1900–1980*. Harvard University Press, Cambridge, Mass.

Pearce, F. (1989) *The Radical Durkheim*. Unwin Hyman, London.

Peck, S. (1963) *The Rank and File Leader*. College and University Press, New Haven, Conn.

Pells, R. (1985) *The Liberal Mind in a Conservative Age: American Intellectuals in the 1940s and 1950s*. Harper & Row, New York.

Perkins, F. (1946) *The Roosevelt I Knew*. Viking Press, New York.

Perlo, V. (1973) *The Unstable Economy*. Lawrence and Wishart, London.

Pfeffer, J. and Baron, J. (1988) 'Taking the Workers Back Out: Recent Trends in the Structuring of Employment', *Research in Organizational Behavior*, 10: 257.

Phillips, J. (1969) 'The Economic Effects of the Cold War', in Horowitz (1969).

Phillips, K. (1981) *Post-Conservative America: People, Politics and Ideology in a Time of Crisis*. Vintage, New York.

Phillips, K. (1990) *The Politics of Rich and Poor*. Random House.

Piore, M. and Sabel, C. (1984) *The Second Industrial Divide*. Basic Books, New York.

Piven, F. and Cloward, R. (1971) *Regulating the Poor*. Vintage, New York.

Piven, F. and Cloward, R. (1982) *The New Class War*. Pantheon, New York.

Plunkert, L.M. (1990) 'Job Growth and Industry Shifts in the 1980s', *Monthly Labor Review*, 113 (9): 3.

Polenberg, R. (1966) *Reorganizing Roosevelt's Government*. Harvard University Press, Cambridge, Mass.

Poster, M. (1989) *Jean Baudrillard: Selected Writings*. Stanford University Press, Stanford, Cal.

Potter, J. and Wetherell, M. (1987) *Discourse and Social Psychology: Beyond Attitudes and Behaviour*. Sage, London.

Preis, A. (1975) *Labor's Giant Step*. Pathfinder, New York.

President's Research Committee on Social Trends (1933) *Recent Social Trends in the U.S.* McGraw-Hill, New York.

Pursell, C.W. (ed.) (1972) *The Military Industrial Complex*. Harper & Row, New York.

Quadagno, J. (1984) 'Welfare Capitalism and the Social Security Act of 1935', *American Sociological Review*, 49 (5): 632.

Quadagno, J. (1985) 'Two Models of Welfare State Development: Reply to Skocpol and Amenta', *American Sociological Review*, 50 (4): 575.

Quick, P. (1975) 'Rosie the Riveter: Myths and Realities', *Radical America*, 9 (4) and 9 (5).

Radosh, R. (1972) 'The Myth of the New Deal', in Radosh and Rothbard (1972).

Radosh, R., and Rothbard, M. (eds) (1972) *A New History of Leviathan*. E.P. Dutton and Co., New York.

Reagan, M. (1972) *The New Federalism*. Oxford University Press, New York.

Reich, C. (1964) 'The New Property', *Yale Law Journal*, 73: 733.

Reichley, A. J. (1981) *Conservatives in an Age of Change*. The Brookings Institution, Washington.

Resnick, S. and Wolff, R.D. (1987) *Knowledge and Class: A Marxian Critique of Political Economy*. University of Chicago Press, Chicago.

Rieder, J. (1989) 'The Rise of the "Silent Majority"', in Fraser and Gerstle (1989).

Riesman, D. (1950) *The Lonely Crowd*. Yale University Press, New Haven.

Rifkin, J. and Barber, R. (1978) *The North Will Rise Again*. Beacon Press, Boston.

Rimlinger, G. (1971) *Welfare Policy and Industrialization in Europe, America and Russia*. Wiley, New York.

Roberts, P.C. (1984) *The Supply-Side Revolution*. Harvard University Press, Cambridge, Mass.

Robertson, J.O. (1980) *American Myth, American Reality*. Hill and Wang, New York.

Robertson, R. and Turner, B. (eds) (1991) *Talcott Parsons: Theorist of Modernity*. Sage, London.

Roby, P. (ed.) (1974) *The Poverty Establishment*. Spectrum Books, Englewood Cliffs.

Rogers, J., Rogers, T. and Rogers, C. (1985) *By the Few for the Few: The Reagan Welfare Legacy*. D.C. Heath, Lexington.

Root and Branch Collective (eds) (1975) *The Rise of the Workers' Movements*. Fawcett, Greenwich, Conn.

Rose, R. (1977) *Managing Presidential Objectives*. Macmillan, London.

Rosen, S. (ed.) (1975) *Economic Power Failure: The Current American Crisis*. McGraw-Hill, New York.

Ross, R.J.S. and Trachte, K.C. (1990) *Global Capitalism: The New Leviathan*. State University of New York Press, Albany.

Rostow, W.W. (1983) *The Barbaric Counter-Revolution: Cause and Cure*. University of Texas Press, Austin.

Rothbard, M. (1970) 'The Hoover Myth', in Weinstein, J. and Eakins, S. (1970).

Rousseaus, S. (1989) 'Can the U.S. Financial System Survive the Revolution?', *Challenge*, March/April: 39.

Roustang, F. (1989) 'On Reading Again', in Kavanagh (1989).

Rowan, H. (1972) 'The Big Steel Crisis: Kennedy vs. Blough', in Latham (1972).

Sale, K. (1974) *Power Shift: The Rise of the Southern Rim and its Challenge to the Eastern Establishment*. Random House, New York.

Samuelson, P. (1973) *Economics*. McGraw-Hill, New York.

Saville, J. (ed.) (1965) *The Socialist Register*. Merlin, London.

Sawhill, I. (1988) 'What About America's Underclass?', *Challenge*, May/June: 27.

Sawyer, M.C. (1989) *The Challenge of Radical Political Economy*. Harvester Wheatsheaf, New York.

Sayer, A. (1984) *Method in Social Science*. Hutchinson, London.

Schick, A. (1972) 'The Budget Bureau That Was: Thoughts on the Rise, Decline and Future of a Presidential Agency' in Thomas and Baade (1972).

Schlesinger, A., Jr (1957) *The Age of Roosevelt: The Crisis of the Old Order*. Heinemann, London.

Schlesinger, A., Jr (1965) *A Thousand Days*. Andre Deutsch, London.

Schottland, C. (ed.) (1967) *The Welfare State*. Harper Torchbooks, New York.

Schriftgeisser, K. (1967) *Business and Public Policy: the Role of the Committee for Economic Development*. Prentice-Hall, Englewood Cliffs.

Schwarz, J. (1988) *America's Hidden Success*. Norton, New York.

Scitovsky, T. (1976) *The Joyless Economy*. Oxford University Press, New York.

Seidman, H. (1970) *Politics, Position and Power*. Oxford University Press, New York.

Seidman, J. (1953) *American Labor from Defence to Reconversion*. Chicago University Press, Chicago.

Sennett, R. (1973) *The Uses of Disorder*. Penguin, Harmondsworth.

Sennett, R. (1977) *The Fall of Public Man*. Cambridge University Press, Cambridge.

Serrin, W. (1973) *The Company and the Union*. Knopf, New York.

Shapiro, M. (1964) *Law and Politics in the Supreme Court*. Free Press, Glencoe.

Sheahan, J. (1967) *The Wage–Price Guideposts*. The Brookings Institution, Washington.

Silvestri, G. and Lukasiewicz, J. (1989) 'Projections of Occupational Employment: 1988–2000', *Monthly Labor Review*, 112 (11): 42.

Sitkof, H. (1981) *The Struggle for Black Equality 1954–80*. Hill and Wang, New York.

Sklar, M. (1970) 'Woodrow Wilson and the Politics of Modern United States Liberalism', in Weinstein and Eakins (1970).

Sklar, M. (1988) *The Corporate Reconstruction of American Capitalism 1890–1916*. Cambridge University Press, New York.

Skocpol, T. (1980) 'Political Response to Capitalist Crisis: Neo-Marxist Theories of the State and the Case of the New Deal', *Politics and Society*, 10 (2): 155.

Skocpol, T. and Amenta, E. (1985) 'Did Corporations Shape Social Security?', *American Sociological Review*, 50 (4): 572.

Sorenson, T. (1965) *Kennedy*. Hodder and Stoughton, London.

Starr, P. (1982) *The Social Transformation of American Medicine*. Basic Books, New York.

Stearns, L.B. (1990) 'Capital Market Effects on External Control of Corporations' in Zukin and DiMaggio (1990).

Stein, H. (1969) *The Fiscal Revolution in America*. University of Chicago Press, Chicago.

Steiner, G. (1966) *Social Insecurity: The Politics of Welfare*. Rand McNally, Chicago.

Stephens, J. (1979) *The Transition from Capitalism to Socialism*. Macmillan, London.

Sternlieb, G. and Hughes, J. (1976) *Post Industrial America: Metropolitan Decline and Inter-Regional Job Shifts*. Centre for Urban Policy Research, New Brunswick.

Stevens, R. (1976) *Vain Hopes, Grim Realities: the Economic Consequences of the Vietnam War*. New Viewpoints, New York.

Stockman, D. (1986) *The Triumph of Politics*. Harper & Row, New York.

Stone, K. (1988) 'Labor and Corporate Structure', *The University of Chicago Law Review*, 55: 73.

Stub, H. (1972) *Status Communities*. Dryden Press, Hinsdale, Illinois.

Summers, L. (1990) *Understanding Unemployment*. MIT Press, Cambridge, Mass.

Sundquist, J. (1968) *Politics and Policy*. The Brookings Institution, Washington.

Swados, H. (1973) 'The Myth of the Happy Worker', in S. Lynd (1973).

Sweezy, P. and Magdop, H. (1972) *The Dynamics of US Capitalism*. Monthly Review Press, New York.

Taylor, J. (1979) *From Modernization to Modes of Production: A Critique of the Sociologies of Development and Underdevelopment*. Macmillan, London.

Terkel, S. (1974) *Working*. Avon, New York.

Terkel, S. (1988) *The Great Divide: Second Thoughts on the American Dream*. Pantheon, New York.

Thomas, W.C. (1972) 'Presidential Advice and Information: Policy and Program Formulation', in Thomas and Baade (1972).

Thomas, W.C. and Baade, H. (eds) (1972) *The Institutionalised Presidency*. Oceana, New York.

Thompson, H.S. (1989) *Fear and Loathing in Las Vegas*. Random House, New York.

Tilly, C. (1986) 'U-Turn on Equality: The Puzzle of Middle Class Decline', in Eitzen and Baca-Zinn (1989).

Tobin, J. (1974) *The New Economics: One Decade Older*. Princeton University Press, Princeton.

Tobin, J. (1988) 'Reaganomics in Retrospect', in Kymlicka and Matthews (1988).

Tomlins, C.L. (1985) *The State and the Unions*. Cambridge University Press, New York.

Truman, H.S. (1955) *Memoirs*, Vol. II. Doubleday, New York.

Tugwell, R. (1960) *The Enlargement of the Presidency*. Doubleday, Garden City.

Vale, V. (1971) *Labour in American Politics*. Routledge & Kegan Paul, London.

Vatter, H. (1963) *The US Economy in the 1950s*. Norton, New York.

Vernon, R. (1971) *Sovereignty at Bay: The Multinational Spread of U.S. Enterprises*. Basic Books, New York.

Vidich, A. and Bensman, J. (1969) *The New American Society: the Revolution of the Middle Class*. University of Chicago, Chicago.

Wachtal, H. and Sawyers, L. (1974) 'Government Spending and the Distribution of Income', in Roby (1974).

Waldo, D. (1948) *The Administrative State*. Ronald Press, New York.

Wason, J. (1971) 'Labor-Management under Johnson', in Gettleman and Mermelstein (1971).

Waxman, C. (ed.) (1968) *The End of Ideology Debate*. Funk and Wagnells, New York.

Weaver, R.K. (1988) 'Social Policy in the Reagan Era' in Kymlicka and Matthews (1988).

Wedderburn, D. (1965) 'Facts and Theories of the Welfare State', in Saville (1965).

Weidenbaum, M. (1969) *The Modern Public Sector*. Basic Books, New York.

Weiner, H. (ed.) (1966) *Modernization: the Dynamics of Growth*. Basic Books, New York.

Weinstein, J. (1967) *The Decline of Socialism in America 1912–1925*. Monthly Review Press, New York.

Weinstein, J. (1969) *The Corporate Ideal and the Welfare State 1900–1918*. Beacon, Boston.

Weinstein, J. (1975) *Ambiguous Legacy*. New Viewpoints, New York.

Weinstein, J. and Eakins, D. (eds) (1970) *For a New America: Essays in History and Politics from Studies on the Left 1959–1967*. Random House, New York.

Weir, M. and Skocpol, T. (1985) 'State Structures and the Possibilities for "Keynesian" Responses to the Great Depression in Sweden, Britain and the United States' in Evans et al. (1985).

Weir, S. (1973) 'Rebellion in American Labor's Rank and File', in Hunnius, G. (1973).

Weisskopf, T. (1979) 'Marxist Crisis Theory and the Rate of Profit in the Postwar U.S. Economy', *Cambridge Journal of Economics*, 3: 341.

Weisskopf, T. (1988) 'An Analysis of Profitability Changes in Eight Countries', *Review of Radical Political Economy*, 20 (2/3): 68.

Weisskopf, T., Bowles, S. and Gordon, D. (1983) 'Hearts and Minds: A Social Model of U.S. Productivity Growth', *Brookings Papers on Economic Activity*, 2: 38.

White, J.K. (1988) *The New Politics of Old Values*. University Press of New England, Hanover, NH.

White, T.H. (1972) *The Making of the President*. Cape, London.

Whyte, W.H. (1963) *The Organization Man*. Doubleday, New York.

Wildavsky, A. (1964) *The Politics of Budgetary Analysis*. Little Brown, Boston.

Wilensky, H. (1975) *The Welfare State and Equality*. University of California Press, Berkeley.

Williams, W.A. (1966) *The Contours of American History*. Quadrangle, Chicago.

Wolfe, A. (1977) *The Limits of Legitimacy*. The Free Press, New York.

Wolfe, A. (1981a) 'Sociology, Liberalism and the New Right', *New Left Review*, 128: 3.

Wolfe, A. (1981b) *America's Impasse: The Rise and Fall of the Politics of Growth*. Pantheon, New York.

Wolfe, A. (1983) 'Is America Modern?', in Jacobson and Jacobson (1983)

Wolfe, A. (1988) 'Cultural Sources of the Reagan Revolution: the Anti-Modern Legacy', in Kymlicka and Matthews (1988).

Wolff, E. (1986) 'The Productivity Slowdown and the Fall in the U.S. Rate of Profit, 1947–1976', *Review of Radical Political Economy*, 18 (1/2): 87.

Woodiwiss, A. (1990a) *Social Theory After Postmodernism: Rethinking Production, Law and Class*. Pluto, London.

Woodiwiss, A. (1990b) *Rights v. Conspiracy: A Sociological Essay on the History of Labour Law in the United States*. Berg, Oxford.

Woodiwiss, A. (1991) 'Just Another Japanese Cigarette? Class After Postmodernism', a paper given at the annual meeting Canadian Sociology and Anthropology Association, Kingston.

Woodiwiss, A. (1992) *Law, Labour and Society in Japan: From Repression to Reluctant Recognition*. Routledge, London.

Wright, E.O. (1978) *Class, Crisis and the State*. New Left Books, London.

Wright, E.O. (1979) *Class Structure and Income Determination*. Academic Press, New York.

Wright, E.O. (1985) *Classes*. Verso, London.

Wright, E.O. and Martin, B. (1987) 'The Transformation of the American Class Structure: 1960–1980', *American Journal of Sociology*, 93 (1): 1.

Wright, E.O. and Singelmann, J. (1982) 'Proletarianization in the Changing American Class Structure', *American Journal Sociology*, 88 (sup.): 176.

Youstler, J. (1956) *Labour's Wage Policies in the Twentieth Century*. Twayne, Skidmore College.

Zerzan, J. (1974) 'Organized Labor Versus The Revolt Against Work: The Critical Contest', *Telos*, 21: 194.

Zukin, S. and DiMaggio, P. (eds) (1990) *Structures of Capital: The Social Organization of the Economy*. Cambridge University Press, New York.

INDEX

Index compiled by Meg Davies